# ASPECTS OF RACINIAN TRAGEDY

# UNIVERSITY OF TORONTO ROMANCE SERIES

# ASPECTS OF

# RACINIAN

# TRAGEDY

*John C. Lapp*

UNIVERSITY OF TORONTO PRESS

CARL A. RUDISILL LIBRARY
LENOIR RHYNE COLLEGE

COPYRIGHT, CANADA, 1955, BY
UNIVERSITY OF TORONTO PRESS
REPRINTED, 1964, IN THE
UNITED STATES OF AMERICA

842
L31a

48676
Jan. '65

CARL A. RUDISILL LIBRARY
LENOIR RHYNE COLLEGE

*TO MARGARET*

# PREFACE

---

RACINE has been the subject of innumerable critical articles and books since the seventeenth century; of these a small minority have been written in English. If I have been so presumptuous as to add to their number, it is simply because I have felt, ever since I began reading Racine fifteen years ago, not only that much remained to be said about him as a dramatic artist, but that one brought up to consider Shakespeare as the model of tragedy might conceivably bring a fresh approach to a dramatist who has been to a great extent a Gallic monopoly.

Anglo-Saxons—even those with a sound knowledge of French— have in the main felt scant sympathy for Racine. Despite such doughty champions as Lytton Strachey and George Henry Lewes, I would venture the guess that Leigh Hunt's outburst on seeing *Andromaque* in English still sums up fairly accurately the reaction of the literate English reader. "It is French all over," wrote Hunt, "that is to say dramatically speaking—pompous, frigid, and ranting. . . . The French were too much occupied to go to Nature, and so Nature must come to them; and all the 'vasty spirits' of poetry and passion shrink themselves into coats and bag-wigs, as the devils in Milton's Pandemonium did into Pygmies. The persons 'Madam' it away, like the ladies in the Beggar's Opera."[1] If we are tempted to brush away Hunt's reaction as that of a prejudiced Romantic, we have only to harken to the echo of his words provided by a recent critic, who concludes that Racinian tragedy now looks "as grotesquely French and Baroque as Louis himself; wig, laces, high heels, and all."[2] It is to be hoped that the following pages may provide an answer to these animadversions, in particular the suggestion that Racine's tragedy, for moderns, wears only the costume of its time. The first of these quotations, however,

[1]*Leigh Hunt's Dramatic Criticism*, ed. L. H. and C. W. Houtchens, Columbia University Press, 1949, pp. 824–7.
[2]Francis Fergusson, *The Idea of a Theater*, Princeton University Press, 1949, p. 57.

raises a point we might consider at once. Leigh Hunt's comment is comment on translation; Racine's *Andromaque* had become *The Distrest Mother*. Perhaps indeed most Anglo-Saxon antipathy or in-difference to our dramatist is due to the fact that Racine, unlike the Greeks, really doesn't survive translation. His poetry is so essential that when it is gone the work is no longer itself; in each play so delicate a balance prevails, so great is the interdependence of act, scene, and line, that to disturb a single element is to disrupt all. This book is therefore addressed to those who can read Racine in French. Yet even proficient readers of French may, if they do not read with sufficient care, miss much of his power and depth. For despite his apparent simplicity, Racine is a complex poet, and if it is true, as has been said so often, that "il rase la prose," it is also true, as one critic has put it, that "c'est avec des ailes." Readers and critics alike would do well to bear in mind what a professor at the Sorbonne recently told his students: "Il faut faire quand nous le lisons, le même travail que nous faisons quand nous voulons comprendre Sénèque ou Homère. Seulement, quand nous lisons des auteurs anciens, nous n'avons pas, comme lorsque nous lisons Racine, la candeur de croire que nous comprenons la langue."[3]

Thus the main road to any understanding of Racinian tragedy must lead through a careful examination of its form, and it is chiefly as a contribution to the study of Racine's form that I offer this book. That the form is paramount is my continuous argument, and anything which does not involve that argument I have deliberately left out.

For this reason I welcome rather than deplore the fact that we know next to nothing of Racine's personal life. The Romantic idea that an author's career should somehow be a replica of his works has prompted many an incautious remark about Racine's "sadism" and the desire to make of this punctilious courtier a revolutionary has even encouraged critics to find in his plays covert attacks on royal policy or polemics in favour of deposed kings. But Racine was neither a Musset nor a Hugo. Jean Giraudoux says, a trifle pettishly, that "Il n'est pas un sentiment en Racine qui ne soit un sentiment littéraire,"[4] suggesting, I suppose, that his works might have profited from being "sincere" expressions of personal vicissitudes. The same writer shakes his head over the fact that

[3]Charles Bruneau, *Explication de Phèdre, Actes I and II*, Paris, 1945 (mimeographed).
[4]Jean Giraudoux, *Racine*, Paris, Grasset, 1930, pp. 4-5.

the dramatist's love affairs were with actresses. It is really too bad of
Racine! If only he had pursued the Grande Mademoiselle!

Far from regretting that Racine was neither Chateaubriand nor
Vigny, let us be grateful that the paucity of biographical detail, and the
humdrum character of most of the facts that have come down to us
permit us to fix our gaze unswervingly on the only thing that really
matters: the text itself. How can we know Racine? As Jacques Copeau
wisely wrote: "Le texte seul compte; il n'y a que le texte! C'est
seulement par le texte qu'un homme de 1680 pourra faire signe aux
hommes de l'an 2.000. Si c'est un texte dramatique, il leur suffira de
lire. N'attendons rien que du texte."[5]

By thus stressing the importance of form I do not mean to suggest
that I consider Racine a poet alone. This is an error to which recent
critics have not been immune, and one which, because of the peculiar
quality of Racinian verse, lies full in the path of the unwary. True,
Racine was a man of letters, and his plays may certainly be read as
literature, enjoyed as poetry. Has this perhaps led critics to ignore or to
minimize their dramatic quality? We must never forget the picture,
sketched so vividly by the Abbé Dubos,[6] of Racine in the rôle of stage
director, coaching his actresses in the fine points of delivery, schooling
them in the volume and tempo of their lines. If we consider Racine's
psychology, or his imagery, we must not forget that they are also com-
ponents of drama. Such a familiar "talisman" as the line, "Mais tout
dort, et les vents, et l'armée, et Neptune," should be studied not only
for its lyric beauty, but as a line spoken by an officer of Agamemnon's
household to his distraught master, in the exposition of the play.
Phèdre's gasped words, "Vers mon cœur tout mon sang se retire" so
frequently considered to be evidence of Racine's knowledge of physio-
logy, are also significant as part of his system of dramatic gesture.
With these precautions in mind, then, we shall proceed, remembering
always that the play is first, and that in Racine, action is dramatic.

I cannot single out from the many works on Racine any one
from which I have profited most; I owe something to them all.
Besides the inspiration of earlier criticism, I must acknowledge a debt

[5]In *Les Fourberies de Scapin*, Paris, Ed. du Seuil, 1951, pp. 22–3.
[6]J. B. Dubos, *Réflexions critiques sur la poésie et la peinture*, Paris, Mariette, 1719, III, 144–5.

to my former teacher, Professor Emeritus P. G. C. Campbell, of Queen's University, who first stirred my interest in Racine, and to many discussions of the seventeenth-century drama, in letter and conversation, with my friend, Professor Georges May, of Yale University. I should also like to thank Miss Jean C. Jamieson of the Editorial Staff of the University of Toronto Press for her many valuable suggestions. For permission to include here, in somewhat different form, essays which have appeared in *PMLA*, the *University of Toronto Quarterly, Yale French Studies,* and *Studies in Philology,* I am grateful to the editors of those periodicals.

All the quotations from the plays that appear in the text have been taken from *Racine: Œuvres complètes,* edited by R. Picard, R. Groos, and E. Pilon, Editions de la Pléiade, Paris, 1951, volume I. For the reader's convenience I have supplied the line references lacking in this edition.

When referring to the characters in the plays, I have used Racine's spelling, but for their classical antecedents I have used the accepted English version. Place-names have also been kept in their English form.

The following abbreviations have been used for the names of journals in the footnotes:

| | |
|---|---|
| *CL* | Comparative Literature |
| *CR* | Classical Review |
| *FS* | French Studies |
| *MLN* | Modern Language Notes |
| *MLR* | Modern Language Review |
| *RHL* | Revue d'histoire littéraire de la France |
| *RR* | Romanic Review |
| *SP* | Studies in Philology |

J. C. L.

# CONTENTS

—◆—

—◆—

# CONTENTS

ASPECTS OF RACINIAN TRAGEDY

# I. THE THEMES

IF WE BEGIN our study by a discussion of the themes of Racine's tragedies, it is because this has seemed the most convenient way of striking
down into the roots of Racinian drama. Theme in the drama may be
defined as that idea or statement toward which every element in the
structure moves, which such disparate parts of the scaffolding as poetic
imagery and the moment of exits and entrances combine to support
and strengthen. This is not to say that a play must have only one theme;
minor and related themes will frequently develop out of a central
theme. Nor is it to say that a play, in order to be valid dramatically,
must have a theme: the melodramas of Euripides or Cocteau offer
convincing proof to the contrary.

In the case of Racine's tragedies, where, for a multitude of reasons
which we hope to explore in this study, the dramatic structure is so
closely knit, the search for and discovery of a central theme has the
value of illuminating the dramatic apparatus which supports it.
Throughout the Racinian tragedy, themes may vary in intensity; they
may have the power of universal truths; they may consist of a psychological statement on human relationships; they may be nothing more
than the starting-point, the bare foundation upon which the play is
constructed.

About any writer or artist, generalizations are of value, and they
should be made, provided they are based on evidence. As many critics
have found, and as some others should have found, Racine as tragic
dramatist is extremely difficult to generalize about. One of the most
frequently made, yet often most erroneous, generalizations about
literary artists is that they "mature"; that somehow their later work is
infallibly superior to their earlier. This theory we shall reject for
Racine, believing as we do that although in certain respects he pro-
gressed with time, his plays are far from showing an ascending line of
achievement between 1665 and 1691. For this reason, we have not

hesitated in our study of the themes to group together tragedies which are sometimes chronologically rather far apart. The following chapter should help us to arrive at certain valid generalizations, whose validity we may test through the close study of the text in later chapters.

## THE FAMILY IN DISORDER

### La Thébaïde, ou, Les Frères ennemis

In his first tragedy, Racine chose a subject which centred upon family strife. From the rich and varied material provided by the Theban legend of Oedipus, which the dramatist called "the most tragic in antiquity," he selected the struggle between the two sons of the tragic King, Eteocles and Polyneices, whom their father had declared must rule over Thebes in alternate years. Racine's play begins at roughly the same point as Aeschylus' *Seven against Thebes*. Polynice's army is before the city, and the battle is about to start. The events of the play, however, with the exception of the brothers' duel to the death, occur in the palace: they tell, in rapid succession, of Jocaste's efforts to reconcile her sons, her failure, her suicide and the suicide of Antigone, followed by the suicide attempt of Créon.

As the alternate title indicates, the brothers' hatred is the core of the play, and this explains, I think, why the other characters, Antigone, Hémon, and Créon, unlike their illustrious forebears in Greek tragedy, are here scarcely more than *figurants*. Their emotions pale beside those of the brothers, so that nothing remains of the characteristics they had in the Greek plays; Antigone's fraternal love, Hemon's noble defiance, Creon's fierce single-mindedness. The brothers' hatred in *La Thébaïde* is not only deeper and more frenzied than in any of the sources; it becomes almost pathological. Acting perhaps on a suggestion in Seneca's version,[1] Racine makes his tragic action essentially the result of human agency; his theme is thus a disorder in that human relationship where the bonds of affection should be firmest: the family. I say "should be firmest" because the chief irony lies in the fact that Jocaste bases her pleas on a criterion of normal love and affection that we, the audience,

---

[1] *Phoenissae*, ll. 451–4:

> Error invitos adhuc
> fecit nocentes, omne Fortunae fuit
> peccatis in nos crimen: hoc primum nefas
> inter scientes geritur.

know cannot apply to Etéocle and Polynice. As to the brothers themselves, they make no protest against fate; Etéocle, in one of his rare
references to Heaven (the characters allude more frequently to "le
ciel" than to "les dieux") mentions the parental crime and the wrath
it provoked, but in an offhand manner that makes of both hardly more
than a detached simile:

> On dirait que le ciel, par un arrêt funeste,
> Voulut de nos parents punir ainsi l'inceste,
> Et que dans notre sang il voulut mettre au jour
> Tout ce qu'ont de plus noir et la haine et l'amour.
>
> (IV. i. 927–30)

The brothers' violence shows in their clipped, brutal speech; although this is his first tragedy, Racine was never to employ his famous
prosaism with more telling effect. Of the Argive soldiers he has killed,
Etéocle says, "J'ai fait mordre la poudre à ces audacieux" (I. iii. 53),
and when he temporarily transfers command to Jocaste, there ensues
the following brief dialogue with Créon, unparalleled for its brusqueness:

> Et vous, vous me suivrez.
>
> CRÉON
> Quoi ! Seigneur...
>
> ÉTÉOCLE
> Oui, Créon, la chose est résolue.
>
> CRÉON
> Et vous quittez ainsi la puissance absolue ?
>
> ÉTÉOCLE
> Que je la quitte ou non, ne vous tourmentez pas:
> Faites ce que j'ordonne, et venez sur mes pas.
>
> (I. iv. 183–6)

Both brothers express impatience with their mother's entreaties;
Polynice says roughly, "Madame, au nom des Dieux, cessez de
m'arrêter" (II. iii. 449) and Etéocle cries in exasperation as he yields
to her request that he receive his brother,

> Hé bien, Madame, hé bien ! qu'il vienne, et qu'on lui donne
> Toutes les sûretés qu'il faut pour sa personne.
>
> (III. v. 811–12)

It will be recalled that in Euripides' *Phoenician Maidens* enmity has
replaced what had been the brothers' natural affection for one another.

As Euripides' Eteocles says, "Loved he became my foe; but loved, yet loved" (l. 1447). Racine, however, dates their hatred from beyond the cradle:

> Elle n'est pas, Créon, l'ouvrage d'une année;
> Elle est née avec nous; et sa noire fureur
> Aussitôt que la vie entra dans notre cœur.
> Nous étions ennemis dès la plus tendre enfance;
> Que dis-je ? nous l'étions avant notre naissance.
>
> (IV. i. 916–20)

And in an image of surprising audacity, Racine portrays the brothers clasped together in mortal struggle within their mother's womb:

> Dans les flancs de ma mère une guerre intestine
> De nos divisions lui marqua l'origine.
>
> (IV. i. 923–4)

In this *ambiance,* Créon's line "[Qu']ils s'étouffent, Attale, en voulant s'embrasser" (III. vi. 890), acquires almost as much force as its better-known counterpart in *Britannicus*: "J'embrasse mon rival, mais c'est pour l'étouffer" (IV. iii. 1314). The ironic metaphor of the embrace of hatred is again suggested in Créon's description of the fight:

> Par l'excès de leur haine, ils semblaient réunis;
> Et, prêts à s'égorger, ils paraissaient amis.
>
> (V. iii. 1315–16)

We are in the presence, then, of an obsession. Etéocle's hymn of hate discounts all such natural causes as ambition and love of power. He fears most of all that his brother will yield, for if Polynice withdrew, leaving him undisputed ruler of Thebes, the hatred to which he clings as to the breath of life might diminish. No, Polynice must flee, must be defeated; their mutual hatred must be allowed to reach its paroxysm.

It is against this flood of passion that Jocaste combats, and Etéocle's paean to hate prepares the most powerful scene in the play: that in which the brothers finally meet. It is from this scene, toward which the action moves with inexorable swiftness, that the fullest irony springs, for Jocaste bases her appeals, her belief in the successful outcome of the meeting, on the assumption that natural affection may thus be awakened in her sons. But Etéocle's words still ring in our ears; the closer he comes, the more hateful he is; he has said: "Plus il approche et plus il me semble odieux," and this is the ironic prelude to Jocaste's cry of thanksgiving as the brothers confront one another. We shall discuss this scene in detail in another place; let it suffice to note here that it summarizes the theme of the play. It is the goal of the action, providing the fatal amalgamation, like the mixture of two chemical elements, which produces the final explosion that brings down all the protagonists.

That the ironic conclusion to Jocaste's agonized efforts should be expressed in her own words:

> N'avais-je tant pressé cette fatale vue,
> Que pour les désunir encore plus que jamais ?
>
> (IV. iii. 1016–17)

is somewhat too explicit. This frequent verbalization of the dramatic action is, as we shall see elsewhere, the chief fault of Racine's first tragedy; his characters are too omniscient, and the action too seldom brings home of itself the tragedy of their situation.

*Britannicus*

The tragic stilling of the voice of nature provides a theme for Racine's fourth tragedy, which in several respects closely resembles *La Thébaïde*. Racine's play describes, not Nero's evil career, but its beginnings; his Néron is a "monstre naissant" who, after ruling for two years, has begun to strain against the bonds of duty and gratitude to the mother who has placed him on the throne and married him to Octavie. In swift succession he abducts Junie, fiancée of his half-brother Britannicus, imprisons the latter, hesitates briefly in his decision to kill him, then plunges on, poisoning him, and driving Junie to escape by becoming a vestal. Agrippine, like Jocaste (although the latter unwittingly) has committed crimes of passion, is spurned by her son and appeals in vain to the bonds of nature. In both plays a scheming villain urges brother against brother, and fratricide is the result. Even the language is similar, with Etéocle's brusque, clipped speech frequently reappearing in Néron's lines. But while *La Thébaïde* showed how the abnormal hatred of the brothers carried all with it to destruction—devoted mother and lovers as well as the enemy brothers—*Britannicus* shows how evil begets evil, how the spurning of parenthood and filial duty "return to plague the inventor." The supreme irony of this play is that

Agrippine, who, like the noble Jocaste, bases her appeals upon a criterion of filial duty, has herself travestied family loyalty; that she who expects gratitude has betrayed her benefactor. In this fact we may see the explanation of Racine's statement that his play is the tragedy of Agrippine as well as of Britannicus.

We have thus a set of relationships far more subtle than those of the early play; in *Britannicus* evil grows with every action of the protagonists. The basis of the chief irony is established early in the words of Agrippine's confidante, Albine, who assures her mistress that she may count on her son's respect and gratitude:

> Quoi ? vous à qui Néron doit le jour qu'il respire,
> Qui l'avez appelé de si loin à l'Empire ?
> Vous qui déshéritant le fils de Claudius,
> Avez nommé César l'heureux Domitius ?
> Tout lui parle, Madame, en faveur d'Agrippine :
> Il vous doit son amour.
>
> (I. i. 15–20)

In *Britannicus* for the first time supporting the central theme there is a constant interplay between appearance and reality. Deception and betrayal infect the whole course of the action; the characters move uncertainly through the heavily charged atmosphere of the court, unable to discover their antagonists' true motives and feelings:

> ... dans cette cour
> Combien tout ce qu'on dit est loin de ce qu'on pense !
> Que la bouche et le cœur sont peu d'intelligence !
>
> (V. i. 1522–4)

This play might indeed be called a drama of watcher and watched; significantly, the rime "lieux-yeux" occurs more frequently than in any other tragedy of Racine, and indeed the very walls of the palace seem to have eyes. As the action progresses, glimpses of true feelings and desires beneath mannered exteriors become more and more frequent; the monster gradually emerges. But to the characters such brief lapses are not enough; their lives depend on how much they can discern. This is why Agrippine must "read" Néron's face. Early in the play she recalls his first suspicious act, which has taken place before the action of the play. He was receiving ambassadors, and as she approached her throne, placed beside his, displeasure flashed over his face. Then, moving swiftly to embrace her, he prevented her from taking her rightful place. Thus the filial embrace thrusts Agrippine from her position as co-ruler. On that occasion, Néron concealed his feelings in a way calculated to disarm not only his mother, but the watching courtiers and ambassadors. At the end of the play, when he has cast off all restraint, he can watch indifferently as Britannicus dies from the poison.

Perhaps the single scene which best translates the theme of human disorder is the famous eavesdropping scene of Act II, in which Junie must interview her lover, making clear to him both by her words and her gestures that she no longer loves him, as Néron watches from his place of concealment. Besides increasing the horror and tension of the play, this scene reveals Néron as both product and agent of disorder, perverting a natural love by turning a lovers' tryst into a horrible charade of deception.

### Mithridate

Racine's seventh tragedy involves conflict within the family. There is again a contest between brothers: Xipharès and Pharnace are both rivals for the love of Monime and rivals in war. They, in turn, are pitted against their father: as the sworn enemy of Rome, the violent and aging Mithridate furiously opposes his son Pharnace, who seeks compromise with the invader; and as a passionate lover he is the rival of his loyal son, Xipharès, who is loved by Monime. If we add to this the fact that Mithridate has already been betrayed to the Romans by Xipharès' mother before the action begins, we have a complex entanglement compared with which the designs of *La Thébaïde* and *Britannicus* seem relatively simple. But just as the development of evil in *Britannicus* acquires greater thematic range through the rejection of natural bonds, conjugal and filial, which "free" the hero to follow his perverse career, so the tragedy of the old King, who is, in his own words, "voisin du naufrage" is reinforced and extended by his emotional disintegration within a network of family conflicts. His love for Monime and his determination to seal the marriage contract become for him the substitute for his vanished power, and it is as if by this last manifestation of virility the reverses of the past will be effaced:

> Ce cœur nourri de sang, et de guerre affamé,
> Malgré le faix des ans et du sort qui m'opprime,
> Traîne partout l'amour qui l'attache à Monime.
>
> (II. iii. 458-60)

When he confronts Monime with the knowledge of her love for his son, he begs that she remember his past glories:

> Ne me regardez point vaincu, persécuté :
> Revoyez-moi vainqueur, et partout redouté.
>
> (IV. iv. 1293-4)

If his love for Monime is a last and desperate manifestation of power to which he clings, his relentless attempts to uncover the hidden motives of the other protagonists appear as a substitute for the violent action he craves, such as his grandiose plan to attack Rome. *Mithridate*, like *Britannicus*, is a play of deception; the entire action consists of the making and disclosing of secrets.[2] The King's first desire, upon arriving in Nymphée, is to discover why his sons have left their assigned posts to come there. Xipharès, on hearing the report of his father's death, had revealed his secret love for Monime, and now must conceal it again. Knowing the King's reputation for guile, both sons fear a trap, and the interpretation he may place on their slightest words:

> Le Roi, toujours fertile en dangereux détours,
> S'armera contre nous de nos moindres discours.
> Vous savez sa coutume, et sous quelles tendresses
> Sa haine sait cacher ses trompeuses adresses.
>
> (I. v. 369-72)

But even when he succeeds in tricking Monime, Mithridate is powerless to act upon his discovery and punish the culprits. Because of his position he can no longer afford to act with his former ruthlessness. Alone on the brink of destruction, his wily stratagems, far from enabling him to act, only bring home to him the more forcibly his final defeat:

> Pourquoi répandre un sang qui m'est si nécessaire ?
> Ah ! dans l'état funeste où ma chute m'a mis,
> Est-ce que mon malheur m'a laissé trop d'amis ?
>
> (IV. v. 1396-8)

---

[2]The word "secret," noun and adjective, occurs eighteen times; "cacher," eleven.

Remembering the old King's historic ruthlessness, his murdering of sons and mistresses, we find his impotency when finally possessed of all the facts the more tragic.

Finally, the tragedy of the "amoureux vieillard" appears in his half-conscious realization of the inappropriateness of his love for Monime. Early in the play, when, in one of the countless *quiproquos* which tend to confuse the action, he had concluded that Monime loved Pharnace, he declared that he might have sanctioned her love for Xipharès:

> Ma honte en serait moindre, ainsi que votre crime,
> Si ce fils en effet digne de votre estime
> A quelque amour encore avait pu vous forcer.
>
> (II. iv. 599-601)

The hesitation in his final monologue of defeat and despair stems from this half-awareness that Monime rightly belongs to "cet autre moi-même," and it is this that prepares his final gesture, redeeming him, and permitting him to die without loss of stature.

These three plays centre upon an unnaturalness in human relationships. The first, *La Thébaïde*, concentrates, however, with too great singleness of purpose upon the brothers' hatred, so that little of the tragic atmosphere remains after the soul-shaking irony of the confrontation scene. *Britannicus* has as its principal theme the ascendancy of evil, which develops through the destruction of natural ties of blood and duty. Unlike the first tragedy, with its single irony, *Britannicus* sets in motion a chain of ironies; the unnatural mother expectant of natural devotion in her son, the poisoner dismayed at the poisoning of her protégé, the ironic clash of freedoms—Néron's struggle for freedom from Agrippine and Octavie, Junie's and Britannicus' struggle to escape from Néron. The disrupted natural relationships in *Mithridate* serve mainly to throw into relief the downfall of the central figure, whose love is an obsessive substitute for his political and military frustrations. The love substitute sets him against his loyal son, and is itself the instrument that reveals his irrevocable failure.

## THE TRAGIC CONCETTO

We said earlier that a play need not necessarily have a central theme. Rather than presenting us with a conception of life, a tragic view which develops out of character and action, it may simply demonstrate, ringing changes on an idea which remains external to the action. Sophocles' *Oedipus* has a theme, which, like most Sophoclean tragedies, reasserts the existence of a universal *logos* or pattern of things through the spectacle of a hero made to suffer, not because of some "flaw" in his nature, but because he has inadvertently disturbed this balance. Jean Cocteau is content, in his *Infernal Machine*, to illustrate the malevolence of destiny by a series of brilliant tableaux.

## Alexandre

After his savage *Thébaïde*, Racine wrote his "tendre" *Alexandre*. Critics who explain this change in direction by the desire to suit the *galant* tastes of his audience are probably right. A facet of those tastes, which has been ably discussed by Professor Mornet,[3] helps to explain the *galant* quality of *Alexandre*. Extremely popular were the "questions d'amour," a kind of game in which the participants developed in verse a given situation involving love. Here are two typical examples: "Si un véritable amant peut être gai et se réjouir pendant l'absence de sa maîtresse?" "Une femme mariée par force ne peut-elle garder son cœur (son cœur seulement) à un amant?" Certain of the questions closely resemble tropes or concetti common in Petrarchan lyric poetry or emblem poetry. One quoted by Professor Mornet is obviously based on one of the more common of the *emblemata*; it asks why love is depicted as a blind and naked child archer. But the concetto-situation which concerns our study of *Alexandre* most closely is that of the "prisoner-of-love." We find this verse beneath an emblem showing a bird in a 'cage in the frontispiece of the *Devises héroïques* of Père Lemoyne:

> Celuy qui le premier m'osta la liberté,
>     Me mit en seureté;
> De sa grâce je suis hors de prise & de crainte.
> Pièges, appas, filets, sont pour moy superflus,
> Pour moy la fraude est vaine, inutile est la fainte,
>     Un prisonnier ne se prent plus.[4]

As Professor Mornet has shown, this conceit admits of many vari-

[3]D. Mornet, *Histoire de la littérature française classique, 1660-1700*, Paris, Colin, 1942, p. 33.
[4]Quoted in E. B. O. Borgerhoff, *The Freedom of French Classicism*, Princeton University Press, 1950, frontispiece.

ations. Perhaps the most common of these is the situation in which the captor becomes a captive (Achilles-Briseis), and a further development of it, the allegorical war of love fought by the characters of *L'Astrée* and in a stream of books with such titles as *Le Combat de l'amour et de la fierté* and *La Revue des troupes d'amour*.[5] Evidently Racine's second play, rather than evolving a theme with universal implications, is built around the elaborate metaphor of the warrior-lover's attack on the citadel of his lady, who has been his prisoner and whose prisoner he becomes. The preliminaries would be something like this. Quite probably, as has been suggested, the idea of writing a play about Alexander was an outright bid for the favour of the young Louis XIV. Such a subject would naturally suggest the war-of-love as well as the concetto of the captor-a-captive. There had to be a rival, not in love—for Alexandre-Loüis must be irresistible—but in war, so that he may display his magnanimity. The enemy, Porus, must have a love interest, and this necessitates another rival, who becomes the brother of Alexandre's beloved.

Almost any scene of the play rings changes on the two related concetti. Taxile has promised to help his ally Porus resist Alexandre; for some reason, however, Alexandre has hesitated so far to attack. We learn gradually that this is because of his love for Taxile's sister, Cléofile, who has been urged by her brother to look upon his suit with favour. The vocabulary of war provides a metaphorical language of love. You need not hesitate to yield to such a conqueror, says Taxile,

> Vous pouvez, sans rougir du pouvoir de vos charmes
> Forcer ce grand guerrier à vous rendre les armes;
> Et sans que votre cœur doive s'en alarmer,
> Le vainqueur de l'Euphrate a pu vous désarmer.
>
> (I. i. 57–60)

The associative quality of the rimes further illustrates the love-war imagery; "charmes" calls almost inevitably for "armes."[6]

That the dramatic situation is nothing more than a symbol of the battle of love is evident from the characters' readiness to admit that

---

[5]D. Mornet, *Histoire de la littérature française classique*, pp. 138–9.

[6]Cléofile, urging Taxile to yield to Alexandre without a struggle, calls Axiane's love "une conquête," producing another version of the concetto (I. i. 101–2):

> Pourquoi dans les combats chercher une conquête
> Qu'à vous livrer vous-même Alexandre s'apprête ?

love takes precedence over all obligations, either to the nation or to personal honour. Love for Axiane is by far the greatest of the motives that govern the attitude of the two rivals, Porus and Taxile, toward the waiting Alexandre. On one occasion, this love keeps Taxile from capitulating: "... l'amour le retient quand la crainte l'entraîne" (I. iii. 290). The "gloire," the concern for honour and reputation of the ferocious Porus, melts away before the attractions of Axiane:

> La gloire y peut beaucoup, je ne m'en cache pas;
> Mais que n'y peuvent point tant de divins appas !
>
> (I. iii. 323–4)

The captor-a-captive conceit is developed by the heroine herself with remarkable virtuosity:

> Des captifs comme lui brisent bientôt leur chaine...
> Tandis que ce héros me tint sa prisonnière,
> J'ai pu toucher son cœur d'une atteinte légère;
> Mais je pense, Seigneur, qu'en rompant mes liens,
> Alexandre à son tour brisa bientôt les siens.
>
> (II. i. 365, 369–72)

Far more important to Alexandre than the conquest of Porus' territory is the conquest of Cléofile. Even the spatial aspects of the setting—the two camps, drawn up before one another, prior to the clash of arms—serve primarily to provide delicately erotic metaphors rather than to widen poetically the area of the action. Ephestion's plea to Cléofile, with its frequent use of the possessive modifying such words as provinces, entrenchments, banners, lends itself to the kind of *double entendre* so favoured by the *précieux*:

> Il ne cherchait que vous en courant aux combats.
> C'est pour vous qu'on l'a vu, vainqueur de tant de princes,
> D'un cours impétueux traverser vos provinces,
> Et briser, en passant, sous l'effort de ses coups,
> Tout ce qui l'empêchait de s'approcher de vous.
> On voit en même champ vos drapeaux et les nôtres;
> De ses retranchements il découvre les vôtres;
> Mais, après tant d'exploits, ce timide vainqueur
> Craint qu'il ne soit encor bien loin de votre cœur.
> Que lui sert de courir de contrée en contrée,
> S'il faut que de ce cœur vous lui fermiez l'entrée ?
>
> (II. i. 376–86)

Cléofile's love is thus a fortress, against which the conqueror of the world is powerless unless she deigns to open it to him. The concetti are similarly employed by participants in the secondary love triangle. Porus, successful rival of Taxile, thus expresses the reasons for his valour:

> Il faut vaincre, et j'y cours, bien moins pour éviter
> Le titre de captif que pour le mériter.
>
> (II. v. 647-8)

As we shall show in later chapters, there is certainly more in *Alexandre* than the dramatic development of the two principal concetti, those of the prisoner-of-love and the warrior-of-love. But just as the central theme illuminates the action of *La Thébaïde* or *Britannicus*, so in this play the concetti, though always exterior to the play, help to explain the action. It is thus that profounder questions such as patriotism, treason, and so on, scarcely arise. Taxile, it appears, must die as much because he is unworthy of love as because he is a traitor: he is "ce traître à sa patrie, à sa maîtresse." Porus is victorious in defeat, and Alexandre, because he is victor in love as well as war, remains the supreme figure, capable of bestowing clemency from his heights.

*Andromaque*

Perhaps the one line in *Andromaque* that has caused the most critical ink to flow is Pyrrhus' plaint that he is "Brûlé de plus de feux que je n'en allumai." This line is explainable, however, as a development of the prisoner-of-love conceit, for upon Pyrrhus, hero of Troy, the love of his Trojan captive, Andromaque, metaphorically inflicts the very tortures he has visited upon her compatriots. The "fiercer fires" that burn him are only one aspect of the retribution he suffers through love, and his famous line must be read in relation to the two just preceding it:

> Je souffre tous les maux que j'ai faits devant Troie.
> Vaincu, chargé de fers, de regrets consumé.
>
> (I. iv. 318-19)

Racine's point of departure seems once again to be the concetto, and it would be easy to demonstrate how the action of this play evolves a series of variations on the paradox of the captor-a-captive. We must recognize at once, however, an important difference between *Andro-*

*maque* and *Alexandre*. The paradox in the later play develops into a series
of reversals in rôles, producing ironies and complexities which bring a
depth and a reality to the characters' dilemma which is almost totally
lacking in *Alexandre*.

So it is that Andromaque not only conquers her conqueror, enchains
her captor, but her powers make the once proud and dominant Hermione, who had been chosen as Pyrrhus' bride, a prisoner herself, and
eventually a suicide. As Pyrrhus puts it, blaming fate,

> Le sort vous y voulut l'une et l'autre amener :
> Vous, pour porter des fers, elle, pour en donner.
> Cependant ai-je pris quelque soin de lui plaire ?
> Et ne dirait-on pas en voyant au contraire
> Vos charmes tout-puissants, et les siens dédaignés,
> Qu'elle est ici captive, et que vous y régnez ?
>
> (I. iv. 347–52)

As complexities further develop from the paradoxical situation,
irony and suspense are the result. Oreste, the discarded lover, enjoys
a momentary reversal of his rôle, and suspense arises as we wonder
how long this will be maintained. Pyrrhus' position shifts frequently
because of his inability to be the "parfait amant," and the precarious
teetering that results provides much of the dramatic interest of the play.
In his lack of grace, in his discomfort in the rôle of love's prisoner, we
may see an indication of Racine's tendency to return to the realism of
*La Thébaïde*; certainly the rôle aroused the displeasure of the critics.
That Pyrrhus' lack of resemblance to an Alexandre or a Porus was
deliberate is suggested by Racine's contemptuous reference to the
pastoral hero in the first Preface.[7]

A further innovation is the interpenetration of the fate of all the
characters: they rise or fall together. Oreste is maintained in his new
rôle only as long as Hermione is convinced of Pyrrhus' infidelity; when
she is convinced that the position has changed, Oreste is dashed down
from his heights, only to be promised reinstatement in return for killing
the King, and to be cast down again into despair and madness by the
wild "qui te l'a dit?" of Hermione.

---

[7]"Pyrrhus n'avait pas lu nos romans. Il était violent de son naturel. Et tous les héros ne sont pas
faits pour être des Céladons." It is true, as R. Picard points out (*Œuvres*, I, p. 1102), that some
critics had also found Pyrrhus "trop tendre et galant," and he suggests "habileté" as the reason for
Racine's replying only to those who criticized his hero for his violence. I would prefer as a
reason Racine's bias against the artificiality of the novel.

But *Andromaque* differs from the preceding plays in another and far more significant fashion. As Paul Bénichou has shown, at about the time Racine was writing this play, an atmosphere of moral pessimism, producing as an offshoot that doctrine of man's worthlessness we know as Jansenism, coincided with the triumph of monarchic absolutism and the fading of the aristocratic ideal.[8] The *Pensées* of Pascal (in so far as they concern human character), the *Maximes* of La Rochefoucauld, and similar works, reflect the prevailing tendency to deny human value. For a Pascal or a La Rochefoucauld, man was no longer the invincible creature he had been in Corneille's drama, but the weakest, the most inconstant, the most unfaithful and irrational of beings. The great abstractions, "gloire" and "vertu", so familiar to readers of seventeenth-century literature, lose their mystical and transcendent nature, the one becoming *amour-propre*, and the other, in La Rochefoucauld's celebrated phrase, mere "vice in disguise." Nature—what M. Bénichou calls "the domain of morally indifferent, brute necessity"—submerges the aristocratic sublimation of self; the concept of heroism disappears, the hero is "demolished," becoming mere man, whose every action is explainable in terms of base desires.

*Andromaque* reflects this "demolition" of the hero. The constant presence, in the memories of the characters, of the events at Troy, provides a scale against which they are measured and found wanting. In contrast with the mighty heroes of the past, Achilles and Agamemnon, Pyrrhus and Oreste diminish in stature. Racine shows this in various ways, ranging from the depiction of Pyrrhus' "heroism" at Troy as senseless brutality to the ironic use of the patronymic. In the sarcastic exchange between Pyrrhus and Oreste in the first act, the latter deliberately contrasts the exploits of Achilles and the less clearly defined rôle of the "fils d'Achille":

> ... je montre quelque joie
> De voir le fils d'Achille et le vainqueur de Troie.
> Oui, comme ses exploits nous admirons vos coups :
> Hector tomba sous lui, Troie expira sous vous.

> (I. ii. 145–8)

In the lines immediately following, Oreste stresses that to shield Hector's son from the vengeful Greeks, as Pyrrhus is doing, is unworthy

[8]P. Bénichou, *Morales du Grand Siècle*, Paris, Gallimard, 1948, pp. 97 ff.

of his great father. In reply, Pyrrhus hurls back the scornful patronymic: who would have thought, he exclaims, that such a mission would
be considered worthy of the son of Agamemnon!

As Bénichou has shown, the word "gloire" on Hermione's lips is
no more than a pretext to conceal her chagrin. But she is not alone in
her equivocations on "gloire"; Andromaque herself appeals to Pyrrhus'
"grand cœur," which, she pleads, ought to be truly magnanimous,
truly "généreux":

> Faut-il qu'un si grand cœur montre tant de faiblesse ?
> Voulez-vous qu'un dessein si beau, si généreux,
> Passe pour le transport d'un esprit amoureux ?
>
> (I. iv. 298–300)

The irony is that his action is not motivated by "générosité" or "gloire,"
but passion and self-interest.

The heroic figure degenerates further through his own remorse and
in the attitudes of the other characters toward his past actions. Pyrrhus
excuses his slaying of Priam and his family by pleading the intoxication
of victory and the excitement of the night. His exploits are valueless
because they lack a constant value in the minds of the characters: they
are seen in the light of Hermione's changing moods, brought on by
fluctuations in her amorous fortunes. At first, when all goes well
between her and her lover, she praises his deeds. They "outmatch" she
says, those of his great father. When he proposes to return to her,
she forgets vengeance and exclaims ecstatically:

> Sais-tu quel est Pyrrhus ? T'es-tu fait raconter
> Le nombre des exploits... Mais qui les peut compter ?
>
> (III. iii. 851–2)

But when he has finally abandoned her, she denounces these same acts
as cowardly and vile in an eloquent description of the slaughter of old
Priam and his women:

> Du vieux père d'Hector la valeur abattue
> Aux pieds de sa famille expirante à sa vue,
> Tandis que dans son sein votre bras enfoncé
> Cherche un reste de sang que l'âge avait glacé;
> Dans des ruisseaux de sang Troie ardente plongée;
> De votre propre main Polyxène égorgée
> Aux yeux de tous les Grecs indignés contre vous :
> Que peut-on refuser à ces généreux coups ?
>
> (IV. v. 1333–40)

Once again the contrast is clear; Achilles had killed in glorious combat the mighty Hector; it remained for Pyrrhus to slaughter Hector's helpless father. Just as the abstractions "gloire" and "vertu" break down with the revelation of how complex and unstable human emotions are, so the grandeur of Pyrrhus fades when he is seen in the changing light of Hermione's moods or Andromaque's distress.

*Bérénice*

The prefaces of both *Alexandre* and *Bérénice* boast that the plays contain the barest minimum of incident and detail. Of the first, Racine wrote that it was made of "peu d'incidents et peu de matière"; in his latter play, he says, he has made "quelque chose de rien," which, as he concludes with some arrogance, demands consummate skill. The "action simple" of Bérénice consists of a sentence from Suetonius: "Titus reginam Berenicen, cui etiam nuptias polliticus ferebatur, statim ab urbe dimisit invitus invitam"—"Titus, who had promised to wed the Queen Berenice, sent her forth from the city against both his and her will." It can be seen at once that the "invitus invitam" lends to this sentence all the earmarks of one of those "questions of love" that the habitués of seventeenth-century salons delighted in asking and answering with the utmost ingenuity.[9] This concetto, then, provides Racine with his point of departure, and his play is the subtle developing of the paradoxical situation it so succinctly describes. Once again, ironies develop. When the play opens, Titus has been ruling for a week, but he who before his rule was a free agent, a young libertine of the court, is no longer master now that he has become emperor:

> Maître de mon destin, libre dans mes soupirs,
> Je ne rendais qu'à moi compte de mes désirs.
>
> (II. ii. 457–8)

Ruler of a mighty empire, he implores pity:

> Plaignez ma grandeur importune.
> Maître de l'univers, je règle sa fortune;
> Je puis faire les rois, je puis les déposer :
> Cependant de mon cœur je ne puis disposer.
>
> (III. i. 719–22)

[9]Actually Racine combined two sentences from chapter vii of Suetonius' *Divus Titus*, achieving greater epigrammatic quality than the original.

The conventional warrior-lover's submission to his *dame*, the ruling theme of *Alexandre*, in this play bows to the exigencies of rule. From this stems a further irony: Titus, as a young debauchee who had acquired his habits at the court of Néron, has learned virtue and valour from Bérénice, and thus owes to her the very constancy and resolve upon which he must now lean to renounce her:

> Je lui dois tout, Paulin. Récompense cruelle !
> Tout ce que je lui dois va retomber sur elle !
>
> (II. ii. 519-20)

And in a new variation on the captor-a-captive conceit, Titus tells how the brave and generous deeds he performed "to conquer his conqueror," now make him worthy of the throne and the position which demands that he repudiate her. As in *Andromaque*, the love triangle of Titus-Bérénice-Antiochus offers the possibility of shifting relationships. Like Pyrrhus, though for different reasons, the despairing Titus decides to entrust his rejected mistress to his rival, and the sorrowful King of Comagène declares in a briefly hopeful moment, "J'accepte avec plaisir un présage si doux." But all hope vanishes in the triple renunciation of the dénouement.

We have seen how, in *Alexandre*, the concetto at the basis of the play's action assumes that the victory of love overshadows that of war; in Racine's "tendre" play, the mighty conqueror is the *galant homme*, happy to be vanquished by his captive. Although *Andromaque* and *Bérénice* have similar concetti or concetto-like paradoxes as points of departure, in both plays we see the beginning of a development from paradox to theme. The action no longer consists of piquant variations on the concetto, but instead, the situation based upon it is extended and deepened. That things should be as they are is questioned, and acquires tragic implications. Pyrrhus the warrior-hero is all lover, yet in *Andromaque* the situation differs from that of *Alexandre* because of the uneasiness of his position. The concetto is no longer merely a sturdy basis for the action; it is no longer taken for granted that a king *should* be lover first and hero afterward, and Pyrrhus' passion in a wider context illustrates the disintegration of the hero-concept on which an earlier society had relied.

In *Bérénice* for the first time the baroque theme of the dilemma of majesty rises to the surface. Mr. Martin Turnell has based his generally adverse criticism of this play on what is for him the characters' oppressive consciousness of the public quality of their actions, summed up in the concluding lines of the play:[10]

> Adieu : servons tous trois d'exemple à l'univers
> De l'amour la plus tendre et la plus malheureuse
> Dont il puisse garder l'histoire douloureuse.
>
> (V. vii. 1502–4)

But it is precisely through their realization of the universal purport of their actions that the characters acquire stature. Titus is obsessed with his need for exemplary action: "Me croyez-vous indigne," he asks,

> De laisser un exemple à la postérité
> Qui sans de grands efforts ne puisse être imité ?
>
> (IV. v. 1173–4)

And his counsellor, Paulin, promises him "the applause of the universe." For Titus, the alternative to renunciation is to become a vile spectacle before the entire world, and indeed, cries the young King, echoing Corneille's Rodrigue, you would despise me if I acceded to your wishes:

> Vous-même rougiriez de ma lâche conduite :
> Vous verriez à regret marcher à votre suite
> Un indigne empereur sans empire, sans cour,
> Vil spectacle aux humains des faiblesses d'amour.
>
> (V. vi. 1403–6)

Bérénice's parting words, then, must be taken, not as an isolated expression of overweening self-satisfaction, as Mr. Turnell suggests they should be, but in connection with Titus' frequently reiterated expression of responsibility to a universe which in a geographical and historical sense looks upon his every move for guidance. For Titus no longer belongs to himself; his renunciation, unlike the "mastery of self" of Corneille's Auguste, appears as the penalty, the pain of greatness. That Titus' responsibility rises above that of ordinary mortals is shown spatially by the contrasts between the "cabinet superbe et solitaire" where he broods, the court that surrounds it, and the wide universe

[10]M. Turnell, *The Classical Moment*, New York, New Directions, 1947, p. 191.

subject to the emperor that forms the real background against which the triangle drama is played. Yet Titus' renunciation does not, as with the Cornelian hero, involve personal fortitude, but the awareness that a king is not his own man. His mastery of the universe is tempered by the awesome responsibility hinted at in *La Thébaïde*:

> Un roi sort à l'instant de sa propre personne.
> L'intérêt du public doit devenir le sien,
> Il doit tout à l'Etat et ne se doit plus rien.
>
> (I. iii. var. 1664)

## "Awake, Poor Slave!"

### Bajazet and Phèdre

*Bajazet* and *Phèdre* each have as subject the fateful passion of a queen for one who convention and morality rule should not be the object of her love. The setting of the former is the seraglio where Bajazet is kept under close guard by order of his absent brother, Sultan Amurat, who considers him a threat to his throne. The disgruntled vizier, Acomat, has succeeded in bringing Bajazet and the Sultana, Roxane, together; Roxane has fallen in love and willingly agrees to Acomat's plan to place Bajazet on the throne as her husband. Since Amurat, before leaving for Byzantium, has given his favourite full power over his brother's life, the "aimable Bajazet" has found it politic to encourage Roxane's passion, at least verbally. But he loves Atalide and cannot bring himself to continue feigning affection for the Sultana, and so he is killed, to be followed in death by the implacable heroine.

This play seems in many ways to be a preliminary sketch for *Phèdre*, although the latter is far more complex, with its sub-themes of incest and the interplay of unnatural forces. The subject also recalls the prisoner-of-love cliché; in the first case Bajazet is Roxane's captive and is physically in her power. In the second, although Hippolyte is not Phèdre's prisoner, she inherits her husband's throne when he is reported dead, and for the brief moment of her declaration of love, she is all powerful at Troezen.

The two plays under discussion share with *Iphigénie*, at least implicitly, that fusion of biblical and classical legend which was to culminate in *Athalie*. Variations on the *Phèdre* story occur frequently in the literature of the time; Heliodorus' *Theagenes and Chariclea* is perhaps

most frequently cited in this connection. But like *Iphigénie*, which
has a biblical parallel in the sacrifice of Abraham, *Bajazet* and *Phèdre*
suggest the story of Potiphar's wife. The conflict in both French plays
is succintly stated in Bossuet's *Sermon sur l'ambition*, in his comment
on the biblical story. "Qui ne voit," he asks, "que dans cette femme la
puissance est liée bien plus fortement qu'elle n'est dans son propre
esclave?" Bossuet's whole peroration depends at this point upon the
paradox of the ruler-a-slave; he even seems to be thinking of the confession scene in *Phèdre* (which he might have known through Seneca):

Ah ! sans doute, à moins que d'avoir un front d'airain, elle avait honte en son cœur
de cette bassesse; mais sa passion furieuse lui commandait au dedans comme à un
esclave : Appelle ce jeune homme, confesse ton faible, abaisse-toi devant lui, rends-toi
ridicule. Que lui pouvait conseiller de pis son plus cruel ennemi ? C'est que sa passion
lui commande.

And he concludes his peroration with the admonition, "Eveille-toi,
pauvre esclave!"

At first glance, Bossuet's formulation suggests the concetto-paradox
of earlier plays. Yet neither *Bajazet* nor *Phèdre* has the thinness of the
underlying concetto. From both there emerges a profound theme:
the tragedy of the noble and powerful figure who is the victim of an
uncontrollable force. One is aware, moreover, of a compelling difference between the characters of these plays and those of *Andromaque* or
*Bérénice*: the agonizing lucidity with which they face the reality of
this force. Certainly, in *Andromaque*, love is destructive: Hermione's
frenzy ends in violent death and Pyrrhus lies slain by the altar. Yet
Pyrrhus' dilemma appears less tragic, since he nowhere questions the
rightness of his position as Andromaque's suitor, nor envisions any
grave consequences of his position. Hermione's love is legitimate; her
suicide the result of despair. The prisoner-of-love, the warrior-lover,
the king who must choose between kingdom and love, are involved in
melancholy and even tragic events, but true citizens of "le pays du
tendre" know that this must be so, and are consoled that thus true
lovers present "un exemple à l'univers."

In *Bajazet* and *Phèdre*, however, both heroines are agonizingly
conscious of the impossibility of their position; in both there is the
awareness that despite their power, despite the criminal nature of their
love, they must continue to act as they do. In *Bajazet*, there is a heavier

emphasis on the paradox of power and enslavement. The words "esclave," "esclavage," "puissance," and "pouvoir" recur frequently. In
Amurat's absence, Roxane has absolute power, while Bajazet is impris-
oned and disarmed; this situation, as we shall see in another chapter,
is amply reinforced by the character of the play's setting, the im-
penetrable seraglio of the Sultan. Earlier in the play, Roxane vaunts
her power to Bajazet:

> ... je tiens sous ma puissance
> Cette foule de chefs, d'esclaves, de muets,
> Peuple que dans ses murs renferme ce palais.
> (II. i. 434–6)

Yet she realizes the superior power of love, and the futility of her
claims. Almost simultaneously with her attempts to assure herself that
Bajazet will love her for the benefits she has bestowed on him, comes
the awareness that gratitude must always bow to passion, an awareness
based upon her own example:

> Et pourquoi dans son cœur redouter Atalide ?
> Quel serait son dessein ? Qu'a-t-elle fait pour lui ?
> Qui de nous deux enfin le couronne aujourd'hui ?
> Mais, hélas ! de l'amour ignorons-nous l'empire ?
> Si par quelque autre charme Atalide l'attire,
> Qu'importe qu'il nous doive et le sceptre et le jour ?
> Les bienfaits dans un cœur balancent-ils l'amour ?
> Et sans chercher plus loin, quand l'ingrat me sut plaire,
> Ai-je mieux reconnu les bontés de son frère ?
> (III. vii. 1082–90)

She is even aware that she is deceiving herself. At first she excuses her
betrayal of Amurat on the grounds that he has refused to marry;
suddenly, however, in swift revulsion she cries out:

> ... que sert-il de me justifier ?
> Bajazet, il est vrai, m'a fait tout oublier.
> (I. iii. 307–8)

It is this terrible lucidity, by which Roxane sees both her own true
motives and the futility of her hopes, that distinguishes her from earlier
heroines, like Hermione, who in her wavering, her fits of hope alternating with rage or despair, never really rises to the consciousness of
her position. Such clarity of vision subtly alters the nature of the dra-

matic irony: unlike Agrippine, the poisoner and faithless wife who expects her son to be virtuous and loyal, Roxane knows she ought really to expect nothing from Bajazet, and that human motives have their roots in passion. Such acuity of insight has the further purpose of making clear to the audience that the hero's doom is inevitable, when instead of mentioning love to Roxane, he harps continually on gratitude, the very feeling that Roxane has recognized as powerless before the onslaught of passion.[11] Yet while aware of his duplicity, Roxane cannot resist her desperate desire to believe: her agony is double because the consciousness of futility cannot abate her hopefulness, and she is carried along, providing Bajazet with one opportunity after another despite the most obvious proofs of his love for Atalide.

In *Phèdre* the central figure outshadows all the other characters, as Roxane did not. Roxane's rôle, in numbers of lines, is scarcely greater than Atalide's; Phèdre's dominates the play. The political motives remain in the plot, but they are now unobtrusive, although to some degree they serve the heroine as a pretext as they do in *Bajazet*. Phèdre, like Roxane, nourishes hope in the midst of despair and dreams of winning the hero's love in exchange for material benefits. She instructs her servant:

> Cherchons pour l'attaquer quelque endroit plus sensible...
> Œnone. Fais briller la couronne à ses yeux.
>
> (III. i. 794, 800)

But Phèdre is incapable of such calculation for long; such brittle pretexts crumble under the weight of her passion. What were mere "faiblesses" in Roxane become in Phèdre a physical and spiritual debility. Her passion takes on the power of a vital force, since from it alone springs whatever animation she shows, and in her despair she lapses into the twilight state between life and death in which we found her at the beginning of the play: "une femme mourante et qui cherche à mourir." Like Roxane, she sees clearly the hopelessness of her position,

---

[11]Cf. Bajazet's letter (IV. i. 1140–2):
> Par de nouveaux serments de ma reconnaissance,
> J'apaiserai, si je puis, son courroux;
> N'exigez rien de plus.

but where the former recognizes her betrayal of her husband as merely unscrupulous, Phèdre sees her love for Hippolyte as a monstrous taint. Both heroines lose their lucidity in the hero's presence; in the case of Roxane, pathos is achieved by her almost mechanical repetition of appeals she has earlier recognized as hopeless,

> Malgré tout mon amour, si je n'ai pu vous plaire,
> Je n'en murmure point; quoiqu'à ne vous rien taire,
> Ce même amour peut-être, et ces mêmes bienfaits
> Auraient dû suppléer à mes faibles attraits.
>
> (V. iv. 1473-6)

But that she should thus, in the midst of her distress, persist in her rationalistic argument, makes her, despite the irony, a less tragic figure than Phèdre, whose abandonment in the presence of Hippolyte is total: "J'oublie, en le voyant, ce que je viens lui dire."

Phèdre is not only a victim, she is a victim of destiny. The single theme of "passion's slave" is skilfully combined with the theme of perversion in nature we have encountered in earlier plays, and the whole appears as the mocking of man's aspirations by malevolent and universal forces. In the earlier play there is no feeling of destiny: the love affair has been instigated by the wily Acomat, and the heroine, in her exploration of every last possibility of success suggests rather a gambler frantically tossing the dice in throw after throw than a tragic heroine. In the later play, however, all the protagonists' aspirations are turned against them. Not only is the heroine destroyed by love, but Hippolyte's physical prowess, Thésée's obsession with honour, bring about their ruin and despair, so that all appear as the victims not of events, but of supernatural harassment.

## MAN AND GOD

### Iphigénie and Phèdre

In our discussion of Racine's themes, we have seen that certain ideas recur throughout, whether they are expressed in an elementary fashion and so fail to have universal application, or whether in our minds they arise out of the immediate dramatic situation to become identified with some eternal human problem. From the beginning, Racine seems to have been struck by the intensity of the emotions unleashed through family conflict. His choice of La Thébaïde as the subject of his first tragedy seems, when we consider *Britannicus, Bajazet, Mithridate,* and *Phèdre,* not so much the result of a desire to emulate Corneille's *Œdipe,* as has been suggested, but rather the outcome of a conviction that grew with the poet's experience. In support of this view, we may note that the marginal comments on Euripides' *Phoenician Maidens* in the Estienne edition read less like the record of a discovery than that of a confirmation found in the Greek play of observations he had already made about human life.[12] We have also seen that Racine is concerned with the concept of human power, its effect on the individual and those who surround him. His plays present various angles of the problem: the struggle for power at the expense of blood ties in *La Thébaïde* and *Britannicus,* the decline of royal power in *Mithridate,* the inability of power to shape emotions in *Bajazet* and *Phèdre.* One is tempted to see, in all these variations on the theme of power and frailty, the result of the dramatic dichotomy Racine and his fellow courtiers had constantly before their eyes in the person of the Sun-King, that symbol of divinity who was also a man possessed of a full assortment of human frailties.

But in none of the plays before *Iphigénie* do the motives or actions leave the human plane; even in those with Greek sources, references to the gods are hardly more than incidental, nor are they really woven into the fabric. We have already seen how, in *Phèdre,* the action acquires greater thematic depth than in *Bajazet,* with its similar structure, through the spectacle of a universal force bringing disaster to its victims.

The first tragedy which implicates the gods, *Iphigénie,* was composed three years before *Phèdre.* The story as Racine found it in his sources admitted either a tragic or a happy ending; Racine chose the latter, but ended his play with the suicide of Eriphile upon the altar, instead of Euripides' miraculous intervention of Artemis who substituted a hind for the maiden in the Greek play. In his sparing of Iphigénie, it is probable that not only the Aristotelian precepts concerning the fate of the tragic hero, but Racine's recollection of the benevolent deity's rôle in the sacrifice of Abraham strengthened his resolve not to "stain the stage," as he put it, with the blood of an innocent victim.

As the action begins, the Greeks are becalmed at Aulis. Agamemnon, having heeded the oracle which demands the death of his daughter

[12]These marginalia suggest that Racine read Euripides before writing *La Thébaïde.* For a discussion of the question, see R. C. Knight, *Racine et la Grèce,* Paris, Boivin, 1950, pp. 248–58.

in exchange for friendly winds, has sent for Iphigénie on the trumped-up pretext that she is to marry Achille. But, harried by conscience, he is now resolved to prevent Clytemnestre and Iphigénie from setting foot in Aulis, and in the first scene he despatches a messenger to meet them with his new orders. But Achille, who has been absent, arrives unexpectedly, the messenger misses the Queen's party, and Agamemnon is forced to prepare the sacrifice. In the climactic scene, which of course occurs offstage and is simply reported by messengers, Achille and his men face Agamemnon and the Greeks across the altar. Swords are unsheathed, and arrows fly, but suddenly the High Priest reveals that Eriphile is the "daughter of Helen" demanded by the oracle. She stabs herself upon the altar, as the thunder roars and the wind rises.

*Iphigénie* portrays in most striking fashion the "joug suprême"— that supreme yoke of responsibility before God under which the ruler must bow. Agamemnon is the first Racinian character to be in close relationship with the gods. He addresses them, they threaten him in dreams; he manœuvres to outwit them as he would a human adversary. Yet he is a sceptic; not so much sceptical of the gods' existence, as of their power and of the actual extent of their implication in human affairs. His conflict is not a conflict between religion and his paternal feelings, but between his desire to retain power through Iphigénie's death and his awareness of the terrible injustice of such a step. When he sends Arcas to forestall her arrival in Aulis, he tells him, "Va . . . sauve-la de ma propre faiblesse." He fears his own weakness, prompted by ambition, to resist the gods' edict, and later, when he tells his daughter how he had revoked the order for her death, he clearly shows what was at stake: "Je vous sacrifiais mon rang, ma sûreté."

When he accedes to the gods'demand, his action appears, not as the homage of a religious man, but as an appeasement of the Greek soldiers' superstition, that "zèle indiscret" of which he is so scornful. For him, as for the devious vizier of *Bajazet*, Acomat, religion is a means of manipulating the ignorant masses. It is the power of religion, rather than that of the gods, that he sees as a constant menace:

> ... la religion, contre nous irritée,
> Par les timides Grecs sera seule écoutée.

$$(I. i. 137-8)$$

In the end it is "tout le camp aveugle" with the high priest at its head, that demands the sacrifice:

> La piété sévère exige son offrande.
>
> (V. iii. 1626)

In the final scene, Agamemnon stands by the altar, his face shrouded in his cloak, in a last attempt to dissociate himself from the proceedings.

It is, however, the fatalistic Achille, rather than the rationalistic Agamemnon, who finally triumphs. Unlike the King, he is completely indifferent to the gods, and indeed realizes that too close inquiry into their purposes may be fatal; as he tells Agamemnon, "vous lisez de trop loin dans le secret des dieux." In his famous declaration of independence, while acknowledging the power of divine forces, he claims the right to pursue his destiny regardless of divine edict. His words are spoken with all the assurance of a hero who knows himself to be half divine, and who does not hesitate to consider himself a candidate for Olympus:

> L'honneur parle, il suffit : ce sont là nos oracles.
> Les Dieux sont de nos jours les maîtres souverains;
> Mais, Seigneur, notre gloire est dans nos propres mains.
> Pourquoi nous tourmenter de leurs ordres suprêmes ?
> Ne songeons qu'à nous rendre immortels comme eux-mêmes,
> Et, laissant faire au sort, courons où la valeur
> Nous promet un destin aussi grand que le leur.
>
> (I. ii. 258–64)

Thus oblivious of divine dictates, Achille stands by the altar, ready to parry the sacrificial blade. And when the danger has passed, Clytemnestre's gratitude goes both to Achille and to Heaven, in equal proportion:

> Par quel prix, quel encens, ô ciel, puis-je jamais
> Récompenser Achille et payer tes bienfaits ?
>
> (V. vi. 1795–6)

Are we to consider then, that Achille's course, the impetuous drive toward valorous deeds, despite dire predictions and celestial warnings, is the one preferred by Racine? Certainly in the final scene the glory is all Achille's, while the rationalistic and contemplative Agamemnon has failed, and stands a pitiful figure beside the altar as Iphigénie's champion prepares to defend her. The intervention of the god in her behalf actually appears as a confirmation of Achille's stand.

In a wider sense the play is deeply fatalistic. There is frequent mention of the careers of the characters, both prior and subsequent to the action, and although the play suggests only the possibility of divine injustice, the future destruction of almost all the characters is taken for granted. The moral of the play would seem to be that expressed in the lines of Achille quoted above: unquestioning submission to fate and the pursuit of an independent course of action. Achille's earlier warning to Agamemnon is reiterated in the death of Eriphile, doomed through an Oedipodean curiosity to know her origins.

In *Iphigénie* the *potential* injustice of the gods echoes and re-echoes only to die away in Diana's benevolent thunder. To Clytemnestre's cry, "Les Dieux ordonneraient un meurtre abominable?" Racine's answer is still in the negative. He still clings to the concept that virtue must go unscathed, asking, "quelle apparence que j'eusse souillé la scène par le meurtre d'un personne aussi vertueuse et aussi aimable?" The gods cannot claim an innocent victim; to deserve her fate, Eriphile must betray the heroine, and die by her own hand of unrequited love.

In *Phèdre*, Racine takes a further step; the gods destroy both the guilty Phèdre and the innocent Hippolyte. The mythological apparatus is complete. Phèdre is the descendant of Helios, on whose line Venus has sworn vengeance; Hippolyte's purity and chastity are sacred to Diana, but his equestrian prowess brings him under the aegis of Neptune, who is also his father's protecting deity. His wife and son destroyed, Thésée is left to ponder the god's perfidy; as Leo Spitzer has shown, the play might have as its theme a parody of Vergil's line, "timeo deos et dona ferentes."[13] The gods crush those whom they favour most. In this light the dramatic rightness of the rendezvous of Hippolyte and Aricie at the temple of his ancestors, a temple where sacred oaths are taken, becomes at once apparent; it is the final irony that Hippolyte should meet his death near the cemetery of his ancestors, in the shadow of a temple sacred to all the gods, on whose protection he had called just before setting out. It is the gods in concert that destroy hero and heroine and betray Thésée; Venus and Neptune make perfidious answers to the prayers of Phèdre and Thésée; Diana replies not at all.

[13]Leo Spitzer, *Linguistics and Literary History*, Princeton University Press, 1948, p. 92.

## Esther and Athalie

*Esther* is a slight play, rather quickly passed over by most critics, who have been content to reiterate Racine's own deprecating judgment of it as "une espèce de poème où le chant fut mêlé avec le récit." Its theme is the victory of divine over temporal force, the changing of the fierce Assuérus, "le lion rugissant," into "un agneau paisible." Racine has grafted somewhat precariously on to the biblical story the familiar love conceit of the captor-a-captive:

> Le fier Assuérus couronne sa captive,
> Et le Persan superbe est aux pieds d'une Juive !
>
> (I. i. 27–8)

But the beauty of the heroine now appears as the instrument of divine, rather than temporal, power. This power is demonstrated in the two climactic scenes which provide the chief dramatic interest. In the first, Esther comes unsummoned into the monarch's presence, to plead for the Jews, knowing that if he fails to extend his sceptre for her kiss, she must die. In the second scene, confronting Aman in the presence of the King, she reveals her Jewish origin, and although she receives no direct reply from the King (surely a structural error) he condemns her enemy to death.

In the first of the two scenes, as she appears, the King cries out in anger at the intrusion, but when she faints, his wrath vanishes, and he promises to grant her wish, declaring that she is "du cœur d'Assuérus souveraine maîtresse." Her beauty only *seems* to affect the King; in reality the divine power alone inspires his favour:

> De mes faibles attraits le roi parut frappé.
> Il m'observa longtemps dans un sombre silence;
> Et le ciel, qui pour moi fit pencher la balance,
> Dans ce temps-là sans doute agissait sur son cœur.
>
> (I. i. 70–3)

And although Esther's grateful reply to the King is another formulation of the captive-a-captor concetto,

> Hé ! se peut-il qu'un roi craint de la terre entière,
> Devant qui tout fléchit et baise la poussière,
> Jette sur son esclave un regard si serein,
> Et m'offre sur son cœur un pouvoir souverain ?
>
> (II. vii. 661–4)

her conquest of the conqueror is shown, not as the triumph of passion, but as the victory of the weak over the powerful, the triumph of docility over ferocity that symbolizes the conquest of the temporal by the divine. Words like "docile," "timide," "faible," "innocent," "sereins," "paisible," contrast with "puissant," "majesté," "terrible," "fier," "sévère," "colère." The paradox of docility in power is expressed by Assuérus, who calls Esther's beauty "doux et puissants attraits."

So in *Esther*, the love conceit, as in the poems of St. John of the Cross, or in Corneille's *Théodore*, expresses the triumph of divine love; Esther, the concubine, is only the docile instrument by which God transforms the ferocious oriental despot, so that "tel qu'un ruisseau docile," he "obéit à la main qui détourne son cours."

The theme of *Athalie* is the renewal, the revitalizing of the race through divine intervention; it centres around the ancient myth of cleansing and rebirth through the death of a sacrificial victim. Racine says in his Preface that the events of the plot were supposed to have taken place on some unnamed holy day, and that he has chosen Pentecost, the festival of the harvest, because it permitted him to give some variety to the songs of the Chorus. These songs, it is true, celebrate and reiterate God's bounty, the fruits of the earth and its beauty, but I think we may go beyond the playwright's explanation to see a significant link between the sacrifice of Pentecost, when the first fruits of the harvest are offered up, and the killing of Athalie, which assumes ritual proportions. In the play, God's intervention is made to depend on the action of the protagonists, the divine power remaining suspended until the victim has been offered up. This abstention is summed up in the first scene when Abner declares that God has withdrawn from the Hebrews: "Il voit sans intérêt leur grandeur terrassée . . . ." The Ark of the Covenant is silent, the miracles have ceased. But the way for the return of God to the people is open: their sacrifices, their customary observation of the law, have become perfunctory and inadequate; they must gird themselves for a battle of the faith to be followed by a sacrifice which will by then have acquired full meaning:

> Du zèle de ma loi que sert de vous parer ?
> Par de stériles vœux pensez-vous m'honorer ?
> Quel fruit me revient-il de tous vos sacrifices ?

*Ai-je besoin du sang des boucs et des génisses?*
*Le sang de vos rois crie et n'est point écouté.*
*Rompez, rompez tout pacte avec l'impiété,*
*Du milieu de mon peuple exterminez les crimes,*
*Et vous viendrez alors m'immoler des victimes.*

(I. i. 85–92)

Only Joad is aware that God's intervention awaits the people's action: "Il sait quand il lui plaît, faire éclater sa gloire." His "profond silence" will be broken when the signal of battle is given; only then will His arm, "pour un temps suspendu," fall upon His enemies.

The theme of revival and resuscitation is linked to metaphors of vegetation. Abner calls the royal line of Judah "cet arbre séché jusque dans les racines." The young King Joas, "chère et dernière fleur d'une tige si belle," who has been kept hidden in the temple for eight years, will emerge as from out of the tomb in answer to Abner's disbelief. Joad's parting words at the end of the first scene are more than an announcement of dawn; they suggest the glow of the warm sun, in which a revived Juda is burgeoning:

Allez : pour ce grand jour il faut que je m'apprête,
Et du temple déjà l'aube blanchit le faîte.

(I. i. 159–60)

Symbolizing the relationship of God and His people is the contrast between, on the one hand, Abner and Josabet, united in their fear of the temporal power of Athalie, and their doubt of divine intervention, and on the other hand, the High Priest, with his unswerving faith. Joad's certainty is based on his prophetic awareness that resuscitation is at hand, that the reappearance of Israel in its former glory is part of a God-willed cycle. In this faith in divine control of human events, in the immeshing of human activities with the divine plan, lies the essential difference between Racine's attitude toward deity or supernatural force in this and the earlier plays. In *Iphigénie*, Achille's indifference toward the prophecies seems to have the playwright's endorsement. Agamemnon, like the sceptic who might accept Pascal's wager, wavers between attempts to outwit or ignore the gods, and bitter submission to their "injustice." *Phèdre* distils and clarifies the idea of the perfidy of the gods nascent in *Iphigénie*. But the clash of deities in *Phèdre* represents the disastrous opposition of forces unleashed in the universe; the horrible granting of Thésée's prayer is evidence of the irony of man's fate as a subject of these forces, and the course of Achille still appears as the soundest alternative.

*Athalie*, however, not only posits the need for faith in the one God of the universe, but it stresses that man is incapable of foreseeing, without God, the portent of his actions. Joad's words of remonstrance to Josabet when she loses hope on hearing that a formidable army is surrounding the temple, evoke the history of the race, inextinguishable through the will of God alone, subject to defeats and disasters, and now once more resurgent. For the temple that will be the scene of regeneration, the sanctuary where the flower of David has grown in tomb-like darkness and secrecy, stands upon the very mountain where Abraham stood willing to sacrifice his son, although fully aware of the divine promise that his line would survive:

> Et quand Dieu, de vos bras l'arrachant sans retour,
> Voudrait que de David la maison fût éteinte,
> N'êtes-vous pas ici sur la montagne sainte
> Où le père des Juifs sur son fils innocent
> Leva sans murmurer un bras obéissant,
> Et mit sur un bûcher ce fruit de sa vieillesse,
> Laissant à Dieu le soin d'accomplir sa promesse,
> Et lui sacrifiant, avec ce fils aimé,
> Tout l'espoir de sa race, en lui seul renfermé ?
>
> (IV. v. 1436–44)

The unquestioning faith of an Abraham could not have been matched by Agamemnon in a similar situation; the latter, we remember, analyses the god's command as pure caprice: "tes oracles sans doute ont voulu m'éprouver." An Abraham or a Joad could only reason thus after the fact.

*Athalie* seems thus to abandon reason in favour of faith; to demonstrate the feebleness and aimlessness of rational seventeenth-century man before the divinity that shapes his ends. The frustration of a single passionate character, as expressed in Phèdre's "Comme on voit tous ses vœux l'un l'autre se détruire" assumes a wider scope, broadening, in the dramatist's gaze over the centuries, to reveal an endless panorama of man's persecution, regeneration, falling away from God, and return to Him.

This shifting of the interest from the tragic character to the race itself and to the successive eras through which the race must pass had begun to become apparent in the earlier plays. The increased distance between spectator and play which this diminishing in stature and stress on divine instrumentality produces, accounts, in part at least, for the "Greek" quality in *Athalie*, and is far more important than the structural innovations which Racine admitted having drawn from Greek drama.

But if a gradual change in emphasis between *Britannicus* and *Athalie* can be discovered through an examination of the themes, a similar development is evident in Racine's structure, which everywhere reinforces and underlines his themes. It will be the purpose of chapter II to examine this aspect of Racinian tragedy.

# II. THE UNITIES OF TIME AND PLACE

HISTORIES of French seventeenth-century drama give unfailing prominence to the "rules" to which dramatists were subject. It has become traditional to point out that the first great playwright, Corneille, proved an uneasy thrall, and of this his own jealous allusions to the "freedom" of novelists have frequently been adduced as proof. Racine, on the contrary, so the story goes, was able to adapt himself effortlessly to these shackles chiefly because his themes were psychological, while Corneille's were full of action, *espagnolisant*, impatient of constraint, and so on. It is interesting to find even André Gide, whose comments on great writers are so often incisive, reiterating this view in so far as it concerns Racine:

Quelles œuvres n'eût-il pas produites si son génie eût pu se donner libre cours, ne se soumettre à d'autres lois que celles qu'il se serait données lui-même? Question vaine. Et l'on peut se demander tout aussi bien, tout aussi vainement : qu'eût donné Shakespeare dans la contrainte ? Mieux vaut penser que la contrainte convenait au génie de Racine, tandis que celui de Shakespeare n'eût peut-être pas gagné en perfection ce qu'il aurait perdu en aisance.[1]

Vain indeed the question is, as Gide acknowledges, but perhaps for other than the reason he advances. His remark is significant, however, because readers of Shakespeare and Racine often have made similar conjectures: if only Racine had had Shakespeare's freedom! The point that I shall try to make in the following pages is not that Racine's genius bowed gracefully beneath the yoke of superimposed rules, through some quirk of personality or because of his subject-matter, but rather that he assimilated and transformed dramatic convention so as to produce a drama particularly his own.

Actually the picture of Shakespeare the unconventional, the "barbarous," firmly fixed in French minds since Voltaire, is exaggerated because it fails to go beneath the surface. Shakespeare may have cried out against the limited range of his stage in the Prologue to *Henry V*,

[1]André Gide, *Journal* (1939–42), Paris, Gallimard, 1946, pp. 138–9.

but he nevertheless submitted to a framework of convention, and indeed one might say that he could scarcely have written without it.[2] In a way, he even had his *bienséances*. Earthy remarks could be put in the mouths of eye-rolling nurses and servant-girls, but not young ladies; when Ophelia sings her bawdy song of Saint Valentine's day, she is mad. One would never say that Shakespeare makes her mad so she can sing that song; her madness stems naturally from the action, but the marvellous thing is that he gave her the song at this juncture. Its content startles us because of the break-down that the bawdy words on virgin lips reveal.

But for our purpose here, it is revealing to consider the effect of an action in Shakespeare which is not dictated by any convention. It is well known that the dramatic proprieties in France—*les bienséances*—frowned upon onstage death.[3] Shakespeare bowed to no such rules, but in *Macbeth*, Duncan is murdered behind the scenes. Certain tangible effects result from this concealment of a violent action from the eyes of the spectators. The differing descriptions of the King as he lies dead increase the tension in various ways. There is first of all the strained quality, the "studied hypocrisy" of Macbeth's own speech.[4] This ornate language reveals here and elsewhere in the play, the speaker's weakness, the shattering effect of the crime upon his whole being, since such artifice denotes a failure to come to grips with reality. His wife's grim words, with their callous pun, offer the contrast of her much harder fibre, and lastly, in their plain grief, Macduff and Lenox react like the representatives of sanity and order that they are.

Now had we seen Macbeth plunge the dagger, and his wife smearing blood on the hands of the sleeping grooms, our concentration upon these different accounts would have had to be shared with our remembrance of the scene as we had watched it on the stage; the contrasts would have been blunted. With the murder chamber located offstage, the deed itself, the dead King, and the frightened grooms remain, as it is proper they should, in the grey background, abstract entities.

That Duncan's death occurs offstage thus produces a specific dramatic effect. In Shakespeare offstage death is infrequent; in Racine it is the

[2]See M. C. Bradbrook, *Themes and Conventions of Elizabethan Tragedy*, Cambridge University Press, 1935.

[3]Racine transgressed in three instances: Atalide, in *Bajazet*; Mithridate; and Phèdre.

[4]Critics from Dr. Johnson on down have noticed this.

rule. Is this any reason why we should not consider the device as used by the French playwright on its own merits, just as we have now briefly done for Shakespeare? But the tendency in Racinian criticism has rather often been simply to label this or that element in the structure "required by the rules" and to go no further into the matter. Surely it is possible that these dramatic conventions were not encumbrances to Racine, but were simply accepted and sublimated in the course of the creative process. Believing this, let us consider those conventions which every schoolboy can quote as essential elements of seventeenth-century drama: the unities of time, place, and action.

It has always been clear that the first two meant that the dramatic action must not take more than twenty-four hours, and that it should be confined to the place represented by the setting. The third is somewhat more complex. It required that none of the several actions should be fortuitous, that the secondary plot should be so essential that to suppress it would be to obscure the main plot. The various actions had all to begin with the opening of the play and continue until the *dénouement*.[5] The first two unities answer much better than the third to the concept of the seventeenth-century rules as hindrances or checks to the playwright. I shall thus confine my discussion in this chapter to the first two, believing that ample evidence of how Racine observed the third will emerge from the book as a whole. Our consideration of the unities of time and place is concerned, not with demonstrating how scrupulously he observed them, but how he developed from them concepts of time and space which we may call peculiarly Racinian.

## UNITY OF TIME

In early seventeenth-century plays, specific references to time seem often to have been made for no other reason than to show that the rule was being observed. So in Corneille's *Horace*, Curiace says carefully that the champions of Rome and Alba will be selected "Dans deux heures au plus," and in *Le Cid*, the hero's battle with the Moors takes only three hours.

Such references are obviously self-conscious in the extreme. Similar statements of the actual length of time elapsed serve a quite different

[5]For an excellent discussion of the conventions of action, see J. Schérer, *La Dramaturgie classique en France*, Paris, Nizet, n.d., p. 91 ff.

purpose in Racine, and I shall begin our discussion of Racinian time by considering them. For the sake of convenience, they may be divided thus: references to the past (whether the pre-dramatic past, or the inter-dramatic past); references to the future (whether the interdramatic future or the post-dramatic future).

Let us begin with exact periods of time stated to have elapsed in the pre-dramatic past. In *La Thébaïde* an unusual precision is already evident. Jocaste has spent *six months* of entreaty and prayer, six months during which Polynice has been besieging Thebes. Hémon has been away *one year*; the brothers meet after a separation of *two years*. In *Andromaque* Oreste encounters Pylade after a separation of *six months*; he has waited a year to ask Hermione's final decision (II. ii. 501). Andromaque has resisted Pyrrhus for the same length of time. This kind of measurement becomes even more precise in *Britannicus*. Albine, defending Néron in the first scene, asks Agrippine:

> Depuis trois ans entiers, qu'a-t-il dit, qu'a-t-il fait
> Qui ne promette à Rome un empereur parfait ?
> Rome, depuis deux ans par ses soins gouvernée,
> Au temps de ses consuls croit être retournée.
>
> (I. i. 25–8)

In the third line of the above quotation, Racine had first written "trois ans." It has been suggested that he changed this so as not to depart too far from historical exactitude, since Nero had actually been reigning only one year at the time of Britannicus' death. But why, one feels obliged to ask, did he leave the first line untouched? It could hardly have been inadvertence when the two references occurred so close together. Furthermore, if the historical time should have been one year, why change it to two? We find the answer in a later scene, as Néron is telling Narcisse what hinders his pursuit of Junie:

> Octavie, Agrippine, Burrhus,
> Sénèque, Rome entière, et trois ans de vertus.
>
> (II. ii. 461–2)

Three years of virtue. Racine's alteration shows that of these three years, one preceded Néron's ascent to the throne. Néron goes on to mention that Octavie has prayed in vain for children for *four* years. Agrippine, who recognizes the façade for what it is, says Néron showed gratitude for *six months* only. All these references to exact periods of time seem a conscious effort to show a series of steps in Néron's immediate past leading to the dramatic action. His marriage and his exemplary conduct appear as part of the preparation for his ascending the throne.

The same careful delineation of the time of past events appears in *Bérénice*. Antiochus, the sorrowful King of Comagène, has loved in vain five years. We are told so twice within twenty lines of Act I, Scene i, and shortly afterward we learn that of those years, three have been spent in silent adulation at the court of Titus, and that for five years the love of the principals has flourished, never waning:

> Depuis cinq ans entiers chaque jour je la vois,
> Et crois toujours la voir pour la première fois.
>
> (II. ii. 545–6)

In the more recent past, Titus has just ended a week of fasting and meditation in mourning for his father, but admits that during this "retraite austère" he has thought frequently of Bérénice and the sad news he must impart to her. Once again, precise measurement of time is made:

> Vingt fois, depuis huit jours,
> J'ai voulu devant elle en ouvrir le discours.
>
> (II. ii. 473–4)

In *Bajazet*, Amurat's messenger bearing the order for the hero's death has been sent three months before; Roxane has been in love for six months. In *Mithridate* the old King's forty years of resistance to Rome are mentioned four times; when he appears for the first time he tells Arbate: "Enfin, après un an, tu me revois." His confidant tells him that Pharnace has been at Nymphée a week. The Greek army in *Iphigénie* has languished at Aulis three months and Achille has been away for a month of that time. In *Phèdre*, Thésée has not been heard from for over six months, Phèdre has fasted three days. In the religious plays, Esther has sought Elise for six months, Athalie has reigned for eight years, and for two days prior to the action has appeared distraught and fearful; Josabet has spent three days and nights in prayer.

*Britannicus* is the first play to mention the immediate past. Néron has seized Junie in the night preceding the action, and we first see this

event through Agrippine's and Britannicus' eyes, then hear Néron
tell, with sadistic relish, how he spent the time between the abduction
and daylight:

> Voilà comme, occupé de mon nouvel amour,
> Mes yeux, sans se fermer, ont attendu le jour.
>
> (II. ii. 405–6)

In *Bérénice*, the night preceding the action has flashed with the fires
of the sacrifices in celebration of Titus' elevation to the throne. Agamemnon has been forced to a decision because of Achille's unexpected
arrival "hier, avec la nuit."

References to future time as precise as these are considerably rarer,
and almost totally confined to the time within the dramatic action.
The murder of Britannicus takes place at night, so that the action of the
play lasts almost a full twelve hours. Junie has reason to fear the coming
of night. She wonders, "Si . . . Néron avait choisi la nuit pour cacher
sa vengeance," although the Emperor has declared, "Avant la fin du
jour je ne le craindrai plus." Titus' marriage to Bérénice may take
place, we learn, "avant la nuit." Acomat hopes that

> aujourd'hui
> Bajazet se déclare, et Roxane avec lui.
>
> (I. i. 96–7)

Calchas announces mysteriously that in an hour, the gods will be
appeased, and Eriphile confirms the time of the sacrifice: "Quand je
devais comme elle expirer dans une heure." At the beginning of
*Athalie*, Joad gives the hour of reckoning in a periphrasis that has the
effect of concentrating our attention on the exact time:

> quand l'astre du jour
> Aura sur l'horizon fait le tiers de son tour,
> Lorsque la troisième heure aux prières rappelle,
> Retrouvez-vous au temple...
>
> (I. i. 153–6)

There are a few exact references to time beyond the play. Bérénice
thinks of a future without Titus in terms of months and years:

> Dans un mois, dans un an, comment souffrirons-nous,
> Seigneur, que tant de mers me séparent de vous ?
>
> (IV. v. 1113–14)

Mithridate's grandiose plans for a march on Rome include precise notation of the time required for his exploits, ironically based on the swiftness of his past achievements. Have not his people seen him

> ... chassant les Romains de l'Asie étonnée,
> Renverser en un jour l'ouvrage d'une année ?
> (III. i. 771–2)

So he will cross the Black Sea in two days, and accumulating allies as he goes, reach the capitol in three months; he will launch his vessels, like catapults, with the dawn. In *Esther*, the Jews are to be massacred in ten days' time; Esther orders three days of fasting. In *Athalie*, Abner, unaware that Joad's plans are on the point of materializing, promises to garrison the temple, "demain, dès cette nuit."

But if past and future are summoned up by precise measurement in hours, days, months, and years, other devices, no less prominent, constantly cast us backward into the past, or forward into the future. For the past, these are appeals to the memory, either of audience or protagonists, by means of recitals or mnemotechnic tricks; for the future, predictions or prophecies, premonitions or foreshadowings, voiced by the protagonists or hinted at by various poetic means.

Appeals to memory are of course an important element of the exposition. One of the characters will begin, "Do you remember?" or simply, "You remember..." and proceed to summarize events leading up to the play, or to describe scenes of the past. In *Andromaque*, Hermione's poignant lines recalling the awakening of her love for Pyrrhus are of this type:

> Tu t'en souviens encor, tout conspirait pour lui.
> Ma famille vengée, et les Grecs dans la joie,
> Nos vaisseaux tout chargés des dépouilles de Troie.
> (II. i. 464–6)

In the same play, Oreste's evocation of the past in the first scene (ll. 38–104) deserves rather close study because it reveals for the first time Racine's ability to lend movement and variety to his description of past events. The sixty-eight lines fall into five recognizable divisions: the first eighteen come as a direct answer to his friend's reproach, "Vous me trompiez, seigneur." They are a revelation, the baring of one's soul that can only be made to a bosom friend. Directly addressing Pylade throughout, Oreste asks: "T'ai-je jamais caché mon cœur et mes désirs?" and continues,

> Tu vis naître ma flamme...
> Tu vis mon désespoir et tu m'as vu depuis
> Traîner de mers en mers ma chaîne et mes ennuis.
>
> (I. i. 40, 43–4)

He goes on to speak of his friend's faithfulness, his efforts to protect him, how he alone knew of his wrath at Hermione's love for Pyrrhus.

The second part of the speech goes beyond the recapitulation of events known to both, beyond the expanding and confirming of Pylade's protest, "Vous l'abhorriez," to a summary of events in the more recent past. The third part (arrival in Greece), the fourth part (alarm of the Greeks and revelation of the survival of Astyanax), and the fifth part (Oreste's embassy and its aim), follow swiftly one upon the other.

The straight narrative is linked by pauses in which, as it were, the speaker turns from his story to his listener. As we shall see later, this implication of the listener was to become characteristic of Racine's *récits*.

Furthermore, as Oreste's story continues, Racine effects an increase in the tempo by a skilful juxtaposition of the past definite and present indicative tenses. The verbs in the first twenty-eight lines are all in the past definite; a series of historic actions promptly succeed one another. But when the speaker reaches the fourth part, the alarm of the Greeks, he switches to the present historic; a tense which lends feverish rapidity to the narrative. This continues for eighteen lines. Then, following the words

> Je triomphe; et pourtant je me flatte d'abord
> Que la seule vengeance excite ce transport,
>
> (I. i. 83–4)

which describe his strange and secret joy at the Greeks' distress, the past definite is resumed and thereby the lines in which he reveals awareness of his true motives, his helpless enslavement to Hermione, achieve a dying fall:

> Mais l'ingrate en mon cœur reprit bientôt sa place :
> De mes feux mal éteints je reconnus la trace.
>
> (I. i. 85–6)

Oreste's historical reconstruction now acquires a two-dimensional character; he in fact *recollects* the *recollection* of his dormant passion leaping into flame. After these four lines, a reflective interruption of the *récit*, the present tense reappears, and the tempo, which had fallen, picks up again with the linking word "Ainsi," the events following one another in rapid sequence:

> Ainsi de tous les Grecs *je brigue* le suffrage,
> On *m'envoie* à Pyrrhus : *j'entreprends* ce voyage,
> *Je viens* voir si l'on peut arracher de ses bras
> Cet enfant...
>
> (I. i. 89–92)

The dual purpose of his visit, the one motive so far transcending the other, is revealed by the echoing "je viens" seven lines later:

> ... je viens chercher Hermione en ces lieux.
>
> (I. i. 99)

The *récit* ends with a return to the direct address, and the command "dis-moi ce qui se passe."

Our analysis of Oreste's speech shows that in his descriptions of events preceding the dramatic action, Racine is concerned, not simply with summing up the events of the past, but with indicating a *movement in time*, the progression from one happening to another. His use of varying tempi, by alternating present and past tenses, lends depth and complexity to the spectacle of the past. We receive the impression, not only of a series of events, but of a simultaneity of events in the course of Oreste's long-lasting love, of a past recollected within the past. The present tense is also skilfully used to bring the action up through the various layers of narrative to the dramatic present, with Oreste's final "J'aime," (l. 99) becoming an affirmation of his earlier, submerged, "je sentis que je l'aimais toujours" (l. 88).

But Oreste's evocation of the past, of course, functions first and foremost as part of the exposition. Throughout *Andromaque*, memories of the past stir constantly, and, for dramatic purposes, memories of the same event often wear different colours. Thus, against Oreste's memory of Hector and the might of Troy:

> Ne vous souvient-il plus, Seigneur, quel fut Hector ?
> Nos peuples affaiblis s'en souviennent encor,
>
> (I. ii. 155–7)

are set in reply the magnificent lines in which Pyrrhus evokes the ashes of a devastated city:

> Je ne vois que des tours que la cendre a couvertes,
> Un fleuve teint de sang, des campagnes désertes,
> Un enfant dans les fers...
>
> (I. ii. 201-3)

We have already seen how Hermione first praises, then denounces, Pyrrhus' exploits; in turn, Andromaque offers her version of the bloody events at Troy. "Dois-je les oublier," she asks piteously, "s'il ne s'en souvient pas?" The obsessive phrase "Dois-je oublier?" is repeated twice; the spectacle of the conqueror, in the midst of the eternal night of Troy pierced by flames and the shouts and moans of victors and vanquished, has fixed itself ineradicably upon her mind: "Voilà," she recalls, "Voilà comme Pyrrhus vint s'offrir à ma vue."

A further appeal by Céphise summons the memory of Andromaque's last interview with Hector in an example, unique in Racine, of a scene from the pre-dramatic past which relates, not only events, but the actual words of a speaker:

> Ah ! de quel souvenir viens-tu frapper mon âme !...
> Hélas ! je m'en souviens, le jour que son courage
> Lui fit chercher Achille, ou plutôt le trépas,
> Il demanda son fils, et le prit dans ses bras :
> *Chère épouse, dit-il, en essuyant mes larmes,*
> *J'ignore quel succès le sort garde à mes armes;*
> *Je te laisse mon fils pour gage de ma foi :*
> *S'il me perd, je prétends qu'il me retrouve en toi.*
> *Si d'un heureux hymen la mémoire t'est chère,*
> *Montre au fils à quel point tu chérissais le père.*
>
> (III. viii. 1014, 1018-26)

It is through these constantly varied versions of the spectacle of Troy in conflict and defeat that Racine shows to what extent his characters are haunted by the past. The obsessive past has another rôle: that it should, in all its glory and awesomeness, take such precedence over the frenzied and passionate present of the play itself, underlines the theme of the disintegration of the hero.

There are further products of this multivalency of past events and scenes. Like the different letters, which, in the epistolary novel, can present various facets of a single character or action, such "prismatic" treatment endows the past with depth and vitality. Just as, paradoxically, the presentation of a character or event through the eyes of different letter-writers may convey a stronger illusion of reality than a "realistic" description by Flaubert or Zola—since no character or event is ever seen in exactly the same way by different persons—so Racine's different versions of the pre-dramatic past lend it a reality and a prominence hardly secondary in importance to the dramatic action itself. This technique, revealed in *Andromaque*, recurs in succeeding tragedies, especially those which draw on Greek or Roman legend. Agrippine, moments after *Britannicus* begins, recalls the first sign of Néron's coldness with the words, "Ce jour, ce triste jour, frappe encor ma mémoire." Néron's three years of virtue are seen very differently by the characters who discuss them, and the magnificent speech of Agrippine to her son in Act IV consists of a lengthy "harking back" intended to awaken his sense of gratitude, evoking with startling effect the atmosphere of intrigue, corruption, and fear in the Roman court.

In *Bérénice*, Paulin recalls the history of the ill-timed amours of Roman emperors and heroes; Titus, under Bérénice's guidance, has cast off the corrupting influence of Nero's court, and now attempts to extirpate the imprint left by

> Monstres dont à regret je cite ici le nom,
> Et qui ne conservant que la figure d'homme,
> Foulèrent à leurs pieds toutes les lois de Rome.
>
> (II. ii. 398–400)

Of all the plays *Bajazet* contains the fewest references to the past; here the playwright commanded nothing like the wide knowledge he had of Greek and Roman history, nor could he count on the evocative power of proper names as in his plays drawn from classic sources. There is of course the necessary summary of events leading to the action: the Sultan's order, Acomat's planning, the complexities of the Bajazet–Atalide–Roxane triangle. The mystery of the seraglio, with its rigorous laws; the marriage customs of the sultans; a few titles or functions such as "vizir," "sultan," "muets": these establish the atmosphere. But there is no hint of a succession of events stretching far back beyond the opening scene.

In *Mithridate*, however, the vista of the past serves to contrast the old King's former glory and his present eclipse:

> Jusqu'ici la fortune et la victoire mêmes
> Cachaient mes cheveux blancs sous trente diadèmes.
> Mais ce temps-là n'est plus.
>
> (III. v. 1039–41)

Xipharès long speech in the expository first scene sketches events in a past that knew only victory for his father—

> Tout reconnut mon père; et ses heureux vaisseaux
> N'eurent plus d'ennemis que les vents et les eaux —
>
> (I. i. 77–8)

but a past that for him, because of Monime's engagement to the King, was "ce temps odieux."

Besides the events preceding Xipharès' arrival we hear a hint of Mithridate's cruelty in a brief reference to his earlier treatment of his concubines:

> Tu sais combien de fois ses jalouses tendresses
> Ont pris soin d'assurer la mort de ses maîtresses.
>
> (I. i. 87–8)

Another event in the past, brought into sharp focus by two different views, is Mithridate's defeat by Pompée. We hear first Xipharès' expository statement, quite devoid of colour or surprise, with its interjected "en effet" giving it a matter-of-fact quality:

> Rome en effet triomphe, et Mithridate est mort.
> Les Romains, vers l'Euphrate, ont attaqué mon père,
> Et trompé dans la nuit sa prudence ordinaire.
> Après un long combat, tout son camp dispersé
> Dans la foule des morts, en fuyant, l'a laissé,
> Et j'ai su qu'un soldat dans les mains de Pompée
> Avec son diadème a remis son épée.
>
> (I. i. 2–8)

The King's words at the beginning of II. iii. balance perfectly the earlier report, but now the same scene is presented with a richness of tone, with a new combination of visual quality and evocation; the soldiers' helpless struggle in the dark suggests the futility of Mithridate's own perseverance in a fight in which valour counts for little. His words,

"Que pouvait la valeur dans ce trouble funeste?" could serve as a summary of his own plight, in which will and bravery are insufficient arms against old age and the might of Rome:

> Pompée a saisi l'avantage
> D'une nuit qui laissait peu de place au courage.
> Mes soldats presque nus, dans l'ombre intimidés,
> Les rangs de toutes parts mal pris et mal gardés,
> Le désordre partout redoublant les alarmes,
> Nous-mêmes contre nous tournant nos propres armes,
> Les cris que les rochers renvoyaient plus affreux,
> Enfin toute l'horreur d'un combat ténébreux :
> Que pouvait la valeur dans ce trouble funeste ?
> Les uns sont morts, la fuite a sauvé tout le reste;
> Et je ne dois la vie, en ce commun effroi,
> Qu'au bruit de mon trépas que je laisse après moi.
>
> (II. iii. 439–50)

But the dark scene of Pompée's victory is crowded out by the exalted crescendo of Mithridate's speech to his sons, in which he announces his plans for a descent on Rome (III. i. 755–862). The accumulated references to the past suggest that the King, by reiterating old successes, is attempting to thrust aside the unhappy present. So, after the resigned statement, "je fuis: ainsi le veut la fortune ennemie," comes the admonitory, "Mais vous savez trop bien l'histoire de ma vie." The twenty lines that follow attempt to prove the temporary nature of the statement "je fuis". More than once, he says, the enemy has been deceived by his flight, and he has reversed "en un jour l'ouvrage d'une année." A new effort in place of the old is called for—"d'autres temps, d'autres soins,"—and finally, the pathetic "je fuis" of the first lines has become the defiant "moi seul, je leur résiste."

By thus evoking "l'histoire de ma vie," Mithridate turns awareness of his own position, defeat and flight, into the wishful concept of resistance; the memory of strategic withdrawals that became victories transforms in his imagination his actual predicament. Once again references to the pre-dramatic past serve a wide dramatic purpose, revealing the tragic self-delusion of a king who is in reality only "un chef de malheureux bannis," as Pharnace insinuates. As we have shown elsewhere, this clinging to the past forms the core of the play's theme, with the pursuit of victory-in-love a desperate substitute for victory-at-arms; Mithridate's final appeal to Monime is to see him, not as he is, but as he was:

> Ne me regardez point vaincu, persécuté,
> Revoyez-moi vainqueur et partout redouté.
>
> (IV. iv. 1293–4)

We turn now to the "Greek" plays, *Iphigénie* and *Phèdre*. In these plays, the spectacle of the past is not simply a backward vision related to the fortunes of the characters, as in *Mithridate* and *Britannicus*. The drama now unfolds against the wide panorama of Homeric legend. In *Iphigénie*, the ordering of the past into successive layers, still tentative in *Andromaque*, has now become a part of the play's action. To illustrate how this has come about, we may begin by examining the famous opening scene of *Iphigénie*, where Racine's modifications stand out all the more clearly since he followed his source in Euripides so closely.

In both the Greek and the French play, the action begins before dawn, with the King awakening his servant. In both, the action takes less than twenty-four hours, so that unity of time is observed. The first significant change we note is Racine's evoking of different areas in the past: distant, recent, and immediate. These allusions take two forms. They are first expounded from the external point of view of the servant, Arcas, in the form of remonstrances at Agamemnon's bitter reference to his "joug superbe," which prompts the servant to mention the divine origins of the King, his high position as leader of the Greeks, Achille's love for his daughter, and the becalming of the fleet. The recent past—the time elapsed since the attempted departure from Aulis—is specifically given as three months.

This impervious, somewhat rationalistic recital is broken off when Arcas notices the letter in the King's hand, and asks, "Votre Oreste au berceau va-t-il finir sa vie?" locating in time the point at which Agamemnon has arrived in his career. In his answer, the King elaborates and extends each event, uncovering one by one the underlying causes and results, and linking his explanations to Arcas' memory by such familiar phrases of exposition as "tu te souviens du jour?" or "Tu t'en souviens?" He then tells of Calchas' prophecy, his own hesitation followed by the decision to send for his daughter after the gods have threatened him with destruction, and finally, Achille's unexpected return to Aulis only a few hours earlier.

The events prior to the dramatic action, which is precipitated by Achille's return, appear, in these double references to the past, as a series of steps on the way to tragedy at Aulis: the affront to the Greeks, their assembling and attempted departure, the summoning of Iphigénie, and the arrival of Achille.[6] In the same manner, at the beginning of I. iii, Ulysse once again recalls and interprets the events preceding the three months of inaction at Aulis.

In *Phèdre*, as in *Iphigénie*, the memory of the earlier careers of the protagonists colours the dramatic canvas. Thésée's exploits, heroic and amorous, enrich the exposition with some of the most famous gems in the Racinian lode: "la Crète fumant du sang du Minotaure"; "Salamine témoin des pleurs de Péribée"; "Ariane aux rochers contant ses injustices." In vain Œnone urges her mistress to forget the fatal memories of the past:

> Oublions-les, Madame; et qu'à tout l'avenir
> Un silence éternel cache ce souvenir.
>
> (I. iii. 251-2)

But the harking back to her fatal encounter with Hippolyte continues, a shrill threnody with its recurrent "i" sounds, suggesting her obsession, her *delectatio* of the past, into which she projects us with the conjurer's mystic formula "mon mal vient de plus loin."

> Mon repos, mon bonheur semblait être affermi;
> Athènes me montra mon superbe ennemi.
> Je le vis, je rougis, je pâlis à sa vue;
> Un trouble s'éleva dans mon âme éperdue;
> Mes yeux ne voyaient plus, je ne pouvais parler;
> Je sentis tout mon corps et transir et brûler.
>
> (I. iii. 271-6)

In the confession scene, her veiled allusions to her passion take the form of a series of reproaches that the past did not turn out differently: her desperation, her inability to accept reality are nowhere more effectively demonstrated than in the plaintive "why's" and "would have's" of these lines:

> Il [Thésée] avait votre port, vos yeux, votre langage,
> Cette noble pudeur colorait son visage,

[6]This "harking back" in the exposition scene, first by the servant (external, rationalistic), then by the master (internal, analytic), reminds one of the baroque "echo" technique which occurs so frequently on the linguistic level in Racinian tragedy. Cf. H. Hatzfeld, "A Clarification of the Baroque Problem in the Romance Literatures," *CL*, I (1949), pp. 130-1.

Lorsque de notre Crète il traversa les flots...
Que faisiez-vous alors ? Pourquoi sans Hippolyte,
Des héros de la Grèce assembla-t-il l'élite ?
Pourquoi, trop jeune encor, ne pûtes-vous alors
Entrer dans le vaisseau qui le mit sur nos bords ?
Par vous aurait péri le monstre de la Crète...
Et Phèdre, au labyrinthe avec vous descendue,
Se serait avec vous retrouvée ou perdue.

(II. v. 641-3, 645-9, 661-2)

In *Phèdre* it is the past which haunts and fascinates the heroine; it is the past which she condemns and which has condemned her. The lucidity with which she sees that past events might have followed a quite different pattern increases our awareness of the inevitability of her fall, and the triumph of the "feu fatal à tout mon sang."

The aura of legend was lacking for the biblical plays; in *Esther*, the scarcity of references to the past may in part account for the play's episodic quality. In *Athalie*, however, an important use is made of allusions to the history of the Jews, the primary purpose being to show the extent of their present degradation by comparison with their past glory. Abner, in the first scene, is almost a lone observer of "l'usage antique et solennel," and he prefaces his memory of the festivities of the pentecostal celebration with a sigh: "Que les temps sont changés!" Joad's violent reproof of Abner's defeatism and despair consists of a series of allusions to miraculous events in the *recent* past: "Des prodiges fameux accomplis *en nos jours*." These are the disgrace of the Israelite kings, the destruction of Ahab and the horrible death of Jezebel, the flame upon the altar, the three years of drought, and the resuscitation of the dead by the prophet Elisha. Joad concludes this awesome list by summoning Abner to see in it a proof that his God has lost none of His power, and is indeed, "Un Dieu tel aujourd'hui qu'il fut dans tous les temps." The miracles of the past are evoked then, not merely as evidence of the former Israelite glory, but as an illustration of God's might, and thus as a prediction of what is about to occur. Rather than providing the poetic aura of legend as in *Iphigénie* and *Phèdre*, or indicating a relentless march toward a final outcome, Joad's summoning up of the past shows that the tragic moment is at hand; as he says, "les temps sont accomplis." Jehovah's "bras vengeur pour un temps suspendu" is about to descend again in favour of his chosen people.

This treatment of the past serves to give the impression of a historic cycle of recurring suffering and redemption, not the tragic cycle of a series of tragic events as in *Iphigénie* and *Phèdre*. Joad's reference to the past contains a promise for the future, and as we shall see later, the stress on the future sharply decreases the finality of the play's close.

As Thierry-Maulnier has said, Jocaste's despairing cry, "Nous voici donc, hélas! à ce jour détestable" might serve as a formula for the Racinian canon.[7] The fateful and hateful day, long prepared, has arrived; the imposthume is about to break. The actual duration of the action therefore seems reduced to a minimum, what Francis Fergusson has aptly called "a pinpoint on the spectrum of action."[8] Nevertheless an illusion of duration is created by frequent references to the inter-dramatic past. These frequently take the form of *récits* describing off-stage actions shortly after they occur. The same "prismatic" effect we observed as resulting from multiple references to pre-dramatic time is obtained by these varied accounts. For example, Créon's description of the brothers' duel is preceded by Olympe's report of the same event, a report which is, however, both vague and erroneous.[9]

This "double vision" which underlines the sequence of events in time, develops in the later plays. A similar technique is employed in *Andromaque*, when Cléone reports that the wedding procession is nearing the temple, and that Oreste and the Greeks have entered it. In the next scene, Oreste begins his narrative from that point. In *Mithridate*, the time sequence is made strikingly evident by the device

[7] Thierry Maulnier, *Racine*, Paris, Gallimard, 34th ed., 1947, p. 238.

[8] Francis Fergusson, *The Idea of a Theater*, Princeton University Press, 1949, p. 53.

[9] Incidentally, this is one of the rare cases in Racine of deliberate misrepresentation, the kind of false lead that Corneille frequently used. But Racine's approach already differs from Corneille's. In *Horace*, Julie reports that Horace has taken flight, and as a result we witness the splendid wrath and despair of the old father. Such deceptions are legion in the work of the older playwright, who leaned heavily for effect on "surprises" like the one created when the report is shown to be false, and the flight a ruse. But Olympe's statement: "Le Roi n'est plus, Madame, et son frère est vain-queur," was almost true *at the time* she left the scene to make her report; the King was really dying. Créon describes the situation at the moment she left with the words, "Le Roi, qui semble mort...." and he knows that the King was not yet dead only because he has seen the outcome. Moreover, Olympe says her information comes only from "mille bruits confus"; the lack of specific quality in her narration is further increased by the use of the indefinite pronoun. Thus, even though the device of the false report is the same in both *Horace* and *La Thébaïde,* the final result in Racine's play is totally different. In the former, the anger, and then the surprise, are dramatic ends in themselves. In the latter, both the progress from vagueness to clarity and the appearance of two characters who succeed one another with different versions emphasize the sequence in time rather than the reaction of the listener.

of the two messengers sent in succession by the King to Monime. On learning of the Roman attack, he despatches Arcas with poison for Monime *at the end of Act IV*. Arcas appears in Act V, Scene ii, and as Monime is about to take the poison, the second envoy, Arbate, rushes in crying, "Arrêtez!" He then proceeds to describe the events leading to the revocation of the suicide order. But the appearance of the two envoys, one after the other, gives physical support for the impression of a continuity in time of the events that begin with the end of Act IV: the arrival of the Romans, Mithridate's resistance and mortal wound, and his command to save Monime "s'il en est temps encore."

But perhaps the most striking example of this technique of double narration occurs in *Iphigénie*, when Arcas and Ulysse relate in succession the events that have taken place at the altar. The sense of urgency is now greater than in any of the preceding plays, however, for the entire movement of the play is directed toward the altar as the scene of the climax. The two eye-witness accounts convey the rapid movement of successive events because they dovetail so completely. The death of Eriphile has taken place *after* Arcas left the altar to enlist Clytemnestre's help, as his words show when he rushes in crying: "Le fatal sacrifice est encor suspendu." Ulysse, in the following scene, echoes Arcas' account of the action before the altar, then goes on to tell of Eriphile's suicide.

Characters often recapitulate earlier onstage actions which they have witnessed, or in which they have participated. This may impart new information to one of the characters or it may recall to the audience an earlier action, thus investing it with a kind of existence independent of mere chronological sequence. An example of this is Junie's explanation to Britannicus of her actions during the scene in which Néron, the hidden witness,

> Témoin de tout notre entretien,
> D'un visage sévère examinait le mien.
>
> (III. vii. 989–90)

In this scene, the lines in which she tells how she feared even her own paleness, or how she sighed and avoided his glance—

> De combien de soupirs interrompant le cours,
> Ai-je évité vos yeux que je cherchais toujours...
> De mon front effrayé je craignais la pâleur —
>
> (III. vii. 1001–2, 1009)

are related to actual moments, already enacted before the audience in the eavesdropping scene, when Britannicus cried in despair, "Vous ne me dites rien? Quel accueil! Quelle glace!" and "Que vois-je? Vous craignez de rencontrer mes yeux?" By thus recalling the visual through the verbal, the poet increases the illusion of reality. Monime, in like fashion, tells Xipharès how she was tricked into betraying their secret:

> ... avec quelle adresse
> Le cruel est venu surprendre ma tendresse !
> Quelle amitié sincère il affectait pour vous !
> Content, s'il vous voyait devenir mon époux !
>
> (IV. ii. 1231-4)

And we recall the earlier scene in which we watched her as Mithridate exercised his "dons empoisonnés."

Although we have been concerned with this type of repetition chiefly for its effect on the time scheme, it may frequently clarify other aspects. On occasion, it helps to emphasize the isolation of the characters, their need to interpret word, gesture, or even lack of gesture. So Hermione, recasting in her soliloquy her interview with Pyrrhus, correctly sees his embarrassed silence as proof of indifference:

> L'ai-je vu se troubler et me plaindre un moment ?
> En ai-je pu tirer un seul gémissement ?
> Muet à mes soupirs, tranquille à mes alarmes,
> Semblait-il seulement qu'il eût part à mes larmes ?
>
> (V. i. 1399-1402)

But such évaluations may as easily err, with tragic results. After Phèdre's confession, Hippolyte is petrified with shock, but she takes his immobility for callousness:

> Hélas! quand son épée allait chercher mon sein,
> A-t-il pâli pour moi ? Me l'a-t-il arrachée ?
>
> (III. i. 748-9)

We are always aware when these are misunderstandings, and this increases our feeling of impotency in the face of impending catastrophe.

The repetition may also be a tool of exegesis. The double account of the altar scene in *Iphigénie*, referred to above, may also explain how Racine achieved the unusually bold personification in Arcas' line, "On se menace, on court, *l'air gémit*, le fer brille" (V. v. 1705), which one would expect rather from a Hugo, who wrote of a storm in *Masferrer*, "L'air gronde." But Racine could not have meant the storm, which only begins with the death of Eriphile. If we compare Arcas' with Ulysse's version of the abortive struggle around the altar, we see how the personification was born:

> ... Achille furieux
> Epouvantait l'armée et partageait les Dieux.
> Déjà de traits en l'air s'élevait un nuage,
> Déjà coulait le sang, prémices du carnage.
>
> (V. v. 1739–42)

"Gémir" in line 1705 means the sound of the arrows that rose in a cloud; the air "whirs" or "whines" with them. (Racine's precedent is probably Latin rather than French; in Vergil, for example, "stridere," the equivalent of "gémir," means not only "groan," or "roar," but also, when used with "sagitta," the whirring of arrow or spear through the air.)

References to the future take various forms; in seventeenth-century drama the most conventional of these are veiled predictions made through oracles or dreams, or vaguely felt premonitions of events that are to take place within the action. We shall consider first the oracle, of which only two examples occur in Racine. Georges May has carefully distinguished between Racine's and Corneille's use of this device.[10] The older dramatist wanted it to deceive or disarm the spectator, and thus it became an important factor in his "dramaturgy of curiosity." Mr. May has refuted the possible objection that once we have seen a play of Corneille, our "surprise" at the false oracle is necessarily blunted. One might add to his analysis at this point the observation that after we have seen the play a number of times, "curiosity" decreases, but irony increases, because the deception, the false security, are felt only by the protagonists.

As Racine uses the device, it inspires despair rather than hope, uncertainty rather than certainty. Antigone interprets the pronouncement of the oracle in *La Thébaïde* to mean that her whole family is doomed. At Ménécée's death (he alone, a character who does not

[10]G. May, *Tragédie cornélienne, tragédie racinienne*, University of Illinois Press, 1947, pp. 102–4, 149–51.

appear, takes the oracle to apply to a single member of the family)[11] she has a fleeting moment of hope, but this is immediately dashed by Jocaste's gloomy admonition: "Connaissez mieux du ciel la vengeance fatale."

In *Iphigénie*, no sooner are the words of the oracle uttered than we hear allusions to "une autre Hélène" and to the mysterious origins of Eriphile. These clues, coupled with later references to a daughter of Helen and Theseus, urge the audience to doubt the oracle, and to foresee the outcome,[12] at least dimly. Racine's characters never feel the confidence in the oracle that Corneille's Julie expresses when she urges Camille, "pour le moins, croyez-en votre oracle"; as Racine uses it, it serves primarily to project our thoughts into the future rather than to foster puzzlement or deception.

The premonitory dreams in Racine, as in the two examples in Corneille, warn of catastrophe. The older playwright, however, makes his dreams ambiguous so as to preserve a balance of possibility: "C'est en contraire sens qu'un songe s'interprète," says Julie of the dream that appears to contradict the cheerful forecast of the oracle; Polyeucte and Néarque agree that Pauline's dream is a product of "woman's fancy."

Only one dream forms an integral part of a Racinian tragedy.[13] This is Athalie's vision of her mother, Jezebel, who appears to her "pompeusement parée" only to dissolve in a horrible mass of bones and rotting flesh. Corneille's two dreams present, in truly baroque fashion, a confusion of images; Camille sees only

> Mille songes affreux, mille images sanglantes,
> Ou plutôt mille amas de carnage et d'horreur.
>
> (I. ii. 216–17)

Pauline, although she sees Sévère in her dreams and watches her father stab her husband, tells her confidante that her "douleur trop forte a brouillé les images." By contrast, Athalie clearly sees her mother and receives a specific warning. In the second part of the dream, she sees

---

[11]See my article, "The Oracle in *La Thébaïde*," *MLN*, LXVI (1951), pp. 93–8.

[12]While I would not agree that such hints "reveal the dénouement explicitly," as G. May thinks (*Tragédie cornélienne, tragédie racinienne*, p. 151), it is clear that Racine reacted against the Cornelian surprise effects.

[13]In *Esther*, Assuérus' "songe étrange" which reveals that (III. ii. 922–3):

> ... la main d'un perfide étranger
> Dans le sang de la reine est prête à se plonger,

is, at most, incidental to the action. For a detailed analysis of Athalie's dream, see chapter v, pp. 179–87.

Joas plunge a dagger into her breast. Thus, the dream clearly predicts the outcome, and furthermore, by taking the audience and the speaker back to the day of Jezebel's death, summons up with the past the knowledge that the seeds of vengeance will bear fruit. So in the one instance in which he uses the dream device, Racine invests it with his own time-concept, which, as we have seen, involves a continual contemplation of the past in conjunction with thoughts of present and future.

If, at this point, as I suppose all Racinians must, we have been led into the sempiternal parallel with Corneille, it has helped us to reveal Racine's approach to time-worn devices already employed by Corneille with sure sense of purpose. Both oracle and dream serve Corneille's desire to create an "agréable suspension"; they are devices of action. Racine, on the other hand, assimilates them to his time-concept; his oracles, like Athalie's dream, evoke both past and future.

The same contrast is evident in the two dramatists' use of premonitions. These are frequently quite gratuitous in Corneille. In *Le Cid*, Chimène, despite Elvire's good news, feels strangely ill at ease:

> Il semble toutefois que mon âme troublée
> Refuse cette joie et s'en trouve accablée.
>
> (I. i. 53–4)

Such unexplained feelings of impending calamity are frequent. In Racine, however, such premonitions are prepared for by the preceding action. Jocaste's forebodings are fully justified by her past experience, and when Iphigénie feels a "secrète horreur" this is occasioned by the evident embarrassment and cryptic language of her father: "Je crains, malgré moi, un malheur que j'ignore." In the case of Junie, we can well understand that she should be "D'un noir pressentiment malgré moi prévenue."

All these devices reach toward the crisis within the play. Frequently this obsession with the future is expressed by the impatience of the characters to make an end, harried as they are by the knowledge that time is running out. In *Bajazet*, the implacable Roxane sets the limits of the action:

> ... si, dans cette journée
> Il ne m'attache à lui par un juste hyménée...
> J'abandonne l'ingrat.
>
> (I. iii. 318–19, 323)

In explaining what had seemed to be an exchange of vows between himself and Roxane, Bajazet declares:

> Soit que le temps trop cher la pressât de se rendre,
> A peine ai-je parlé que, sans presque m'entendre,
> Ses pleurs précipités ont coupé mon discours.
>
> (III. iv. 985–7)

Weighing upon the characters is the knowledge or suspicion that the Sultan is soon to arrive. Acomat dreads his return, and plans to avert it, but the arrival of Orcan at the end of Act III increases the pace even more. Now Roxane cries, "L'ordre, l'esclave, et le vizir me presse." The question of how much time they have is forever in the minds of the characters. "D'un jour si précieux perdez-vous les moments?" asks Acomat two scenes later, and he sees Roxane's decision to defer her vengeance as a brief respite provided by love:

> ... j'ose te répondre
> Qu'il n'est pas condamné, puisqu'on le veut confondre;
> Que nous avons du temps.
>
> (IV. vii. 1409–11)

But the time is ticking relentlessly away; Bajazet is seen leaving his room "avec empressement," and as he enters Roxane's presence for the last time, we hear her say coldly, "Les moments sont trop chers pour les perdre en paroles."

Even more significant than this preoccupation with the future within the play, as far as our study of the rôle of time in the tragedy is concerned, is the bursting of the play's terminal point so that the action embraces the post-dramatic future. In his Preface to *Athalie*, Racine discusses Joad's prophecy of the destruction of the temple and the fall of Jerusalem, events that come later than the action of the play, as if it were an innovation in his theatre. It is true that *Athalie* is the only play in which a prophecy plays such a prominent part. Yet at least the mood of prediction hovers over most of the tragedies. Since so many of his characters are legendary figures, we cannot help feeling that if they are not destroyed by the end of the play, their existence continues afterward. An Oreste, an Agamemnon, an Agrippine, have thus a kind of supra-dramatic existence, which Racine is not only careful to preserve (he would never, for example, take such liberties as Euripides, whom

he cites with horror in the Preface to *Iphigénie*) but which he deliberately emphasizes in order to project us in imagination beyond and above
the action. This technique is perhaps most strikingly illustrated in
*Britannicus, Iphigénie,* and *Athalie,* but it also figures prominently in
*Bérénice* and *Mithridate,* and comes briefly into play in *Bajazet.*

In *Britannicus,* the bold resolve to depict, not the famous matricide
that had provided dramatic material since the Middle Ages, but a
"monstre naissant," at the moment of his self-realization and resolve
to pursue evil, reveals the dramatist's interest in projecting tragic
careers beyond the play. Agrippine's "prediction" is explicit:

> Tu n'as pas fait ce pas pour reculer;
> Ta main a commencé par le sang de ton frère;
> Je prévois que tes coups viendront jusqu'à ta mère.
>
> (V. vi. 1674–6)

These lines are a pendant to her reply to Albine in the first act when she
visualizes Néron's career as a reversal of the natural process whereby
age brings wisdom and measure to foolhardy youth:

> ALBINE
> Enfin Néron naissant
> A toutes les vertus d'Auguste vieillissant...
> AGRIPPINE
> Il commence, il est vrai, par où finit Auguste;
> Mais crains que, l'avenir détruisant le passé,
> Il ne finisse ainsi qu'Auguste a commencé.
>
> (I. i. 29–30, 32–4)

Néron's criminality is thus symbolized temporally: the future engulfing,
or in Racine's remarkable phrase, *destroying* the past, because his actions
will obliterate all trace of Augustan virtue. Agrippine's hope on hearing
of Néron's collapse at the loss of Junie, her eager desire to learn "S'il
voudra désormais suivre d'autres maximes," only increases the irony
as Burrhus' fervent cry, the last line in the play, echoes through the
sinister corridors and out into the future:

> Plût aux Dieux que ce fût le dernier de ses crimes !

Frequently, as with the evocation of the past, the projection into the
future takes two forms: the immediate or near future and the more
distant destiny that lies far ahead of the characters. Often we are aware

of an uneasy equilibrium in which the characters are poised, like sprinters at the starting-line. At the beginning of a play, or early in the action, they will announce their intention to leave; they are awaiting some outcome or other, not at rest, but rather pausing expectantly in a kind of arrestation of flight. Hermione, in her dilemma, is "toujours prête à partir, et demeurant toujours," and in *Bérénice*, Antiochus has made his preparations for departure; his ships lie at anchor ready for flight. In the long scene at the beginning of Act III in *Mithridate* the King announces his plans:

> Demain, sans différer, je prétends que l'aurore
> Découvre mes vaisseaux déjà loin du Bosphore.
>
> (III. i. 855–6)

Hippolyte's plans are announced in the first line of *Phèdre*: "Je pars, cher Théramène." In *Iphigénie*, Achille reveals his own and the Greeks' eagerness to rush toward their fate by the frequently recurring use of the verb "courir":

> Et laissant faire au sort, courons où la valeur
> Nous promet un destin aussi grand que le leur;
> C'est à Troie, et j'y cours.
>
> (II. i. 265–7)

This aspect of Racine's time-concept: violence in precarious equilibrium, is curiously reflected in a metaphor which recurs with surprising frequency: that of the torrent, the torrent momentarily checked, then bursting its banks and rushing on. In *La Thébaïde*, the limit set upon each brother's reign is compared to the damming of a torrent:

> Pareils à ces torrents qui ne durent qu'un jour,
> Plus leur cours est borné, plus ils font de ravage,
> Et d'horribles dégâts signalent leur passage.
>
> (I. v. 218–20)

The same metaphor evokes Alexandre's conquering sweep:

> C'est un torrent qui passe, et dont la violence
> Sur tout ce qui l'arrête exerce sa puissance.
>
> (I. ii. 189–90)

In later plays the metaphor becomes submerged; in *Bérénice* the pressure of public opinion upon Titus is "le torrent qui m'entraîne"; a moment later, speaking of Bérénice's anger and despair, Arsace advises Antiochus: "Laissez à ce torrent le temps de s'écouler" (III. iv. 942). In *Mithridate* the same figure describes the Roman hordes destined to overrun Europe: "Ce torrent, s'il m'entraîne, ira tout inonder" (III. i. 810); in *Iphigénie*, Agamemnon asks resignedly of the impetuous Achille who precipitates the action, "Mais qui peut dans sa course arrêter ce torrent?" (I. i. 107). And finally, in *Athalie*, there is the child Joas' sublime reply to the Queen's offer: "Le bonheur des méchants comme un torrent s'écoule" (II. vii. 688).

Despite the long interval of silence separating *Esther* from the secular plays, one is surprised that Racine did not take advantage of this "motion-in-equilibrium" device which had imparted such violent urgency to the earlier plays. The action would certainly have lent itself admirably to this technique, since the peril of the Jews is known at the beginning. Yet strangely, the day of extermination, far from sharing the imminence of Sultan Amurat's arrival or the sacrifice of Iphigénie, is not to take place until ten days have passed. It is true, however, that *Esther* is the only one of Racine's plays that does not observe the unity of time. The author does not mention this fact in his Preface, although carefully justifying his neglect of the unity of place. Perhaps the ten days' delay before the execution of the order was intended to show the far-reaching extent of the fatal order—"Toute la nation à la fois est proscrite"—which applies in all of Assuérus' kingdom. This length of time may be necessary for the command to reach into its farthest corners. Such a linking of time and space, the delay in time which suggests the vast area over which the order must travel, is also implicit in Esther's order that "tous les Juifs dans Suse répandus" must fast three days and nights. It must I think be admitted, however, that in regard to space and time, as in so many other aspects, *Esther* has to be set apart from the other plays. There is no doubt that it has merits, chiefly lyrical; these will be touched on elsewhere. It remains a frankly occasional piece, loosely constructed and operatic in form; one we can hardly call "Racinian."

But these examples involve the near future; what other works besides *Britannicus* create a final irony through the vision of eventual catastrophe at the end of the play? *Athalie* springs immediately to mind, with Racine's own remark that Joad's prophecy in the third act "sert beaucoup à augmenter le trouble dans la pièce." One critic has even found *Athalie* to be, like the *Agamemnon* or the *Eumenides*, a kind of fragment of a tragic cycle.[14] And indeed a very convincing case can be made to show how the ultimate tragedy of Joas is made explicit throughout the play. Lines such as those of Josabet's:

> Et c'est sur tous ces rois sa justice sévère
> Que je crains pour le fils de mon malheureux frère,
>
> (I. ii. 235–6)

as well as Joad's stern prayer that, should Joas err,

> Qu'il soit comme le fruit en naissant arraché,
> Ou qu'un souffle ennemi dans sa fleur a séché,
>
> (I. ii. 285–6)

help to prepare the great prophecy which dimly foresees Joas' crime.[15] And, as Mr. Williams has remarked, the introduction (quite unnecessary on any other grounds) of the young Zacharie, Joas' future victim, provides a living symbol of the future catastrophe. Athalie's final anathema on the house of David evokes the tragic cycle, both past and future, and Joad's prayer, just before the play's close, reaffirms the irony:

> Faites que Joas meure avant qu'il vous oublie.

Not only is there a striking resemblance, because of such references to the future, between *Athalie* and the Aeschylean cycles, but the treatment of time helps to express the play's theme, the dramatist's view of the changing destinies of the race, ever tragic, yet ever renewing itself in time. In Racine's mind a part of this destiny is not only the murder of Zacharie by Joas, but the destruction of the temple, the fall of Jerusalem, the coming of "ce consolateur, après lequel tous les anciens justes soupiraient," and perhaps even the founding of the Church of Rome. The tragedy of *Athalie* reaches into the future, joining, in the ebb and flow of destiny, the tragic history of the Jews to the march of Christendom.

[14]E. E. Williams, "*Athalie*: The Tragic Cycle and the Tragedy of Joas," *RR*, XXVIII (1937), pp. 36–45.

[15]The High Priest himself does not understand the full meaning of the prophecy. For an interesting exploration of this question, see Annie Barnes, "La Prophétie de Joad" in *The French Mind: Studies in Honour of G. Rudler,* ed. W. Moore, R. Sutherland, and E. Starkie, Oxford University Press, 1952, pp. 90–108.

It would be incorrect to infer,[16] however, that Racine gave his play this "cyclic" quality simply because he found himself in a situation similar to that of the Greek tragedians with regard to plot and the beliefs and traditions of his audience. The technique appears much earlier than *Athalie*. We have noted how, in *Britannicus*, the future career of Néron is constantly before the audience's mind. In this case, of course, only the future career of an individual is concerned, and one can hardly consider the murder of Agrippine part of a tragic cycle. But beginning with *Mithridate*, the playwright seems to have felt that an essential part of tragedy was the suggestion of an ultimate catastrophe, counteracting the comparative calm of the ending. The progression in time, so clearly begun before the play, will thus continue into the future, and the compression of the tragic present between past and future serves to increase the frenzied haste and *malaise* of the characters. In *Mithridate*, two parallel forces converge toward the *dénouement*: the King's resolve to set sail against Rome, and the threatened arrival of the Roman army summoned by Pharnace. A similar menace from without, drawing ever closer to the sphere of action, had occurred in *Bajazet*, where the thought of the avenging Sultan's approach haunts the protagonists. In *Mithridate*, however, the coming of the Romans is known only to Pharnace:

> Mithridate revient ? Ah ! fortune cruelle !
> Ma vie et mon amour tous deux courent hasard,
> Les Romains que j'attends arriveront trop tard.
>
> (I. v. 336-8)

The arrival of the Romans, so eagerly awaited by Pharnace, thwarts the King's departure, and thus the two lines of force converge, producing a momentary suspension in time which is the final act of the play. But the movement recommences in the final prophecy of the dying Mithridate, who foresees the ultimate defeat of his triumphant son, Xipharès. The predicted defeat of Rome itself, mentioned earlier in Mithridate's speech to his sons, had already imparted a cyclic quality, suggesting the inevitable fall of empires, however great:

> Annibal l'a prédit, croyons-en ce grand homme :
> Jamais on ne vaincra les Romains que dans Rome.
>
> (III. i. 835-6)

[16]As Mr. Williams' essay seems to do, pp. 37-8.

The King's dying words, like Joad's prediction, serve to "augmenter le trouble dans la pièce," or rather, at the end of the play, revive the feeling of fear that had momentarily subsided:

> Mon fils, songez à vous; gardez-vous de prétendre
> Que de tant d'ennemis vous puissiez vous défendre.
> Bientôt tous les Romains, de leur honte irrités,
> Viendront ici sur vous fondre de tous côtés...
> Cachez-leur pour un temps vos noms et votre vie.
>
> (V. v. 1679-82, 1687)

The still somewhat tentative handling of post-dramatic time in *Mithridate* is a preparation for the firm and confident treatment in *Iphigénie*. The external structure of the two plays is similar at many points. In both there is a portentous and dreaded arrival, in both a straining for departure by sea toward conquest. In some respects, indeed, *Mithridate* seems like a *stage*, a testing-ground, for the following play. Nowhere is the time element as significant as in *Iphigénie*, nowhere does it so firmly support the theme. We feel constantly that the characters are pausing temporarily in a movement toward a destiny awaiting them after the play. Ulysse visualizes both the departure and the defeat of Troy:

> Voyez tout l'Hellespont blanchissant sous nos rames,
> Et la perfide Troie abandonnée aux flammes.
>
> (I. vi. 381-2)

He predicts the lasting glory of the legend:

> ... ce triomphe heureux qui s'en va devenir
> L'éternel entretien des siècles à venir.
>
> (I. vi. 387-8)

That Ulysse not only predicts, but actually describes the impending departure by sea and the burning of Troy, lends prominence to the vision of the future.

The dramatic advantages of presenting the familiar characters of Greek legend have frequently been pointed out. For one thing, the names alone of the descendants of Atreus call to mind in a general way their subsequent career. In *Iphigénie*, as always, Racine exploits his advantages in his own way. The two allusions to Oreste serve two specific purposes: Arcas mentions him as being a babe in the cradle, thus locating the exact point in his father's career, and also projecting our vision beyond the play to the death of his father and the murder of his mother; and Iphigénie makes an unconsciously ironic prediction similar to the last line in *Britannicus* when she comforts her mother with the words:

> Vos yeux me reverront dans Oreste mon frère,
> Puisse-t-il être, hélas ! moins funeste à sa mère !
> (V. iii. 1661–2)

In Euripides' version of the play, the child Orestes is present, and Iphigeneia says simply, "May your maternal care rear Orestes to manhood."[17] The increased irony in Racine's alteration depends on the audience's visualizing the future destiny of all the protagonists. Through this repeated evoking of the future we seem to be witnessing the process by which things become "fatal," and we come finally to believe that they must indeed have happened thus.[18] Racinian fatality lies in the irreversibility so often expressed by the characters: "le mal est sans remède." And a not inconsiderable result is that the characters acquire a kind of supra-temporal reality; Racine's Ulysse, his Agamemnon and Clytemnestre rejoin and even replace the figures of history and legend.

## UNITY OF PLACE

We turn now to the second established convention confronting Racine, unity of place. His first tragedy, *La Thébaïde*, is unique because, of the many versions of the Theban drama, it is the first to observe this unity. We can see in this play, despite its imperfections, the same kind of development that we have been discussing with regard to time. Almost from the beginning, out of the prescribed "unity" new spatial relationships develop. The palace where the characters must now meet is the potential haven of reason and reconciliation, the scene of the brothers' childhood that Jocaste hopes will arouse feelings of brotherhood. The plain beyond the ramparts, flashing with the arms of the

[17]As Lancaster suggested (*A History of French Dramatic Literature in the Seventeenth Century*, Johns Hopkins University Press, 1929–42, IV, pp. i, 90), Racine's reason for not showing Orestes on the stage may in part have been that he thought a queen on a journey would normally leave her child with a nurse, but a more impelling dramatic motive would be the playwright's feeling that the presence of Orestes as a child might distract the audience from the memory of the horrible deed that his name at once evokes.

[18]G. Poulet, *Le Temps humain*, Edinburgh University Press, 1949, p. 145.

opposing hosts, is the terrain of violent death. Jocaste's efforts to reconcile her sons are realized spatially in the endless pull between palace and plain, and her failure looms larger when the palace, hitherto the locus of reason, becomes the scene of self-imposed death.

This constant balance between the confined space of the action and the unseen areas beyond provides evidence of a new awareness of the vast poetic and dramatic potentialities involved in a wider scene than that of the circumscribed stage. This awareness is apparent in Racine's treatment of the death of Ménécée. In his commentary on the *Phoenician Maidens*, he had criticized Euripides for skimping the description of this event, declaring "cela devrait être préparé avec bien plus d'éclat."[19] His immediate predecessor, Rotrou, had been content to describe the event in a few lines; Racine took advantage of the opportunity to evoke the breadth of the scene of battle. In Antigone's forty-three line description of the suicide, he makes unusually skilful use of spatial effects of intensification, in order to sharpen the contours of the scene. It is as if, in our mind's eye, we viewed the death through a telescope. The vastness of the scene is first established by Antigone's vain pursuit of her brothers; in their haste they have already outdistanced the sound of her cries. She then joins the people on the city wall, and we watch, through her eyes, the tiny figures below. In the complete silence of the onlookers, "[glacés] d'effroi," and of the soldiers below, who fall motionless at the young prince's shout, Ménécée's words acquire a tremendous resonance. The fatal blow falls in this deathly silence, the scene shifts momentarily to the effect on the spectators above ("les Thébains . . . regardent en tremblant ce noble sacrifice"), then, maintaining the telescopic perspective, swings back again to the gestures of Hémon and Créon and the two armies.

Such an indelible mental picture could only be painted by recourse to the subtle interplay of spatial contrasts, sound, motion, and immobility, that we have noticed. Racine never lost this awareness of the dramatic effect to be attained through such evocation of space. In *Alexandre*, however, spatial elements are curiously lacking. The descriptions of the two armies facing one another are far less vivid, submerged as they are in a series of variations on an elaborate paradox:

---

[19]*Œuvres*, ed. R. Picard *et al.*, II, p. 875. See my article, cited in n. 11 above, on the use to which Racine puts the oracle. Antigone's *récit* is in III. iii. 619–61.

Alexandre's difficulty in crossing the short distance between him and his beloved in contrast with his ease in sweeping across the vast areas of his conquests. This stylization of space heralds the greater concentration on the interior, on the stage scene, which one finds in the next four plays. Instead of the shifting between exterior and interior which so aptly supports the theme of La Thébaïde, the tragedies that follow Alexandre confine the setting rather closely.

The events in Andromaque, Britannicus, Bérénice, and Bajazet occur almost wholly within the palace. Yet what might appear at first to be merely a strict "observance" of unity of place is actually a deliberate restricting of the scene, resulting in a strengthening and intensification of the total dramatic effect. In Andromaque we first feel the claustrophobic effect which Racine was later to turn to full account:

> Nos vaisseaux sont tout prêts, et le vent nous appelle.
> Je sais de ce palais tous les détours obscurs;
> Vous voyez que la mer en vient battre les murs;
> Et cette nuit, sans peine, une secrète voie
> Jusqu'à votre vaisseau conduira votre proie.
>
> (III. i. 790–4)

The King's palace is thus a maze of dark corridors, through which only an experienced guide can find his way. In the last scene, Pylade pleads with Oreste to escape; the Greeks will hold the gate, but only for a moment; soon it will close on them forever:

> ... sortons de ce palais,
> Ou bien résolvons-nous de n'en sortir jamais.
>
> (V. v. 1583–5)

Despite these suggestions, however, the idea of the palace as a menacing enclosure does not play a prominent part in the action of Andromaque. There does seem to be a deliberate hint that, once outside his palace, Pyrrhus is doomed; in the fifth act various changes of place are linked to fatality; when Astyanax is moved from one of the palace rooms to a fort "éloigné du temple et du palais," Pyrrhus' guards accompany him, leaving their master unprotected. And, as we watch, through Cléone's récit, the joyful wedding procession to the temple, we know that Pyrrhus is going to his death. This account, and Oreste's description of the assassination of the King before the altar, suggest the ironic concept of the temple as a scene of death. An example of the "intensification of perspective" we already noticed in *La Thébaïde* occurs when Pylade witnesses Hermione's suicide. Rushing from the palace, she had encountered the soldiers bearing the body of Pyrrhus; her suicide upon the corpse is seen from the top of the palace steps.

In the three plays that follow, the "within-ness" is more deliberately integrated with the action. Néron's palace is not merely a prison, it is a trap into which the characters are lured. Agrippine appears in the first scene, "sans suite et sans escorte," and the vastness and silence of the palace are emphasized by Albine's comment on her mistress' wandering alone. Like Junie, Britannicus has been living in his own "palais désert," but from the beginning of the action he has, as Agrippine puts it, thrown himself blindly into the hands of his enemies, and he remains in the trap until his death.[20] In contrast to the brilliance of the court, and the penetrating gaze of the watchers there, the outside world appears vague and obscure. Junie has been "dans l'obscurité nourissant sa douleur," and she is frightened at the prospect of passing suddenly into a position

> ... qui l'expose aux yeux de tout le monde,
> Dont je n'ai pu de loin soutenir la clarté.
>
> (II. iii. 616–17)

Frequent mention of doors, rooms, and walls contributes to the feeling of imprisonment. Agrippine waits outside Néron's bedroom, but he has already left by another door, which is secret: "une porte au public moins connue." Later, in *Phèdre*, where the action covers a wider area, it is the woods that echo with the cries of the hunt; in *Britannicus*, hostile palace walls hurl back the young hero's lamentations: "ce palais retentit en vain de vos regrets."

The searching gaze of the watchers, those "témoins assidus," acquires added intensity in these confines. Néron's ironic byplay when he surprises the two lovers together emphasizes this association of place and presence:

> Ce lieu le favorise, et je vous y retiens
> Pour lui faciliter de si doux entretiens.
>
> (III. vii. 1029–30)

In the ensuing dialogue, in which Britannicus denies that the place

[20]With the exception of the visit to Pallas' apartments, which hastens his doom.

intimidates him and Néron retorts that it should on the contrary fill him with obedience and respect, a device which in earlier plays had consisted merely of a rather artificial use of personification, requiring an over-extended and confusing use of subject and possessive pronouns, suddenly acquires new power. One has only to compare Oreste's madrigal on Hermione's eyes—

> Mon désespoir n'attend que *leur* indifférence :
> *Ils* n'ont qu'à m'interdire un reste d'espérance.
> *Ils* n'ont pour avancer cette mort où je cours,
> Qu'à me dire une fois ce qu'*ils* m'ont dit toujours —
>
> (II. ii. 497–500)

with the same stylistic device as it appears in the spirited fencing between Néron and his half-brother to see how different is the result:

> NÉRON
> Et que vous montrent-*ils* qui ne vous avertissent
> Qu'il faut qu'on me respecte et que l'on m'obéisse ?
> BRITANNICUS
> *Ils* ne nous ont pas vus l'un et l'autre élever,
> Moi pour vous obéir, et vous pour me braver;
> Et ne s'attendaient pas, lorsqu'*ils* nous virent naître,
> Qu'un jour Domitius me dût parler en maître.
>
> (II. ii. 1035–40)

It is apparent that the personification which in Oreste's lines verges on the ridiculous, supports, in the above quotation, the rôle of place in the dramatic action. The palace, with its corridors and secret exits, has already taken on a kind of life, so that Junie's warning to her lover that "ces murs mêmes, seigneur, peuvent avoir des yeux," is no mere commonplace. No longer the *précieux* elaboration of a worn-out metaphor as in the quotation from *Andromaque*, the personification now invests the site with the same sinister characteristics as its chief inhabitant. The awareness of the power of place that we have already observed in Jocaste's plea to her sons, and in her pathetic insistence upon their meeting "dans ce même palais où vous prites naissance," and in her plea that they draw feelings of love from contemplating the place of their birth, is now made basic to the tragic atmosphere.

From the palace-trap only Junie escapes, and then only by a ruse. Pretending to go to Octavie's chambers, she makes her way through

the palace gates by "des chemins écartés" and throws herself at the feet
of the statue of Augustus. Agrippine, who has prophesied her own death
at her son's hands, watches from within; Néron, who has followed,
returns, after the foolhardy Narcisse, who had pursued the fleeing girl,
has met death at the hands of the mob. Junie's escape strengthens by
contrast the rôle of the palace as the site of evil: Néron, Agrippine, and
the futile Burrhus remain within to fulfil the dark prophecy; Narcisse,
the loathsome creature who can thrive only within the walls, meets
death when he ventures without.

In *Bérénice*, the treatment of space emphasizes three basic contrasts
which are involved with the play's theme. There is first of all the visible
scene, here more rigidly restricted than ever before, the "cabinet
superbe et solitaire" that lies between the doors leading to Bérénice's
and Titus' apartments. There is secondly the court, where the protagonist must hide his true feelings and from which he must at times
take refuge, and thirdly, "l'univers," the Roman world, before which
the actions of a Titus must appear as an example of greatness and
abnegation.

The contrast between the first two is made in the opening lines,
spoken by Antiochus as he explains in detail how the cabinet adjoins
the rooms of Titus and Bérénice, adding that it is their refuge from the
court:

> C'est ici quelquefois qu'il se cache à la cour,
> Lorsqu'il vient à la Reine expliquer son amour.
>
> (I. i. 5–6)

At one point, Antiochus sends Arsace to beg an interview with Bérénice "sans témoins." When the servant returns with the news that she
is surrounded by courtiers, he cries in dismay, "ainsi donc sans témoins
je ne puis lui parler." Arsace reassures him, however. The Queen will
see him here as soon as she can escape from "une cour qui l'accable."
When she does appear, her first words are, "Enfin, je me dérobe."

Later in the play, when, unable to bear Titus' absence any longer, she
bursts in upon him and Paulin, she apologizes for interrupting his
solitude. In Act IV, the Emperor's courtiers follow him into the
room, but he dismisses them, pleading, "Je veux un peu de solitude.
Qu'on me laisse."

The cabinet, with its doors on either side, symbolizes Titus' dilemma
spatially. In the last scene of Act IV, the Senate and people are waiting

in the royal chambers for his decision; one of the doors leads to them, the other to Bérénice. Titus' hesitation and final resolve are thus portrayed scenically; Paulin, who urges, "passons dans la chambre prochaine," triumphs over Antiochus, who cries, "courez chez la reine."

Finally, as in *La Thébaïde* and *Britannicus*, the setting evokes the past and inspires emotion. Bérénice must flee the painful sight of the rooms prepared with loving care by Titus, who has had them hung with garlands upon which their names' are entwined:

> Je ne vois rien ici dont je ne sois blessée.
> Tout cet appartement préparé par vos soins,
> Ces lieux, de mon amour si longtemps les témoins,
> Qui semblaient pour jamais me répondre du vôtre,
> Ces festons, où nos noms enlacés l'un dans l'autre
> A mes tristes regards viennent partout s'offrir,
> Sont autant d'imposteurs que je ne puis souffrir.
>
> (V. v. 1320–6)

It is upon the wider scene of the universe or Roman world, embracing both the present and the future, that the actions of Titus and Bérénice will be judged. In Titus' long monologue (IV. iv) his repetition of the word "univers" reveals his obsession with the final judgment awaiting him. Neither he nor Bérénice can escape the eye of history; ever present to Titus' mind is the long list of Roman emperors who, in the end, have yielded to the demands of "la patrie et la gloire." Constantly at his elbow is Paulin, urging him to remember "quels applaudissements l'univers vous prépare"; he shrinks at the thought of the spectacle he might provide if he shirked his duty because of love:

> Un indigne empereur sans empire, sans cour,
> Vil spectacle aux humains des faiblesses d'amour.
>
> (V. vi. 1405–6)

Thus the three scenes of action, the visible scene, the unseen setting of the court, and the historical panorama of universal judgment against which the characters must measure themselves, symbolize in their various ways the conflicts of the action. The contrast between cabinet and court serves to underline the constant pressure of responsibilities from which a ruler can find only momentary respite; the vista of the future, and of the world's judgment, stresses the timelessness of these responsibilities, which stretch far beyond the immediate demands of what Titus calls "une foule insensée."

In *Bérénice*, as well as in *Britannicus*, Racine deliberately heightens tension and supports his themes by restricting the scene of action. In *Bajazet*, the action of which takes place in the harem, the physical qualities of the scene are to a great extent already imposed by the plot. The prison-like atmosphere of the play is thus immediately apparent, and requires comparatively little attention from the dramatist. In the opening lines, Osmin and Acomat make clear that their presence in the forbidden place is exceptional, and that events to follow will explain an action heretofore punishable by death. In the seraglio, secret place *par excellence*, the action takes on a special quality of illegitimacy and conspiracy. Acomat tells us how Roxane was at first afraid to show herself,

> Invisible d'abord, elle entendait ma voix,
> Et craignait du sérail les rigoureuses lois.
>
> (I. i. 203-4)

She has finally chosen a secret meeting-place, to which, each day, a slave guides him by a secret passage. The harem, with its secret, winding hallways, encloses a "foule de chefs, d'esclaves, de muets," and it has many rooms, some of them vast, as we learn from Acomat's description of the interview between Roxane and Bajazet, which he watched at such a distance that he could see only their gestures.[21]

*Bajazet* contains an occasional reference to the outside. There is first of all the distance that separates the Sultan and the palace, a distance that he is gradually closing, to the terror of its inmates. As in *Andromaque*, the palace is partially surrounded by the sea, into which recalcitrants are hurled and on which Acomat plans to carry Atalide to safety. But not until *Mithridate*, the scene of which is laid in a Crimean seaport, does the sea appear as a broad expanse beyond the visible setting. Now, for the first time, the palace as setting yields in importance to a wider area, the sea and shore, where important actions occur.[22] "Toute la mer est de vaisseaux couverte!" cries Phœdime, announcing the arrival of Mithridate. Small boats have brought the news, and Arbate has gone out to sea to meet the King. Picturing the excited

---

[21]See chapter III, pp. 121-2.

[22]In this connection, Racine's indicating that the action is "à Nymphée," and not within a specified palace or room, is significant.

throng of people flocking to the shore, Phœdime reproaches Monime for not following them. The battle in the last act is fought over a wide area between the palace gate and the shore. Even more significant, however, is the old King's enumeration of the distances he has covered and those that, with restless energy, he still aspires to cover. The bold synecdoches of his speech to his sons (III. i)—"Le Bosphore m'a vu," "L'Asie étonnée," "l'Orient accablé"—suggesting a giant striding across Europe, contrast ironically with our awareness of his downfall, and with the King's own realization that these vast territories now swarm with Romans who will inevitably triumph. The action of the play, however, oscillates between the palace, where Xipharès and Monime struggle to conceal their love, and the seaport area where the clash of arms takes place. This dual scene supports the essential duality of theme which, as we saw earlier, contrasts the exploits of love and war.

In *Iphigénie*, the vision of the outdoor setting hovers constantly over the action occurring in the visible scene. The place where the altar, set up in the open, awaits its unsuspecting victim, overshadows the tent which is the nominal locus of action. Toward the altar the heroine moves on her journey from Argos; the altar and the wide area around it are poetically visible to the audience throughout the play. Events prior to the dramatic action, and unseen happenings that run concurrently to the onstage action are so important that the invisible setting must be frequently evoked. Racine's description of these events is as pertinent to the theme spatially as it is temporally. In Iphigénie's description of her journey to Aulis the distance seems even greater because she tells us she had sighted her destination two days before arriving:

> Pour moi, depuis deux jours qu'approchant de ce lieux,
> Leur aspect souhaité se découvre à mes yeux,
> Je l'attendais partout; et d'un regard timide
> Sans cesse parcourant les chemins de l'Aulide,
> Mon cœur pour le chercher volait loin devant moi,
> Et je demande Achille à tout ce que je voi.
> Je viens, j'arrive enfin.
>
> (II. iii. 603–9)

As in the exposition speech of *Andromaque* there is here an extremely skilful alternating of the tenses. The present and imperfect, both dependent on "depuis," suggest at once both the earlier and more recent stages of her journey since sighting her destination. The imperfects, "je l'attendais," and "mon cœur volait," convey emotions felt since catching a first sight of the camp. The first present, "se découvre," emphasizes the continuity of the journey, and the second, "je demande Achille," the more recent shift from thought to action as she reached the outskirts. Such phrases as "leur aspect souhaité," and the remarkable metonymy of the heart that looks searching ahead, portray a double movement, the one physical and measured, the other spiritual and rapid, toward her goal. The new sentence, "je viens, j'arrive enfin," takes us back in time to the moment when Eurybate announced in I. iv., "Elle approche."

The many references to the spaces above and around the locus of the visible action create the impression that the action is not confined, that it unfolds upon a wide area, under the sky, of which the King's tent is but a single point. This is borne out by Racine's use of "en" and the definite article with "Aulide," indicating that he thought of Aulis, not as a city, but as an area without clearly defined limits.[23] The elements, wind, lightning, and thunder, join in the action. The sky darkens at Clytemnestre's curse, the sea roars into foam as the suicidal knife descends.

Racine's interest in exterior space may have helped him to find an original device for preventing Iphigénie from receiving the warning letter. In Euripides' version, Menelaus snatches it from Agamemnon's servant. Racine's solution is a topographical one; Clytemnestre and her party become lost for a time in a wood lying near the camp, and so fail to receive the King's missive.

But in this play perhaps the most startling device for focussing our attention on places beyond the visible locus is the thunderclap that announces the death of Eriphile. Iphigénie has left for the altar; Clytemnestre remains alone. Some thirty lines later, the thunder rolls:

> C'est le pur sang du Dieu qui lance le tonnerre...
> J'entends gronder la foudre et sens trembler la terre,
> Un Dieu vengeur, un Dieu fait retentir ces coups.
> (V. iv. 1697-9)

That the roar of the thunder accompanied Eriphile's death is later corroborated by Ulysse. As we have already observed, the dove-

[23]See Œuvres de J. Racine, ed. Mesnard, Paris, Hachette, 8 vols., 1865-73, III, p. 148, n. 1.

tailing accounts of Arcas and Ulysse suggest the time sequence. The latter's words,

> A peine son sang coule et fait rougir la terre,
> Les Dieux font sur l'autel entendre le tonnerre,
>
> (V. vi. 1777-8)

recall the actual sound heard earlier, adding reality to the unseen action by their appeal to auditive memory.[24]

In *Phèdre*, as in *Iphigénie*, topography plays a significant rôle: the forest, that once echoed with the cries of the hunt, and for whose shade the burning heroine longs in vain; the seashore, where the youthful hero raced his chariot and meets the monstrous bull; the temple near the city gates; the cemetery where his ancestors lie, and which becomes the scene of his death. Théramène's speech, giving the itinerary of his search for Thésée (I. i. 10–14), Hippolyte's recital of his father's exploits, warlike and amorous, that covered every corner of the classic world—"la Crète fumant du sang du Minotaure"; "Sa foi partout offerte et reçue en cent lieux"—form a panoramic backdrop for the events at Troezen.

But perhaps the most important element that gives the play spatial depth is Racine's use of light. As in *Iphigénie*, the actions take place beneath the open sky, but in *Phèdre*, the open setting is not merely evoked, it lies before us. A contrast of light and darkness runs through the play: the darkness of the palace chambers providing anonymity and a kind of repose, the light of day to which Phèdre is irresistibly drawn, but which lays bare her guilt. The paradox is observed by Œnone, who tells us, "Elle veut voir le jour," but a moment later, when her mistress recoils from the sunlight, cries wonderingly, "Vous haïssez le jour que vous veniez chercher." The source of the dazzling light before which Phèdre cringes is the accusing eye of her ancestor, the Sun; her gesture toward heaven, "Soleil, je te viens voir pour la dernière fois," and her despairing invocation to Helios, which begins, "Noble et puissant auteur d'une triste famille," ranging in its vision from the heavens and universe teeming with her ancestors to the underworld where her father Minos judges the dead, immeasurably increase the spatial scope of the action.

It is apparent that with the last two tragedies before his long silence,

[24]It is entirely possible that stage technicians produced the sound of the thunder. Cf. S. W. Holsboer, *L'Histoire de la mise en scène dans le théâtre français de 1600 à 1657*, Paris, Droz, 1933, p.145.

a wider field of action became increasingly important to Racine. True, the consciousness of space as an important element in the drama is never absent from his work. But his conscious restricting of the scene in the earlier plays gives prominence to human instrumentality; the reverse is true when the area beyond is widened. In an *Iphigénie* or a *Phèdre*, the will of the gods, like their lightning and winds and all-revealing sunlight, sweep down upon unprotected man and shape his course. As the characters diminish in stature, the instrumentality of the gods, only infrequently evoked before *Iphigénie*, takes on a new precedence as the impetus of the drama.

*Iphigénie* and *Phèdre* were at once a turning-point and a conclusion. When Racine resumed a limited career with *Esther*, the momentum had been broken. In this play, which does not observe unity of place, space nowhere exists dramatically. In this regard, *Esther* seems actually a retrogression, as a single example will show. The word "chemin" had taken on a concrete sense for the first time in *Iphigénie*. We remember the heroine's long journey over "les chemins de l'Aulide," and Clytemnestre's poignant memory of her daughter's triumphant arrival upon

> ... les chemins encor tout parfumés
> Des fleurs dont sous ses pas on les avait semés.
>
> (IV. iv. 1307–8)

In the biblical play, however, almost the identical image, earlier so concrete with its appeal to the visual and olfactory senses, has returned to its abstract metaphorical sense. The chorus sings, warning kings against wicked advisers:

> La fraude adroite et subtile
> Sème de fleurs son chemin.
>
> (III. iii. 981–2)

In *Athalie*, once again Racine makes dramatic use of space. The scene is within the temple, where the Levites exercise mysterious rites that excite the Queen's curiosity, so that she asks,

> Mais tout ce peuple enfermé dans ce lieu,
> A quoi s'occupe-t-il ?
>
> (II. vii. 669–70)

The temple is spacious; a "lieu redoutable" forbidden to non-believers; specific references to its different parts reinforce this impression.

Athalie enters one of the "parvis" and is only prevented from entering "l'enceinte sacrée" by Joad's wrath. In the final *coup de théâtre* the rear of the stage opens, revealing the armed Levites.

Outer spaces are evoked in Joad's reference to the sun which, as the play begins, whitens the roof of the temple, and in Athalie's attempt to lure Eliacin to her palace. The battle between Athalie and the Jews begins as a siege. The temple is surrounded by her soldiers (V. ii); all paths to safety are closed (IV. v). Abner, to enter, must pass through the besieging army. Vaster than the city itself is the historic mountain on which the temple stands; beyond it stretches the desert, to which a secret road leads, and where Josabet offers to take flight with Eliacin:

> Les portes, les chemins lui sont encore ouverts.
> Faut-il le transporter aux plus affreux déserts ?
> Je suis prête. Je sais une secrète issue
> Par où, sans qu'on le voie, et sans être aperçue,
> De Cédron avec lui traversant le torrent,
> J'irai dans le désert.
>
> (III. vi. 1057–62)

Historical references help to suggest that the action takes place in a universe under the eye of God. Joad's recollection of the flame that descended upon the altar, of Elijah commanding the elements, increases the area over which the Israelite destiny is fought out. The hymns of the Chorus, reiterating the effect of God's will upon nature, emphasize the elemental quality of that destiny, not merely confined to cities and temples, but becoming a vast migration.

In studying the means by which Racine bursts the limits of the visible stage, one should note how he lends reality to the invisible scene by making some part of it the physical goal of the characters. In the last act of *Andromaque*, for example, Cléone tells Hermione how she watched the wedding procession as Pyrrhus led toward the temple the unwilling herione who bore even to the altar the memory of her husband Hector. Iphigénie's journey toward the altar, begun before the play, constitutes the chief action. Hippolyte and Aricie set out for the temple near the city gates, and as the action of *Athalie* approaches its climax, Joas is seen by Salomith approaching his hidden goal, the throne of David:

> D'un pas majestueux, à côté de ma mère,
> Le jeune Eliacin s'avance.
>
> (IV. i. 1237–8)

We have seen, in our discussion of time, how the tragic action often seems to poise itself in a kind of precarious equilibrium. This equilibrium, through the contrast between movement and immobility that it suggests, projects our thoughts beyond the spatial confines of the play.

Settings acquire physical and tangible character, not only by the description of forests, hills, seas, and roads, as well as such properties as doors, corridors, and rooms, but by the way in which Racine populates his invisible scenes. From *La Thébaïde* on we are made aware of unseen masses, like the Thebans, who watch trembling as Ménécée stabs himself, or pour down from the walls, weeping their alarm:

> Du haut de nos remparts j'ai vu descendre en larmes
> Le peuple qui courait et qui criait aux armes.
>
> (V. ii. 1237–8)

The temple where Pyrrhus and Andromaque are about to wed acquires a further dimension through Oreste's description of the crowd and the *mêlée* of angry Greeks who surround the King and struggle for the chance to strike him (V. iii. 1499–1500). In *Britannicus*, which depends for so much of its effect on the feeling that Néron is omnipresent, whether he appears on stage or not, the court and its inhabitants are sketched in only briefly. True, the atmosphere of the palace, with its crime and intrigue, pervades Agrippine's long speech in Act IV, and there are scattered references to the "public" and to the brilliance of the court. But during most of the action, the shadow of the Emperor must cover all, and it is to the advantage of the plot that the palace halls, onstage and off, should seem sparsely populated while he is in the ascendancy.[25] Only with the disintegration of the ending, when Néron's power wavers temporarily, does the crowd appear, flocking to Junie's rescue:

> Le peuple cependant, que ce spectacle étonne,
> Vole de toutes parts, se presse, l'environne.
>
> (V. viii. 1739–40)

The unseen courtiers, and beyond them, the Senate and the people

---

[25]The only reference to an action of the courtiers within the play is to their surprise and fear when Britannicus falls dead of the poison; half of those present flee, the remainder Néron dominates (V. v. 1635–6):

> Mais ceux qui de la cour ont un plus long usage
> Sur les yeux de César composent leur visage.

Here Racine is very close to Tacitus, XIII, 5.

of Rome, play a far larger rôle in *Bérénice*, in which the emperor is no longer sole master of his destiny. The "cabinet solitaire" is a refuge for Titus and Bérénice; its doors serve to shut out the inquisitive crowd. Their fickleness is shown when they swarm about Bérénice on hearing the rumour of her marriage; Arsace has difficulty reaching her through the press:

> ... je n'ai percé qu'à peine
> Les flots toujours nouveaux d'un peuple adorateur,
> Qu'attire sur ses pas sa prochaine grandeur.
>
> (I. iii. 52–4)

At the end of Act IV, people, tribunes, consuls, and senators, followed by the mob, await Titus' decision in his chambers. The people's applause signals his choice:

> Le peuple avec transport l'arrête et l'environne,
> Applaudissant aux noms que le Sénat lui donne;
> Et ces noms, ces respects, ces applaudissements,
> Deviennent pour Titus autant d'engagements.
>
> (V. ii. 1271–4)

The crafty vizier of *Bajazet* includes in his plans the people of Constantinople, whom he controls through their priests and by the assiduous planting of rumours; within the palace itself, Roxane commands

> Cette foule de chefs, d'esclaves, de muets,
> Peuple que dans ses murs renferme ce palais.
>
> (II. i. 435–6)

In the end the palace is forced by Acomat's soldiers, who disperse Roxane's "esclaves effrayés." In *Bajazet*, however, as in *Britannicus*, the nameless soldiers and slaves remain unobtrusive, and subservient to the dark power of the heroine.

The fewest references to the unseen throng appear in *Mithridate*. The palace actually seems uninhabited, save for the *dramatis personae*; the people are mentioned only once, when they throng to the shore upon the news of Mithridate's arrival. One might suggest two reasons for this: Mithridate's long absence explains the lack of courtiers, and there is no need for an *ambiance* of court intrigue, since it is his spying and deception alone that Xipharès and Monime have to contend with.[26]

The invisible scene takes on its greatest movement and life in *Iphigénie*, with its mob of nameless soldiers, always called "les Grecs"

[26]Pharnace's intrigues are with the Romans, who are to arrive at the end of the play.

or "les soldats," who are the pawns of Calchas the priest, and who
remain in ignorance of the main course of events throughout most of
the play. At first, when the heroine arrives, they crowd about her,
wondering at her beauty, but when they learn the rôle she is destined
to play, they surround her with their spears. The characters do not
reach or leave the scene through corridors, but through the milling
crowd. "Je n'ai percé qu'à peine une foule inconnue," says Iphigénie
on her arrival, and when she attempts to escape, "Vois comme tout le
camp s'oppose à notre fuite." In *Phèdre*, however, silence predominates;
the sylvan retreat of Troezen, in Hippolyte's words, "ces paisibles
lieux," shelters neither courtiers nor mob; ironically it is seen as a
haven from the squabbles and intrigue of Athens. The characters remain
alone, save for confidant or friend, and Phèdre seeks solitude and darkness when not upon the stage. Although *Esther* has almost no allusions
to the unseen throng, in *Athalie* the people, doubting, fearful, and
finally triumphant, provide depth and variation to the offstage action.

Racine supports the illusion of the presence of invisible masses by
references to the sounds they make, usually in the various accounts of
past actions. In Cléone's description, Andromaque makes her way to
the temple amid the joyful shouts of the populace. In *Britannicus* the
Roman mob takes Junie under its protection "d'une commune voix,"
and the Greeks shout in unison their condemnation of Eriphile in the
last act of *Iphigénie*. The exultant cries of the Jews, mingling with the
trumpets, panic Athalie's troops.

Important offstage sounds are heard in the dramatic present, lending
reality to simultaneous invisible actions. Like the thunderclap, offstage
shouts and cries in *Iphigénie* could actually have been heard by the
audience. It seems logical to suppose so, and indeed we find a strong
hint that they were if we compare a moment in *Alexandre* with the
later plays. Axiane, forced by Taxile to remain in her tent while her
troops battle Alexandre's forces, longs to be with her subjects as they
die for her. "Le cri des mourants," she says, "vient presque jusqu'à
moi." Does not this "presque" suggest that Racine was still too timid
to use actual sounds offstage? Later, however, he has Mithridate tell
Monime: "D'un camp prêt à partir vous entendez les cris."

The presence of courtiers is often made known through sound.
Agrippine hears the noise and confusion as the frightened crowd
rushes from the banquet hall where Britannicus lies dead. "Mais

qu'est-ce que j'entends? Quel tumulte confus?"[27] We hear the buzz of voices as Titus and Bérénice take refuge in the "cabinet solitaire," and Phénice recognizes Titus' approach by the sound of the crowd:

> J'entends du bruit, Madame, et l'Empereur s'approche.
> Venez, fuyez la foule.
>
> (IV. ii. 980–1)

Bérénice hears the people, who a moment before had flocked about her, shouting their joy at her dismissal:

> Ingrat, que je demeure !
> Et pourquoi ?  Pour entendre un peuple injurieux
> Qui fait de mon malheur retentir tous ces lieux ?
> Ne l'entendez-vous pas, cette cruelle joie ?
>
> (V. v. 1312–15)

The cries of the angry soldiers are heard outside Agamemnon's tent; in *Athalie*, Abner's knocking frightens the Levites who guard the temple, and the Queen, hearing the shouts of her army outside ("J'entends à haute voix tout mon camp qui m'appelle") believes they have come to rescue her. A moment later, however, we learn from Ismaël's report that these were cries of terror:

> Et ses sons et leurs cris dans son camp étonné
> Ont répandu le trouble et la terreur subite.
>
> (V. vi. 1754–5)

In the foregoing pages we have seen evidence of the process whereby Racine transforms unity of time and place into his own dramatic realization of time and space. In a very real sense, time is dramatic in Racine; his characters are its prisoners, bearing the onus of the past and confronting a future that brings catastrophe. Though a Pyrrhus may declare confidently, "Je consens d'oublier le passé," that bloody past, that vision of his sword gleaming in the light of burning Troy or plunging into the breasts of helpless victims cannot be conjured away; as Hermione assures him, "Ces Dieux, ces justes Dieux n'auront pas oublié." To forget the past's tragic implications is to ignore a

[27]Here, as when Ulysse describes later the thunder already heard in the last act of *Iphigénie*, Burrhus confirms the source of the tumult heard earlier (*Britannicus*, V. v. 1633–4):
> Jugez combien ce coup frappe tous les esprits.
> La moitié s'épouvante et sort avec des cris.

warning, and part of man's tragedy is that he must so often forget:

> De soins tumultueux un prince environné,
> Vers de nouveaux objets est sans cesse entraîné;
> L'avenir l'inquiète, et le présent le frappe;
> Mais, plus prompt que l'éclair, le passé nous échappe.
>
> (*Esther*, II. ii. 543–6)

We have seen how, in Racine's tragedy, the sense of fatality is increased by his concentration on the past through a precise measurement of the time elapsed, and through the poetic evocation of the distant past and of the earlier careers of his characters. For the Racinian hero, in a very real sense "se sentir vivre, c'est se sentir s'écouler";[28] the dramatic present is in fact a *becoming*, and the characters, with every succeeding moment of the action, feel themselves propelled into the future. This projection extends the scope of the tragedy, giving it a cyclic quality that increases its universality.

The concept of time frequently merges with that of space; just as the tragic action appears as a single moment in a limitless progression, so the dramatic setting becomes the focal point of a wider area, whose vastness is that of the universe. Before *Iphigénie*, the setting is made to exist dramatically, to obtrude upon the consciousness of character as well as spectator. With the later plays the unseen setting increases, dwarfing the visible scene, so that the situation of the tragic figure, conscious of the future rushing to meet him unprotected upon a field of action embracing the surface of the earth beneath the sky, recalls Pascal's fear and wonder at his own existence in time and space:

> Quand je considère la petite durée de ma vie, absorbée dans l'éternité précédente et suivante, le petit espace que je remplis et même que je vois, abîmé dans l'infinie immensité des espaces que j'ignore et qui m'ignorent, je m'effraie et m'étonne de me voir ici plutôt que là, car il n'y a point de raison pourquoi ici plutôt que là, pourquoi à présent plutôt que lors. Qui m'y a mis ? Par l'ordre et la conduite de qui ce lieu et ce temps a-t-il été destiné à moi ? (*Pensées*, 205)

Although we would not suggest that Racine's plays "express" the same feeling as this *pensée* of Pascal, it seems evident that the irony of man's greatness and smallness in space and time had struck the dramatist of *Iphigénie* as well as the recluse of Port-Royal.

---

[28]I borrow this phrase from G. Poulet, who applies it to Fénelon in "Fénelon et le temps," *Nouvelle Nouvelle Revue française*, II (1954), pp. 624–44.

# III. OTHER CONVENTIONS

THE UNITIES are perhaps the best known of the conventions that were imposed upon seventeenth-century dramatists. In addition, however, there existed a flock of minor conventions affecting the characters, both primary and secondary, the moral tone of the play, the dramatic situation, and even the entrances and exits of the actors. I do not propose here to study all of these in their multiple ramifications, but rather to select a sampling for close examination, a group of conventions, which, I believe, when adapted by Racine, helped to invest his plays with the particular mark of his genius.

## THE CONFIDANT

Next to the three unities, the student of French classic drama perhaps calls most readily to mind the confidant. This male or female personage has been rather generally condemned as a pale figure, a "utility character" who accompanies a principal, stimulating him to conversation, offering advice or condolences, and serving as messenger, bearer of information, or chaperon of lovers' tête-à-têtes. It is true that in many plays of our period the confidants do no more than fulfil these functions, and consequently seem dull and monotonous, if not superfluous. But George Saintsbury was wrong when he rather testily labelled this conventional figure "the curse of the French stage."[1] As developed, particularly in Racinian tragedy, the confidant had often a vital and significant rôle to play.

We do not lack critics who have asserted that Racine, unlike Corneille, who considered them "gens sans action,"[2] breathed life into these conventional "comparses." But how he did this is less often ascertained. Georges Le Bidois, one of the very few critics who have treated

---

[1]In his edition of *Horace*, Oxford, Clarendon Press, 1900, p. xxxiv, quoted by H. W. Lawton, "The Confidant in and before French Classical Tragedy," *MLR*, XXXVIII (1943), pp. 18–31.
[2]*De l'utilité et des parties du poème dramatique*, quoted by H. W. Lawton, *ibid.*

the subject,[3] explains the difference between the Cornelian and Racinian confidants by the difference between the kind of characters to which they are attached. The chief purpose of the confidant, he says, is to help reveal the mind or soul of the hero. A Cornelian hero, unswerving and strong-willed, is independent of his confidant; a Racinian hero, weak and torn by passion, leans on his confidant, who by that fact becomes an individual by the influence he exerts. This judgment, however impressive at first glance, is far too general, based as it is upon an assumption that all Racine's heroes are weak and passion-torn.

A view more recently advanced holds that Racine's confidants are projections of his heroes. The advice, good or bad, of the confidant is in reality the voice of the virtuous or wicked side of the principal charac-ter; the confidant becomes simply the "other self" turned by the dramatist into a stage person.[4] This view, like the earlier one, will not stand up to scrutiny if we consider all of Racine's plays, and all of his confidants. The "projection theory" is obviously a literary rather than a dramatic interpretation, since it fails to take into account the stage life of the confidant. Such a character, no matter how small his rôle, acquires a certain reality merely from the fact that he has a rôle to play. Witnessing a scene between Néron and his nefarious adviser, Narcisse (since Narcisse is the prime example offered in illustration of this theory), how can the spectator feel that the latter is a mere symbol of the ruler's evil side? He sees an actor before him, a malign and clever counsellor urging his master on to evil deeds.

This theory further fails to consider the scenes in which the confidant takes part when the hero is not present. And in Narcisse's case, since he is the confidant of both Néron and Britannicus, at what point does he cease to be the projection of the former to become that of the latter? It is surely a capital fact, moreover, that Narcisse is alive enough that he can die! And if, as the projection theory has it, Narcisse repre-sents Néron's evil nature, his death should then symbolize his master's return to virtue.

It is equally fruitless, I believe, to attempt to prove, as a recent critic has done, that confidants are not "unnatural" because they exist in real

[3]G. Le Bidois, *La Vie dans la tragédie de Racine,* Paris, Gigord, 1922, pp. 153-68.
[4]H. W. Lawton, "The Confidant in and before French Classical Tragedy."

life.[5] It is of course of the utmost importance to distinguish carefully between real life and dramatic phenomena. The question is not whether human beings take such confidential rôles in real life, but whether the confidants in a particular drama are dramatically valid. This is the problem that remains to be solved for Racine. If he has made his confidants living figures, and not mere supernumeraries, it is because they have been skilfully created to seem so; it is our business to discover how.

We shall first take the very obvious step of consulting the *dramatis personae* for each tragedy. We find at once that the designation "confident" and "confidente" appears rather infrequently. In *La Thébaïde*, Olympe and Attale are so listed, in *Alexandre* none appear; for each of *Britannicus, Mithridate, Iphigénie, Phèdre*, (Œnone is "nourrice *et* confidente," Arbate, "confident *et* gouverneur de la place de Nymphée"), *Esther*, and *Athalie*, only one character is actually called a "confident." *Andromaque* lists one for each of the two main female characters; *Bérénice* alone has a full complement, with confidants for each of the principals.

This scarcity might signify, however, only that Racine, like Corneille, who often changed the "confidents" and "confidentes" of earlier editions to "gouverneurs" and "gouvernantes,"[6] was simply trying to avoid a term which had acquired some critical disrepute. But it is a fact that Racine, from the beginning, takes pains to break the conventional balance; he makes the traditional duet of principal and confidant-figure the exception rather than the rule. Frequently, regardless of the designations in the *dramatis personae*, a character has no one assigned to him alone as confidant. Some characters confide in more than one person, others share a confidant between them.

The balance is broken in another way. On occasion the confidant no longer retains his traditional rôle as a person of trust; besides the well-known example of Narcisse, there is Arbate, who, although he is listed as "confident de Mithridate" actually fulfils that function for the latter's son, Xipharès. Not only does he speak far more with the latter, he lies, or at least equivocates, to the King concerning Xipharès' feeling for Monime (II. iii. 497–500).

[5] J. Fermaud, "The Confidant in Literature and Life," *MLR*, XLI (1946), pp. 419–22. See also his "Défense du Confident," *RR*, XXXI (1940), p. 334.

[6] See J. Schérer, *La Dramaturgie classique en France*, Paris, Nizet, n.d., p. 47.

And although in Racine, as in Corneille, "tutors" and "friends" act as confidants, they far transcend the traditional confidant-figure in importance. First of all, the various "gouverneurs" are legitimate instructors and mentors, whose rôle as such is called for by the plot. Even in *Andromaque*, where it would seem at first that the traditional pairing obtains—Oreste with Pylade, Pyrrhus with Phœnix, Andromaque with Céphise, Hermione with Cléone—the balance is broken by the imposing stature of the male confidant-figures in comparison with the female.[7] Such characters acquire added dimension when their relationships with the principals have a legendary or historical background; such a background may actually exist, as in the case of Orestes and Pylades, or be invented by the dramatist, as in the case of Phœnix, who has also been tutor to Achilles, Pyrrhus' father, and Théramène, charged with the training of Hippolyte by Thésée himself.

As seems natural, almost invariably the male confidants are strong of purpose, urging the hero to decisions of import; they seem to symbolize the stable world. The females, on the other hand, are less positive, seldom going farther than to proffer advice. In one thing they resemble the men; they are oblivious of the conflicting currents of the heroine's spirit; they are practical souls, pressing a middle course upon characters who know only extremes. They are thus the instruments of dramatic irony. The presence of an Œnone, who can tell Phèdre first that with Thésée's death, her love becomes natural (Racine's word is "ordinaire"), then later, calmly urge her to forget, throws into terrible relief the solitude of the heroine.

But even in the case of a Céphise, a Cléone, an Albine, an Ismène, a Phœdime, or a Doris, who come the closest to the confidante of convention, their being little more than pale shadows of their mistresses is justified by the dramatic situation.[8] Agrippine's having a single lady-in-waiting calls attention to her solitary plight; Andromaque, Hermione, Bérénice, Monime, and Eriphile have in common that they are *aliens*,

---

[7]Note that before the beginning of the play, Pylade has been Hermione's confidant: "Je l'ai vue enfin me confier ses larmes" (I. i. 129).

[8]In the 1954 production of *Andromaque* at the Comédie Française, a remarkably effective use was made of the confidante; Cléone, costumed in brilliant yellow, appeared from the wings a moment *before* her mistress, so that the audience was prepared visually as well as auditively for her entrances. Hearing Andromaque's words in IV. i. "C'est Hermione. Allons, fuyons sa violence" at the same time as Cléone appears, literally forces the audience's gaze toward the place where Hermione is to enter.

come from afar, who must rely on a trusty servitor. And in the few cases where the confidant is almost completely colourless, this again is justified by the situation. The Zatime and Zaïre of *Bajazet*, who speak a bare forty-nine lines apiece, are "slaves," and their muteness accords both with local colour and their rôles as pale and pliable attendants. Yet on occasion, even muteness can bring such a character to life; when Zatime is questioned by the frightened Atalide, she is dumb with fear of her savage mistress.

No longer supernumeraries, Racine's confidants are alive because they are secondary characters participating in the action to whatever degree is necessitated by the plot, no more, no less. In his creation of these secondary figures, Racine seems consciously to have rejected the stability of the hero-confidant relationship characteristic of Corneille and earlier dramatists. The see-saw shifting of relationship between the primary and the secondary characters reflects the uneasy equilibrium of Racine's world.

## Les Bienséances

Earlier in these pages we compared briefly one aspect of Shakespeare's and Racine's handling of death. The Elizabethan taste for battles, suicides, and murders onstage was echoed in French tragedy until after the reign of Louis XIII, but in general, during the latter half of the century, onstage death and combat, as well as certain other types of stage conduct considered shocking or immoral, were proscribed by *les bienséances*, those rules of stage decorum which we may translate, "proprieties." It is not our purpose here to seek out the causes for the prevalence of scenic decency after 1650. The phenomenon has been attributed by more than one critic to the moralistic tendencies of the Counter-Reformation, which interpreted Aristotle's catharsis as a purging of evil and a stimulus to virtue.[9] Others have found the reluctance to show battles onstage an example of the public's growing demand for verisimilitude.[10] Whatever their cause, the proprieties have had an undeniable effect upon the tragedies of Racine. Once again, we must determine what this effect has been, and in what measure he was able to assimilate and recreate them.

[9]See H. Hatzfeld, "A Clarification of the Baroque Problem in the Romance Literatures," *CL,* I (1949).

[10]Cf. Schérer, *La Dramaturgie classique en France,* 410 ff.

Death, to voice a truism, is an all but essential element in tragedy. Propriety required that, if possible, it should occur offstage, and in almost every case Racine bowed to this requirement. What we must first discover is how the observance of this rule affects the plays as a whole, and whether Racine was able, as he was in the case of other conventions, to profit from this observance.

In every tragedy but one, the deaths occur in the last act. The exception is the suicide of Ménécée in *La Thébaïde*, an episode Racine enlarged upon in order to build dramatic irony. But this event is exceptional for other reasons. It is the only *heroic* death in all Racine; because it is a sacrifice, demanded by the gods, it escapes the ignominy of suicide. Every other figure who dies, either commits suicide, or meets an ignoble death at the hands of assassins. Pyrrhus dies beneath the blows of the Greeks, Britannicus is poisoned, Bajazet is strangled, Mithridate stabs himself to avoid capture, after taking poison in vain; Hermione, Eriphile, and Atalide stab themselves; Phèdre takes poison, Roxane is stabbed by the Sultan's slave, and Athalie dies, not at the head of her soldiers, but at the hands of an executioner. Even Hippolyte, who succeeds in wounding the bull-dragon, has the odds stacked against him by Neptune's intervention, and is reduced to an unrecognizable pulp "sans forme et sans couleur."

In general, then, the offstage death is well adapted to Racinian tragedy because the violent end to which his characters come is inglorious, if not ignominious.[11]

There are other specific advantages. Offstage death accords particularly well with plays like *Britannicus* and *Bajazet*, where palace and seraglio are places of mystery, full of hidden corridors and recesses, where summary executions take place in secret. The poison that will kill Britannicus has already been tested on a slave, and we learn from Agrippine herself that mysterious and sudden deaths by poisoning are common. That Bajazet should leave the stage shortly to fall into the hands of Orcan and the waiting eunuchs somewhere in the harem[12]

[11]One may contrast with the ignominious death in Racine, the killing of Camille offstage by her brother Horace. This is an example of strict observance of the convention. Camille dies heroically, in a stream of splendid invective against Rome, and there is no reason other than propriety for Horace to pursue and slay her behind the scenes rather than before the audience.

[12]They are not immediately outside, as some commentators seem to think: Roxane tells her slave to *follow* Bajazet, and to report what happens.

lends far greater force and suspense to Roxane's ultimatum than had he died before our eyes.

The death of a Pyrrhus or a Hippolyte, by occurring offstage, focusses our attention on the fate of more important characters. Of the doomed figures in *Andromaque*, only Oreste, whose subsequent career is known to the audience, remains before us, thus projecting our thoughts into the future. It is true that Hippolyte's fight with the monster could hardly have been shown on the stage, save in an opera, but he might well have been carried on dying, as in the Euripidean version. Instead, Phèdre takes a slow poison, so that she is able to die onstage, before Thésée's and Théramène's accusing gaze, thus reaffirming her position as the central figure of the tragedy.

No violent deaths occur before our eyes; the characters who die onstage are all suicides, and in only one case do we see the act itself committed. In all three cases of onstage death the dramatic necessity is clear: both that the death be self-inflicted, and that the dying characters appear at the end of the play. Unlike Eriphile, Jocaste, and Antigone, whose offstage suicides are acts of desperation, sudden and calamitous, Phèdre and Atalide die in expiation, in a feeling of responsibility for the catastrophe that precedes their deaths. The case of Mithridate is somewhat different, however, He first attempts suicide by poison, and when this fails, attacks the Romans, although heavily outnumbered. On the point of being overwhelmed, he stabs himself to avoid capture. The sudden reversal of the tide of battle, however, makes a final speech by Mithridate necessary, for not only must he cancel his order for Monime's death, he must make restitution by joining her with Xipharès. His tragic stature is increased by the final speech; Racine may also have felt that the prediction he makes acquired greater force on the lips of a dying man.

Like the song of Tristan, the tragedy of Racine eternally balances death and love. The presentation of love upon the stage, the sentimental and sensual relationships of the characters, was also of concern to the proprieties. A significant aspect of convention in this regard that will concern us briefly at this point was the love-confession. A man might confess his love to the lady of his choice, but women had to languish in silence. As D'Aubignac wrote, in his schoolmasterish way, "Il ne faut jamais qu'une femme fasse entendre de sa propre bouche qu'elle a de l'amour pour lui."[13]

Racine did not obey this injunction literally, of course, for one immediately remembers avowals of love by Monime, by Aricie, by Phèdre. Yet, in these confessions, the impact of the convention is felt; they are made only with the greatest difficulty, they are long delayed, they are often ambiguous at first, couched in "Aesopian" terms. Monime, for example, after Xipharès' passionate confession, can only reply,

> Pour me faire, Seigneur, consentir à vous voir,
> Vous n'aurez pas besoin d'un injuste pouvoir.
>
> (I. ii. 221–2)

She tells her servant, to whom she has already confessed her love, of this veiled statement, and of the violence she must do herself to hold back an admission. She has spoken, she says, only "à demi," but such restraint is torture:

> Hélas ! si tu savais, pour garder le silence,
> Combien ce triste cœur s'est fait de violence !
> Quels assauts, quels combats, j'ai tantôt soutenus !
>
> (II. i. 411–13)

Finally, when Mithridate's arrival is announced, and all hope is gone, she lets out the truth with the words: "Ma douleur pour se taire a trop de violence."

Jacques Schérer has pointed out that such confessions are usually made in three steps, first to a confidante, second to the beloved himself, and lastly, to a third party. Where he errs, I believe, is in implying, though citing examples taken almost solely from Racine, that this procedure is common in seventeenth-century tragedy, and in suggesting that it is no more than an example of the observance of the proprieties. Yet what a difference between the few examples occurring in other writers, such as the following gem from Du Ryer, and Racine's subtle gradations:

> Que je dise que j'aime, ha ! Monsieur, nullement.
> Lorsque j'en crois rougir, je parle rarement,

---

[13]*Pratique du théâtre,* ed. Martino, Paris, Champion, 1927, p. 329. Cf. *Troilus and Cressida,* III. ii. 129–32:

> But though I lov'd you well, I woo'd you not;
> And yet, good faith, I wish'd myself a man,
> Or that we women had men's privilege
> Of speaking first.

Et je ne pense pas qu'une fille modeste
Le puisse avec honneur dire, même du geste.[14]

In every case in Racine the reticence, the veiled language, stem from the dramatic situation. Monime has not spoken because she is betrothed to Mithridate; long before the action begins, she has confessed her love for Xipharès to Phœdime, and it is her long habit of repression that serves her so well when he confesses his feeling for her. How much greater because of this is the calamity of Mithridate's arrival, simply because its effect is to startle the heroine into a confession! The case of Phèdre is similar, with its slow uncovering of emotion, step by painful step, until the naked violence of the open confession. Even in the first step in the pattern, the revelation to a confidante, the admission is a tortured one, and to this part of the convention Racine skilfully adapts Euripides in making Phèdre physically unable to pronounce Hippolyte's name. The veiled language itself, as Racine recreates it, is no longer a "façon de parler," but a desperate attempt on the part of the heroine to avoid the shame of a direct avowal. The conventional womanly reserve ordained by the *bienséances* becomes an agonized repression through fear of emotions which appear all the more violent when the confession finally bursts forth. Once again a rule, or rather a codification of dramatic manners, has been woven into the peculiarly Racinian fabric.

## EXPOSITION, RECITAL, AND SOLILOQUY

Concerning dramatic exposition, and probably with Racine in mind, the eighteenth-century critic, J. M. Clément, wrote that

Le grand art est d'exposer le sujet en action: je veux dire que les personnages devraient être mis d'abord en scène par un intérêt pressant qui détermine l'action, et non pour nous donner froidement des instructions préparatoires au sujet. Il faut que ces éclaircissements nécessaires viennent ensuite du [=après le] motif même qui fait agir les personnages.[15]

But no matter what precautions a dramatist may take, an exposition remains an artifice. There is no reason, to take a frivolous example, why the butler and the maid in a hundred plays should discuss the mistress and her plans for divorce at precisely that *juncture* in the action. It is with the exposition as with any other device; the dramatist, comic,

[14]Quoted by Schérer, *La Dramaturgie classique en France,* p. 397.
[15]Quoted by Schérer, *ibid.,* p. 59.

tragic, or other, must decide whether or not to make it plausible, "natural," so that the spectator won't think to ask, "Why are they telling one another all this? Surely both of them are already aware of the facts." If he rejects naturalism, he may, like Euripides or Shakespeare, frankly use a "prologue"—an external piece, pronounced either by a character or an extraneous personage who takes no part in the action. He may, like Molière in *Les Fourberies de Scapin*, spoof the whole idea of exposition, turning it to comic advantage.

Seventeenth-century critics frowned upon the use of patent devices, at least in tragedy. The prologue, at least as a portion of the play detached from the action, was considered as "artificial" as the chorus, and it is understandable that neither Corneille nor Racine (always with the exception of the exceptional *Esther*) ventured to adopt it. Racine, as we might expect, bent all his energies toward assimilating his expository material, making it seem natural. One never finds in Racine, for example, such a flagrantly artificial stimulus for the necessary revelations as Chimène's urging Elvire:

> Dis-moi donc, je te prie, une seconde fois
> Ce qui te fait juger qu'il approuve mon choix :
> Apprends-moi de nouveau quel espoir j'en dois prendre;
> Un si charmant discours ne se peut trop entendre.
>
> (I. i. 7–10)

One characteristic of the Racinian exposition, then, is its rejection of the simple colloquy favoured by Corneille; an impetus, or to borrow Clément's terms, an "intérêt pressant," had to bring the characters on stage and their discussion had to appear to spring from that urgency.

One type of impetus favoured by Racine is the search. A character, accompanied by a confidant, seeks another character, usually at dawn. Significantly, this type occurs in the three "palace" plays, where the enclosed nature of the action plays an important rôle. In the winding corridors of Néron's palace, in the forbidden rooms of the seraglio, the search takes on a peculiar quality of desperation, and the words spoken have a special resonance. Other tragedies (*Andromaque, Bajazet, Esther*) find their impetus in an arrival, others in a decision which is pending and thus requires immediate discussion (*Alexandre, Mithridate, Iphigénie, Phèdre*).

The most skilfully managed "arrival" is that of Oreste. It is surely a touch of genius that while Racine borrowed his traditional friends, Oreste and Pylade, from Greek tragedy and legend, he invented their separation in the events preceding the play, so that the exposition coincides with a long hoped-for reunion. At once all questions and answers, however lengthy and detailed, become plausible, as the excited friends "fill in" the time that has passed since they last saw one another. Of course playwrights had long ago realized that if one of the interlocutors had just returned from a voyage his question concerning well-known facts would appear more natural. But Racine turns the device to much greater advantage than, say, Corneille in his *Médée*. In *Andromaque*, it is the central figure, Oreste, who arrives, and the confidant who apprises him of the situation. Oreste is projected into the action, since he must act on the basis of the events related. In *Médée*, not only is it the chief character, Jason, not the confidant, who gives the information, but he has already taken action before the play has begun.

As to immediate decisions which precipitate action, Taxile must decide whether to accept Alexandre's offer, Xipharès has received confirmation of Mithridate's death and is preparing to pursue his suit of Monime, Agamemnon must send his servant to intercept Iphigénie, and Hippolyte is leaving to search for his father, though in reality to escape from his love for Aricie.

Besides providing an essential impetus, Racine must focus our attention upon the exposition, and he often achieves this by some striking device of setting. Frequently the quiet of early morning serves, not only to set the actual time of the events, as we saw in our discussion of time, but to provide a hushed atmosphere in which action is suspended and narrative takes precedence. That remarkably Shakespearean exposition scene in *Iphigénie* takes place not only in the hush of the sleeping camp, but in the semi-darkness before dawn. This darkness concentrates our minds, not on gesture or appearance, but on speech alone; Agamemnon commands Arcas to recognize, not his face, but "la voix qui frappe ton oreille."

Giraudoux' complaint that "les plus belles métaphores de Racine ne sont pas réservées aux rôles principaux mais à des comparses . . . à des confidents, ou des valets"[16] is of course inexact; furthermore, if a secondary character speaks poetry, there is a reason. The fact that

[16]Jean Giraudoux, *Racine*, Paris, Grasset, 1930, p. 53.

Racine gave to Arcas the most breath-taking line in the play—"Mais tout dort, et l'armée, et les vents, et Neptune"—has a dramatic explanation: the need for our complete concentration on the narrative. And only an Arcas can describe what is external; at this moment Agamemnon's gaze is totally inward.

To prevent his exposition from seeming a prologue-like block of dialogue inserted before the dramatic action, Racine establishes the illusion of its continuity with the pre-dramatic action. Often, when the curtain rises, we seem to be interrupting a dialogue that has been going on for some time. Thus the Racinian exposition is in harmony with the time concept discussed earlier, in which the tragic action is part of a sequence stretching behind the play.

Obviously, then, the first line of a play is of the utmost importance. *Andromaque, Iphigénie,* and *Athalie* all begin with the word "oui," as if in answer to an earlier question. In these plays, however, the conversation is static; the figures stand in an attitude of discussion. Elsewhere a suggestion of continued motion confirms the feeling of continuity. In the first line of Britannicus, Agrippine's confidante cries out, "Quoi?" and begins to expostulate with her mistress for waiting alone at Néron's door. Does this not suggest that Albine has followed her and that her excited "Quoi?" is pronounced as she comes up to the Queen? Other first lines implying that not only conversation, but the physical movement of the characters is already in progress are Antiochus' words in *Bérénice,* "Arrêtons un moment," or Acomat's in *Bajazet,* "Viens, suis-moi."

We have already discussed, in the case of *Andromaque,* some of the advantages Racine derived from the well-known friendship of Orestes and Pylades. And in general he benefits from the fact that his characters are so often legendary figures, who, however much he may change them, still retain a residue of their pre-established characters, and because, like the famous friends, they are so often acquainted. As Georges May has pointed out, for Racine to have had to explain at length the complex relationships binding his characters might have confused and overburdened his expositions.[17] Since "familiar" characters, whose relationships are legendary, appear in the play, the exposition is thereby simplified so that, as Mr. May puts it, the poet can con-

---

[17]*Tragédie cornélienne, tragédie racinienne,* University of Illinois Press, 1947, pp. 157-9.

centrate on "le degré de tension des passions, le niveau emotionnel et comme la température du cœur de chaque personnage."

It is true that this familiarity helps to reduce the amount of necessary detail, but I believe it is less exact to say that the exposition is shortened thereby. Racine usually confines his exposition to the first scene of the first act. Now, with the exception of *La Thébaïde* and *Bérénice*, these scenes contain anywhere from 128 lines (*Britannicus*) to 164 (*Athalie*). Corneille's expositions, even though his characters are rarely familiar to us, seldom exceed 160 lines. Even the exposition of *Rodogune*, crammed as it is with tales of battles, defeats, and the history of the participants, and containing a long recital by Laonice that Corneille felt obliged to interrupt by the entrance of another character, is only 158 lines long, shorter than that of *Iphigénie*.

This point is even clearer if we consider the exposition of *La Thébaïde*, which, as so often is the case, reveals the lines that Racine's technique would follow in later plays. It is true that the dramatist relies on our knowing the relationships between the various members of Oedipus' family. As some critics have pointed out severely, the first scene of 33 lines mentions no names at all except that of Olympe, although when Jocaste cries out, "Ils sont sortis!" or when she tells her confidante to inform "the princess" of what has happened, we know that she is referring to the enemy brothers of the sub-title and their sister. The actual exposition stretches through three scenes, containing a total of 132 lines. Of what do these lines consist? Actually, we find that in this first tragic exposition, Racine's characters suffer from a grave attack of first-act amnesia. Why, if Racine intended to exploit fully his public's knowledge of the Theban legend, is it necessary for Jocaste to expound at length to Etéocle, who is perfectly aware of it, her husband's ruling that his sons should take the throne in alternate years (I. iii. 81–90)? Etéocle continues the game in a twenty-line summary of Polynice's dethronement, his marriage to the King of Argos' daughter, and the raising of troops against Thebes, facts that anyone familiar with the story could be expected to know.

And is it really correct to say, of the exposition of *Andromaque*, that the state of Oreste's and Pyrrhus' passion is in fact "la seule exposition que contienne cette première scène"?[18] But what of Oreste's long dis-

[18]G. May, *ibid.*, p. 159.

course on his past? As we have already shown, this speech establishes a wide panorama in time, showing the characters' progress toward the dramatic action. And although it is true enough that "Oreste n'est presenté à aucun moment, son nom tristement fameux et celui de sa sinistre famille suffisent à l'annoncer," Racine's exposition has other purposes; it must present the character of his new Oreste, who is not the Orestes of Agamemnon, Sophocles, or Euripides, but a man pursued by fate, melancholy by nature; one whose struggle with his love for Hermione is already historical, and who now has reached a point at which, coinciding with the beginning of the play, he has surrendered irrevocably to his hopeless love.

No, the originality of Racine's exposition lies, not in any concision he attained through presenting familiar characters and subjects, but rather in the feeling of urgency, of continuity with the rest of the action, of dramatic tension, that it awakens in the spectator. Thus, the most significant thing about the exposition in *La Thébaïde* is the way Racine adapted the opening lines of Rotrou's play, *Antigone*, to his own purposes:

> JOCASTE (*Antigone*)
> Qu'ils ont bien à propos usé de mon sommeil !
> Ils n'ont pas appelé ma voix à leur conseil;
> Et lorsqu'ils ont voulu tenter cette sortie,
> On a bien su garder que j'en fusse avertie.
>
> JOCASTE (*La Thébaïde*)
> Ils sont sortis, Olympe ? Ah mortelles douleurs !
> Qu'un moment de repos me va coûter de pleurs !
> Mes yeux depuis six mois étaient ouverts aux larmes,
> Et le sommeil les ferme en de telles alarmes ?

It is scarcely necessary to point out that by skilful rearrangement Racine's lines at once establish the note of alarm and fear, the feeling of continuity, the hint of disastrous results to follow, none of which he found in his model.

Also characteristic of Racine's exposition is its mobility. We have already shown, discussing the first scene of *Andromaque*, how a skilful alternating of the tenses lent depth and variety to the recital of past events. The change of pace thus achieved is another means by which Racine prevents the expositional speech from taking on an oratorical and static quality. Another excellent illustration of the way this effect is achieved may be found in the exposition of *Britannicus*, where Agrippine contrasts Néron's present and past practices. The background of Roman history provides examples of past tyranny; Caligula's record foreshadows Néron's (lines 39–42), and following the melancholy recital of vanished power, the past definite, contrasting with the imperfect, brings sharply into focus the scene of Agrippine's disgrace:

> Non, non, le temps n'est plus que Néron, jeune encore,
> Me renvoyait les vœux d'une cour qui l'adore,
> Lorsqu'il se reposait sur moi de tout l'Etat,
> Que mon ordre au palais assemblait le sénat,
> Et que derrière un voile, invisible et présente, 95
> J'étais de ce grand corps l'âme toute-puissante...
> Ce jour, ce triste jour frappe encor ma mémoire,
> Où Néron fut lui-même ébloui de sa gloire, 100
> Quand les ambassadeurs de tant de rois divers
> Vinrent le reconnaître au nom de l'univers.
> Sur son trône avec lui j'allais prendre ma place.
> J'ignore quel conseil prépara ma disgrâce:
> Quoiqu'il en soit, Néron, d'aussi loin qu'il me vit, 105
> Laissa sur son visage éclater son dépit.
> Mon cœur même en conçut un malheureux augure.
> L'ingrat, d'un faux respect colorant son injure,
> Se leva par avance, et courant m'embrasser,
> Il m'écarta du trône où je m'allais placer. 110

With line 97, the setting changes to the more recent past; lines 100–102 situate the scene historically. Lines 97, 104, and 107, in which the speaker gives her own feelings, maintain the balance between present and past, especially line 104, whose present tense, "j'ignore," returns us abruptly to the speaker herself, and her fear of Néron's counsellors. This scene, crystallized out of the past, has marked the first step in Agrippine's continuing disgrace; her words (ll. 111–12)

> Depuis ce coup fatal, le pouvoir d'Agrippine,
> Vers sa chute, à grands pas, chaque jour s'achemine,

take us from that fateful day to the present state of affairs, i.e., a crucial stage in the gradual disintegration of the Queen's prestige.

Racine further achieves mobility by the way in which he implicates both collocutors. The character who delivers an expository speech repeatedly breaks off his narrative to address his listener. Oreste, for example, keeps referring to Pylade's knowledge of his feelings ("Tu vis naître ma flamme," etc.), and calls for his specially close attention at certain points ("Admire avec moi le sort. . . .") Similarly, Hippolyte's mention of Théramène's acquaintance with him since the cradle ("Toi qui connais mon cœur depuis que je respire"), and indeed the way in which his whole recital of the exploits of Thésée takes the form of a recollection of stories told him in his infancy by his mentor, maintains the impression that this is dialogue, not a speech pronounced in another character's presence:

> Tu me contais alors...
> Tu sais combien mon âme, attentive...
> > ... tu me dépeignais ce héros...
> > ... tu récitais des faits...
> Tu sais comme à regret écoutant ce discours.

In this manner, the essential background of legendary exploits and amorous conquests is no poetic *hors-d'œuvre*, but is fused with the dialogue.

On occasion, the characters reflect the playwright's distaste for expositional oratory. In the first scene of *Bajazet*, when Acomat and his confidant Osmin are entering the harem, the vizier replies to his companion's wondering questions in these words (ll. 6-7):

> Quand tu seras instruit de tout ce qui se passe,
> Mon entrée en ces lieux ne te surprendra plus,

but breaks off impatiently (l. 8),

> Mais, laissons, cher Osmin, les discours superflus.

A remarkably adroit way of suggesting that what follows consists of nothing but the bare essentials! In *Mithridate*, Xipharès, revealing to Arbate his long-concealed passion for Monime, says abruptly:

> Mais, en l'état funeste où nous sommes réduits,
> Ce n'est guère le temps d'occuper ma mémoire
> A rappeler le cours d'une amoureuse histoire.
> > (I. i. 42-4)

The five lines that follow are all the more powerful for this self-imposed brevity; especially does the verb "voir," always so pregnant in Racine, take on a brutal force:

> Qu'il te suffise donc, pour me justifier,
> Que je vis, que j'aimai la Reine le premier;
> Que mon père ignorait jusqu'au nom de Monime,
> Quand je conçus pour elle un amour légitime;
> Il la vit.

Despite the fact that 57 lines of exposition follow without a break, such a beginning successfully creates an illusion of terseness and economy.[19]

We have seen how the exposition seems to spring up out of an uninterrupted series of events, but it also thrusts us forward into the ensuing action; in *La Thébaïde* Jocaste tells us that her moment of rest will cost heavily in tears. Indeed one critic has seen, in the unusually explicit exposition of *Athalie*, the final development of the technique, employed in earlier plays, of foreshadowing by the exposition.[20] It should be pointed out, however, that the foreshadowing of the exposition is often ironic. Perhaps the best example of this is *Phèdre*, where the atmosphere of the exposition is at complete variance with what ensues. Troezen is "l'aimable Trézène," the peaceful setting of Hippolyte's childhood that he has always preferred to the bustle of Athens. There is, Théramène tells the youth, nothing to be feared from Phèdre, who no longer gives evidence of hating him. Even the bantering old mentor's plea for love, his knowing talk of Venus and the hearts she has swayed, of Antiope's "modest ardour," prove ironic in the context of the whole play. His portentous statement about love has a double significance:

> Ah ! Seigneur, si votre heure est une fois marquée,
> Le ciel de nos raisons ne sait point s'informer.

> (I. i. 114-15)

Hippolyte's hour has indeed come, but the gods have marked him for a different tryst, and these lines express half-humorously the tragic truth about Venus attached to her prey that we are later to hear from the heroine's lips.[21]

Although we are far from having exhausted the subject, our discussion should by now have shown that Racine's exposition provides yet

[19]Cf. Roxane to Atalide: "Sans vous fatiguer d'un récit inutile."
[20]G. May, *Tragédie cornélienne, tragédie racinienne*, p. 180.
[21]The situation established in the exposition may be reversed; Mithridate is declared dead in the first scene of Act I; his return is announced three scenes later.

another example of his mastery of a dramatic convention. Inevitably, there were flaws. Although after *La Thébaïde* we find no further outbreak of first-act amnesia, there are two occasions on which an interlocutor's questions and reactions resemble those of the "straight man" of radio, whose function is merely to keep the dialogue flowing. Pylade's feverish questioning is quite plausible, for reasons we have already discussed, but in *Bérénice*, Arsace's shocked exclamations are not, for they are too obviously an artifice intended to provide the audience with a thumb-nail sketch of Antiochus.[22] Similarly, Arbate's surprise in the following lines is the surprise of dramatic convention alone.

> L'amitié des Romains ? Le fils de Mithridate,
> Seigneur ! Est-il bien vrai ?
>
> (I. i. 23–4)

It is impressive, however, that lapses of this kind are of the utmost rarity.

We now come to other types of long speeches that have a conventional origin, but that differ in dramatic function from the expositional speech. These are the *tirade*, a vague term sometimes applied to any lengthy speech regardless of its function, the recital (*récit*), which describes events occurring offstage and is delivered by a messenger, and the soliloquy.

Such long speeches, whatever their classification, obviously have some features in common besides length. For example, in analysing Oreste's exposition speech, we have already had occasion to discuss the way in which the playwright contrived to prevent his description of his past career from becoming oratorical. A similar method is employed just as regularly for other long speeches, with one important difference. In the exposition the relationship is that of speaker and listener; the information being delivered is important in itself; the reaction of the listener is less so. This priority was most evident in the exposition of *Iphigénie*, where the scene is in semi-darkness. In the other types of long speech, Racine's technique of "implicating" the silent

[22]"Vous, Seigneur, importun? vous, cet ami fidèle .... Vous, cet Antiochus ...." etc. However, the one instance that Schérer finds overcontrived (*La Dramaturgie classique en France*, p. 57), Arcas' questions on seeing the melancholy of Agamemnon in *Iphigénie* (I. ii), is actually quite plausible. If the old officer is attempting to comfort his King, what better way than to remind him of the honours now in his grasp?

characters takes the form of frequent comments, made by the speakers, on the visible reactions of their listeners.

A type of speech which runs almost as great a risk of appearing static and rhetorical as the exposition is what we might call "the speech from the throne." Such a speech occurs in the triangular scene in La Thébaïde, where Jocaste strives by her entreaties to bring her two sons together. Scenes of like sculptural quality occur when Agrippine meets Néron in Act IV of Britannicus, or in Mithridate's address to his two sons in Act III. In both instances, the first word, "Approchez," has the effect of concentrating our attention on the speaker. In the first case, Agrippine's speech, which sketches at length the sordid story of Néron's ascent to the throne, is nevertheless interspersed throughout with questions and comments directly addressed to the listener. Mithridate's speech (ll. 755–862) would seem inevitably to set up relationships even more static, with the two sons as passive auditors, yet they remain involved in the action through the King's frequent use of direct address, rhetorical questions, or comments on their expressions and gestures:

> Approchez, mes enfants... (755)
> Mais vous savez trop bien l'histoire de ma vie... (760)
> C'est à Rome, mes fils, que je prétends marcher... (786)
> Ce dessein vous surprend... (787)
> Ne vous figurez point que... (791)
> Doutez-vous que l'Euxin ne me porte en deux jours... (797)
> Vous avez vu l'Espagne... (805)
> Et vous les verrez tous... (811)
> Vous trouverez partout l'horreur du nom romain... (814)
> Non, Princes, ce n'est point au bout de l'univers... (817)
> ... En quel état croyez-vous la surprendre... (837)

As Mithridate's zeal mounts, a series of first-person imperatives mark the shift from persuasion to exhortation, enveloping his two sons in his enthusiasm: "Marchons. . . . Attaquons. . . . Croyons-en ce grand homme. . . . Noyons-la dans son sang. . . ." Of all the long speeches in Racine this has perhaps the most sculptural setting, yet by the technique of varying the tone, of ranging in subject-matter from the places described to the career of the speaker and back again, and by the oscillation from Mithridate to his sons, Racine maintains the illusion of mobility, of action in suspension.

In this type of situation, the speaker draws the listeners toward him.

CARL A. RUDISILL LIBRARY
LENOIR RHYNE COLLEGE

Another type of long speech occurs following an entrance, and thus catching the listener by surprise, begins by the speaker's noting the impact of his appearance. Pyrrhus tells Hermione:

> Vous ne m'attendiez pas, Madame; et je vois bien
> Que mon abord ici trouble votre entretien.
>
> (IV. v. 1275–6)

A few lines later he speaks the ominous words that ensure his own death: "J'épouse une Troyenne." His "Oui, Madame," directly following the hemistich, is an evident response to his listener's automatic gesture of recoil. From this point on, Hermione listens in stony silence. The last 8 lines of Pyrrhus' 34-line speech consist of his entreaty that she speak; Racine thus makes even her lack of reaction involve her and prevent Pyrrhus' speech from becoming an oration. "Burst out in curses," he says, in effect, "anything, but speak!" And in the end, instead of the expected outburst, the quiet, almost conversational tone of Hermione's reply marvellously conveys the suppressed fury that is to break out only when he misinterprets her words as "indifference." In his turn, Pyrrhus' silence becomes eloquent, when he absently fails to answer Hermione:

> Vous ne répondez point ? Perfide, je le vois,
> Tu comptes les moments que tu perds avec moi.
>
> (IV. v. 1375–6)

Many other examples could be offered of speakers who see sudden changes of attitude and expression, thus shifting our attention to the listener. In Titus' last speech to Bérénice, he tells her, "Je vois la mort peinte en vos yeux." Bajazet, trying vainly to overcome Roxane's distrust, remonstrates with her:

> Je vois, enfin, je vois, qu'en ce même moment
> Tout ce que je vous dis vous touche faiblement.
>
> (III. iv. 1003–4)

In a scene which may be compared to the interview between Hermione and Pyrrhus discussed a moment ago, Racine insists that even a secondary character be implicated. During the scene in *Andromaque*, although the King's confidant, Phœnix, is on stage, his presence is not recognized by the speakers, but in *Bérénice*, the heroine takes parenthetical note that Paulin is present:

CARL A. RUDISILL LIBRARY
LENOIR RHYNE COLLEGE

... (car je sais que cet ami sincère
Du secret de nos cœurs connaît tout le mystère).

(II. iv. 563-4)

Nor do listeners always stand silent during long speeches; they may weep or sigh, as well as cast eloquent looks. Monime, in the midst of a 37-line speech to Xipharès, remarks (II. vi. 699), "J'entends, vous gémissez. . . ."

The regularity with which Racine employed this technique may be shown by his involving so anonymous a confidante as Zaïre. In I. iv, Atalide's 62-line *tirade* is presented in four movements, each addressed to her servant:

Ah ! Zaïre, l'amour a-t-il tant de prudence ?    (345)
Et que fallait-il donc, Zaïre, que je fisse ?    (354)
Zaïre, il faut pourtant avouer ma faiblesse...    (377)
Mais, Zaïre, je puis l'attendre à son passage.    (398)

Curiously, this particular speech ends in a 5-line monologue, which, by suddenly detaching the confidante, effectively demonstrates the heightening of Atalide's emotions.

Those famous "set pieces" of Racinian tragedy, the *récits*, or passages of epic description, are, like the informative speeches of the exposition, detached from the action by their very nature, since they are delivered to an audience of one or more actors. The *récit* is of course the descendant of the messenger speech in Greek tragedy, which described violent scenes of battle and death. Speaking of the "extraordinary power" of the messenger speeches, which he describes as coming "with supreme glory at critical moments," John Masefield has told of their remarkable success at the time when Gilbert Murray's translations were first being performed:

for the first year or so, some actors were afraid of them: they were "story-telling on the stage." They soon learned what opportunities a Messenger Speech gave to anyone who had any sense. Each Messenger at once has all the attention that has been artfully prepared for him, during the preceding hour or so. He enters upon a stilled house, in which few even dare to cough. He finds a sort of malleable mind in front of him that he can play with as he will. A very few years after the first of these Greek plays in London, an actor said to me, "No one has ever known a Greek Messenger Speech to fail: they are always wild successes."[23]

[23]John Masefield, "The Joy of Story-Telling," *Atlantic Monthly*, CLXXXVII (1951), p. 69.

One may assume that Racine's seventeenth-century audience reacted in much the same way to his *récits* as did the Victorian spectator to the Greek messenger speeches. Our playwright seems to have been well aware of the tremendous dramatic potential of the *récit*; it is frequently the high point of his tragedy, and although essentially static, it develops a variety and sweep which produces a kind of drama within drama. Usually the speech begins with a line or two containing a succinct announcement of the event to be related ("Hippolyte n'est plus"), followed by a rapid sketch of the setting in a few broad strokes, whether it be, as in *La Thébaïde*, the duelling-ground near the city wall, or in *Mithridate*, the seashore and palace grounds, dominated by the palace doors flung open to reveal the imposing figure of the King, or in *Phèdre*, the ancestral cemetery near the temple. Sound, movement, dialogue, gesture; all contribute to the dramatic quality of the scene described. Allusions to the listener, though less frequent than in other types of long speeches, do occur from time to time. But while the exposition speech or *tirade* achieved flexibility through shifts of attention from speaker to listener, in the *récit* this is usually attained by a momentary return from the events described to the speaker himself, often by sudden expressions of wonder or grief, like Arbate's, "J'ai vu, qui l'aurait cru? j'ai vu de toutes parts. . . ." or Théramène's interjection, indicating that he is weeping as he speaks,

> Excusez ma douleur : cette image cruelle
> Sera pour moi de pleurs une source éternelle.[24]

The first of the great *récits*, Créon's vivid description of the duel between Polynice and Etéocle, is worthy of the mature Racine. Beginning with Hémon's vain attempt at intervention, and his death, the recital swiftly increases in tempo. The brothers clash, Etéocle falls; Polynice makes his exultant speech, followed by Etéocle's agonized effort, as, dying, he stabs the triumphant Polynice, and expires, "son âme ravie."[25]

---

[24]L. Spitzer (*Linguistics and Literary History*, Princeton University Press, 1948, pp. 110 ff.) has considered such interjections as Théramène's "digne fils d'un héros," to be a means of playing down the tension, as he calls it, "klassische dämpfung." I prefer to consider such a descriptive phrase, as well as the interjections of the type quoted above, manifestations of Racine's technique of implicating all the actors. He substitutes for the nameless messenger an actual character who is involved with the others, and he employs this device to preserve the impression that one character is addressing others, rather than a supernumerary performing an oratorical function.

[25]*La Thébaïde*, V. iii. This exultancy and joy in death, one may remark parenthetically, are in neither Euripides nor Rotrou; they are found only in Racine.

If we compare this first *récit* with that, say, of Arbate in *Mithridate*, we may however note some important differences. First of all, the brief yet exact announcement of the event to be related ("Le roi touche à son heure dernière"; "Xipharès vit chargé de gloire") replaces Créon's much more veiled statement, which may be a remnant of Cornelian mystification:

> ... les destins contraires
> Me font pleurer deux fils, si vous pleurez deux frères.
> (V. iii. 1297–8)

Créon is far more the orator, seldom referring to his listener or to himself. His description is far less rapid: the brothers' furious duel and Hémon's attempt at halting the combat are related in careful sequence. Créon, moreover, is a kind of omniscient author, able to read Etéocle's thoughts as he lies waiting for the chance to stab his opponent. The earlier *récit* is thus far closer to narrative.

By contrast, Arbate's account is completely that of the onlooker; he becomes, as it were, the eyes of his listeners. To this end, he uses the conditional frequently. When the Romans flee on the appearance of Mithridate, he says, not simply "they retreated," but "you would have seen them retreat"—"Vous les eussiez vu tous, retournant en arrière." Whereas Créon describes at length both actions and expressions—

> D'un geste menaçant, d'un œil brûlant de rage,
> Dans le sein l'un de l'autre ils cherchent un passage;
> Et la seule fureur précipitant leurs bras,
> Tous deux semblent courir au-devant du trépas —
> (V. iii. 1321–4)

Arbate's wonderment serves both as a device of foreshortening and of intensification, leaving the nature of the deeds to the reader's imagination:

> Qui pourrait exprimer par quels faits incroyables,
> Quels coups accompagnés de regards effroyables...
> (V. iv. 1591–2)

But the various elements that make of the Racinian *récit* a tiny play within the play: gesture, movement, sound, are present in both the earlier and the later work. Economy has increased, purely visual quality is now emphasized. The rather conventional description of gesture in *La Thébaïde* ("d'un geste menaçant," "d'une démarche

fière") is replaced in *Mithridate* by the visual evocation, through
gesture, of a dying man too feeble to speak:

> Il soulevait encore sa main appesantie,
> Et marquant à mon bras la place de son cœur,
> Semblait d'un coup plus sûr implorer la faveur.
>
> (V. iv. 1608-10)

But Créon's striking portrait of the dead Etéocle, his expression of
hatred frozen upon his face, had already demonstrated Racine's gift
for plastic description and his way of suddenly halting the violent
action, much as a moving-picture projectionist might stop his machine,
leaving the figures in a scene grouped together in a kind of sculptured
immobility. This is the effect of the scene picturing the dying Mithridate surrounded by dead Romans:

> ... las et couvert de sang et de poussière,
> Il s'était fait de morts une noble barrière.
>
> (V. iv. 1595-6)

Even in such tableaux as this, however, we see evidence of Racine's
developing tendency toward condensation. Bajazet, having heroically
resisted his assassins, is found dead, "de morts et de mourants noble-
ment entouré." The same type of picture, in an earlier *récit*, is sketched
with heavier strokes, as Porus fights on, surrounded in this case by the
bodies of his own men:

> Ses soldats, à ses pieds étendus et mourants,
> Le mettaient à l'abri de leurs corps expirants.
> Là, comme dans un fort, son audace enfermée
> Se soutenait encor contre toute une armée.
>
> (V. iii. 1431-4)

Direct quotation adds to the dramatic effect of all the *récits*. Créon
reports the last words of Hémon, who, like the dying Hippolyte,
thinks of his beloved before he expires. If there is any change or development in this connection, it is once again in the direction of economy.
Créon quotes Polynice as well as Hémon, and in the later *récits*, the
quoted words are those of the central figure alone. The longest quotation (15 lines) is Calchas' announcement of the god's verdict in *Iphigénie*, but in this case the direct quotation serves a special purpose.
Ulysse's account in Act V is so constructed that the high priest's speech,
besides what it communicates, helps to convey the impression of sus-

pended action. Calchas appears "entre les deux partis"—between the opposing forces who had already begun to fight. Both his appearance and his words are thus an effective brake upon the furious Greeks and Myrmidons, who listen in awe:

> Tout le camp immobile
> L'écoute avec frayeur et regarde Eriphile.
>
> (V. vi. 1761–2)

As reported by Ulysse, the high priest's revelation acquires, through the silence and immobility in which it was pronounced, a particular solemnity and resonance. And in fact this *récit*, with its shift from violence to immobility, then to violence and mobility, summarizes the action of the play, which owes so much of its tension to the interplay of movement and equilibrium. With Eriphile's suicide the log-jam is broken; both man and nature are released in a torrent of action.[26]

Finally, we may briefly consider a problem which, although it has to do with the time scheme of the tragedies, we have reserved for this chapter because it arises most frequently in connection with the *récit*. Briefly the question is this: the hero or heroine leaves the stage, and after a few lines the messenger returns with his account of the catastrophe. The events he now relates, it has been objected, have simply not had time to happen. Jean Pommier best formulates this type of objection when he writes, concerning *Phèdre*, that:

Le départ d'Hippolyte, la rencontre du monstre, le combat et ses épisodes, la mort du héros, le retour du messager, il faut que tout cela se passe dans un temps record, le temps de dire soixante-dix vers : quelque chose comme quatre minutes et quart... comme Aricie a pu, elle aussi, atteindre le corps de son amant avant que Théramène ne quitte ce triste spectacle, il faut que ces deux courses (celle d'Aricie à l'aller, puis celle de Théramène au retour) aient duré environ deux minutes, qui est le temps de prononcer les trente-sept vers qui se récitent sur la scène, entre le moment où la jeune fille en sort et celui où le messager y apparaît.[27]

This type of objection has already been anticipated, though somewhat more reverently, by Jebb, who argued that in the *Oedipus Coloneus* the scene of Oedipus' death could not be a mile and a half from the grove, because the intervening ode is so short. Kitto has ridiculed this notion of a rough proportion between choric and linear feet, as well as the generally prevalent impression that a choral ode may indicate the lapse

---

[26]Eriphile's words mark the change from ritual movement to violence. Cf. Ménécée's announcement of his intent to commit suicide, in *La Thébaïde*, discussed above, p. 66.

[27]*Aspects de Racine,* Paris, Nizet, 1954, p. 200.

of some time, but not too much.[28] Such an impression is just as erroneous for the *récit* of Racinian tragedy as it is for the messenger speech or the choral ode of Greek tragedy. For, as Kitto's remarks suggest, there is no reason at all why dramatic time and time of representation should be expected to coincide. If the *entr'acte* can be taken to represent any length of time within the day, why must the time for the offstage action exactly match the few minutes of action onstage?

The fact is that Racine deliberately telescopes offstage time in most of his tragedies, and objections similar to that for *Phèdre* might as easily be made for *Britannicus, Mithridate,* or *Iphigénie.* Whatever may be the seventeenth- or twentieth-century demands for *vraisemblance* in such a case, this kind of "episodic intensification"[29] is a considered part of Racine's technique. In *Britannicus,* the hero's departure for the banquet, the beginning of the feast, and his death, take place before 37 lines have been uttered. In *Iphigénie,* the thunder offstage that signifies Eriphile's death resounds a scant 30 lines after Iphigénie leaves for the altar. And although the *entr'acte* is always elastic, expanding at will to include any number of actions, in *Mithridate* Racine deliberately contracts it. The following events take place between Act IV and Act V. iii, when Arbate arrives to prevent Monime's suicide: Mithridate's fruitless attempt to poison himself, his sally forth from the palace, and battle with the Romans, his second suicide attempt, the victory of Xipharès, Mithridate's order to Arbate to speed to Monime's side ("s'il en est temps encor, cours, et sauve la reine") and Arbate's hurried trip from the dying King's side to Monime. Evidently the time elapsing between acts IV and V is very short indeed, since the King sends Arcas for the poison, which he is then to take to Monime, at the end of Act IV,[30] and he arrives at V. ii. 1511, fifty-eight lines after the beginning of Act V. Since Mithridate was still in the palace when he

---

[28]H. D. F. Kitto, *Greek Tragedy: A Literary Study,* London, Methuen, revised ed., 1950, p. 169, n. 1.

[29]The expression was first used, I believe, by Schücking.

[30]Although none of the editions show them this way, the last two lines of Act IV should be printed thus:

MITHRIDATE

Ciel ! Courons . . .
(*A Arcas*)
Ecoutez...
(*Il lui parle à l'oreille. Arcas sort*)
Du malheur qui me presse,
Tu ne jouiras pas, infidèle princesse.

gave the order, if we are to suppose that there is any appreciable length of time between the acts, Arcas would have to take an unconscionably long time to fulfil his mission. Actually, it appears that most of the actions related by Arbate are supposed to take place *after* the beginning of Act V, since the false report of Xipharès' death comes at V. i. 1461, and the King's first attempt at suicide, his sortie, and subsequent actions occur after he hears the same rumour, as Arbate's *récit* makes clear. Racine's refusal to take advantage of the *entr'acte*, his decision to compress all these violent actions into the brief period of V. i (58 lines), and a small portion of V. ii (28 lines), is even more audacious than his refusal to place Hippolyte's departure, battle, and death between acts IV and V. Monime says:

> Xipharès ne vit plus; le Roi, désespéré,
> Lui-même n'attend plus qu'un trépas assuré;
>
> (I. i. 1461–2)

Arbate emphasizes that both Monime and the King heard the rumour at the same time:

> De sa mort en ces lieux la nouvelle semée
> Ne vous a pas vous seule et sans cause alarmée;...
> Le Roi, trompé lui-même, en a versé des larmes.
>
> (V. iv, 1559–60, 1563)

In only one instance does he seem to have used this technique with a cautious eye on the critics. The rapidity of Britannicus' death after taking the poison was explained beforehand when Narcisse, after the selection of the poison, confided to Néron that "le fer est moins prompt, pour trancher une vie"; as if to drive the point home, Burrhus echoes these words in his description of the death scene.[31] From that time onward, however, Racine made no attempt to excuse or explain his telescoping of time and its concomitant reduction of the *entr'acte*, which increase the pace of the action and, by multiplying the number of simultaneous onstage and offstage actions, add spatial and temporal depth.

Of the tragedies, only *Bérénice* and *Athalie* contain no final messenger speech, since in both all the significant events occur onstage. In *Bajazet*, the fear and confusion of the ending do not permit the relative stability of the formal *récit*; like the action itself, the information comes in

---

[31]V. v. 1630 echoes IV. iv. 1395. Here again, Racine is inspired by Tacitus, XIII, 15.

spasmodic bursts. The breathless Zaïre blurts out the news of the death of Roxane; Osmin's brief account reveals Bajazet's death after only 18 lines. In the frantic concluding moments of this play, such relatively fixed relationships as those of listener and speaker are impossible. Atalide is helpless and alone; Acomat, whose plans have failed, must take flight, and Osmin breaks off with the blunt words, "Mais, puisque c'en est fait, Seigneur, songeons à nous."

Our discussion has concerned only the terminal *récit*, or messenger speech, although *récits* are also found within the play. Some of these, like Mithridate's swift but graphic sketch of his defeat by Pompée, or Thésée's story of his imprisonment and escape, help to broaden the panorama of the past; others, like Néron's description of Junie brought a prisoner to the palace, or Cléone's account of Pyrrhus' wedding procession, provide a background of simultaneous actions. This internal *récit*, like the broader terminal *récit*, not only recounts offstage actions, but also recapitulates actions already seen on the stage, thus adding a third dimensional quality.[32]

What we have already noticed concerning the pace of Racinian tragedy would prevent our expecting to find there the long-soaring soliloquies that form some of the most dramatic and significant parts of Shakespearean tragedy. With Shakespeare the action can grind to a full stop, whereupon the character steps forward to announce, "Now I am alone"; in Racine this is obviously not possible. Indeed, one might expect, in what is so often a drama of watcher and watched, that monologues or soliloquies would be rare or non-existent. It is true that in the play where the atmosphere of suspicion and spying is the most intense, *Britannicus*, there are only two brief monologues, of 4 and 9 lines respectively (II. viii. 757–60; III. ii. 800–8). But every other tragedy (with the exception of *Esther* and *Athalie*, where the Chorus replaces the soliloquizing actor) contains at least one monologue of some length, and a number of short ones.

For purposes of our discussion, we may divide Racine's monologues or soliloquies (I shall use the two words interchangeably) into two types: monologues pronounced by an actor alone upon the stage; and monologues pronounced by one actor in the presence of another or others.

[32]See pp. 45 ff.

What is the dramatic function of the monologue in Racine? He never uses, as did Shakespeare and other Elizabethans, the self-descriptive soliloquy, and nowhere does he use the detached, reflective, or sententious monologue, or the monologue which states, the "moral" or central significance of the play.[33] In Racine, the monologue that is pronounced by an actor alone upon the stage is in almost every case spoken by a major character, and permits us that glimpse of the workings of his tormented soul that can only be revealed in solitude.

Indeed one of the monologue's chief purposes is to stress the terrible solitude of the Racinian tragic character. Hermione, despite her proud refusal to admit to Oreste and even to her confidante that Pyrrhus could ever win back her love, despite the controlled fury of her final scene with him, reveals in the monologue that begins Act V the full extent of her torture and despair. It is in the monologue that the tragic character betrays his hesitancy and distress. Hermione's frenzied self-interrogation:

> Où suis-je ? Qu'ai-je fait ? Que dois-je faire encore ?

is echoed in the long monologue of Mithridate, which shows the breaking up of his resolve. It is no coincidence that Mithridate, alone of Racine's characters, should deliver three monologues, two of them of considerable length (III. iv. 1035–62; III. vi. 1117–26; IV. v. 1379–21). For the proud old King, refusing to admit defeat in either love or war, is the most solitary of figures; distrustful of all, lacking even a faithful confidant, he must blurt out alone his final bewilderment at his strange loss of resoluteness, at the blunting of his implacable purpose by an unaccustomed upsurge of pity. In such monologues of indecision, the speaker asks himself frantically, "will I or won't I?" in a variety of ways. Finally, the terrible wrenching to a halt of the furious outburst, with its painful betrayal of the reason's precarious command of the emotions, typified by Mithridate's cry:

> Mais quelle est ma fureur ? et qu'est-ce que je dis ?
> Tu vas sacrifier, qui, malheureux ! ton fils !
>
> (IV. v. 1393–4)

immediately recalls Hamlet's "About, my brain!"

The briefer monologues usually reveal a decision, or express satis-

[33]M. C. Bradbrook, *Themes and Conventions of Elizabethan Tragedy*, Cambridge University Press, 1935, p. 128.

faction at the turn of events. They seem to provide a moment of suspension before the action plunges on. Often such monologues are instruments of dramatic irony, because of the contrast between the attitude they express and the action directly following. In *Andromaque,* for instance, Oreste in an exultant soliloquy of 14 lines (II. iii), proclaims his certainty that Pyrrhus will consent to his taking Hermione back to Greece; he knows that the King has eyes only for his Trojan captive, and he already visualizes his triumphant return with the fair Hermione as prize. In the scene immediately following, however, Pyrrhus declares that he has changed his mind and will marry Hermione. With Oreste's joyous phrases ringing in our ears, we are all the more acutely aware of his distress as the King is speaking.

In the same play, dramatic irony is achieved through a skilful juxtaposition of monologue and messenger speech. Alone and completely crushed by Hermione's reaction to the death of Pyrrhus, Oreste pours out his despair. At this point, Pylade rushes in with the words, "Il faut partir, Seigneur," and then proceeds to describe the situation. But he is scarcely noticed by the dejected Oreste, who sits with head bowed until he hears Pylade pronounce Hermione's name, at the end of his speech:

> ... tandis qu'Hermione
> Tient encore le peuple autour d'elle arrêté,
>
> (V. v. 1594-5)

at which he springs up, crying, "Non, non, c'est Hermione, amis, que je veux suivre." The dramatic irony lies in the clash between the resoluteness and determination of Pylade and his soldiers, with their clear plan of action, and what we know from the monologue to be the attitude of Oreste.

There are frequent cases in Racine of monologues in the presence of other characters. The most obvious effect of such speeches is to show, by the character's obliviousness of his surroundings, how distraught he is. One of the most striking examples occurs in the first scene of *Iphigénie,* where Agamemnon, although he has awakened Arcas with the express purpose of explaining the straits in which he finds himself, and of sending him with the message to the Queen, lapses frequently into monologue. His distracted lines about the jealousy of the gods (10-13) provoke Arcas' remonstrances, but Agamemnon is evidently not attending to the officer's speech, for the latter breaks off at line 35 to ask why he is weeping and reading the letter in this hand. Instead of answering, the King cries out, from the depths of his despondent reverie, "Non, tu ne mourras point; je n'y puis consentir." The dialogue ceases once again, as he lists his daughter's virtues, and apostrophizes the gods, forgetful of his companion (115–24). This tendency to distraction, revealed through Agamemnon's frequent dropping into monologue in the midst of dialogue, is evidently a device of characterization. Agamemnon's struggle, as we saw earlier, is between his own sense of responsibility and his obligation to capricious deities. His frequent monologues not only suggest his troubled introspection, but since on nearly every occasion they take the form of expostulation with the gods, they clearly indicate his attitude of rebellion.[34]

The same device is used with telling effect in *Phèdre*, where the heroine's debility and anguish appear as she lapses into a kind of incantatory monologue in the presence of Œnone. The famous lines beginning "Dieux! que ne suis-je assise à l'ombre des forêts!" are monologue; submerged in a trance-like reverie, it requires the sharply spoken "Quoi, Madame?" of Œnone before she can struggle painfully to the surface. Her monologues confirm her own pitiful statement:

> Où laissé-je égarer mes vœux et mon esprit ?
> Je l'ai perdu : les Dieux m'en ont ravi l'usage.
>
> (I. iii. 180–1)

This device attains its greatest poetic heights later in the same scene, when Phèdre is brought to reveal her passion to Œnone. The three famous couplets ("O haine de Vénus. . . ." "Ariane, ma sœur. . . ." "Puisque Vénus le veut. . . .") form an incantatory triptych; they are spoken in a trance, the heroine's eyes fixed and unseeing, and all in the same tone, contrasting sharply with Œnone's frightened and unheeded admonitions.

Racine's greatest originality in the use of monologue lies, I believe, in his employment of the device to indicate not merely distraction, but aberration; the lack of control of the tragic figure who slips involuntarily into reverie in what seems a half-conscious effort to escape from the harassment of the conscious world.

[34]The following monologues or asides in the presence of others are addressed to the gods: I. i. 121–5; I. ii. 209–12; I. v. 361–8; II. ii. 551; see also two short monologues, IV. v. 1317–22, and ix. 1462–8.

## LINKING AND QUIPROQUO

In the remainder of this chapter I shall discuss two devices, one of them perhaps the most mechanical of all, since it quite probably sprang from the sheer physical difficulty that the actors had in getting on and off a stage encumbered by a goodly section of the audience. This device we call *liaison*, or "linking." The other is *quiproquo* (I shall call it by its French name, since there is no suitable equivalent in English), a device most frequently found in comedy, but as used by Racine, an important source of dramatic irony.

In a seventeenth-century play, the number of scenes depended on the number of times characters entered or left the stage. Thus, each time the number of persons on stage changed, either by increasing or diminishing, a new scene was indicated by the writer. According to stage convention as it developed after 1650, scenes had to be "linked"; that is, at no time could the stage remain empty between scenes. If, as was the case when what D'Aubignac called "liaison de fuite" occurred, the characters in one scene left the stage as other characters entered, it was felt that there should be no interval, and that the departing characters should, in some way, announce the new arrivals. More common than this "linking through flight" was the "liaison de présence"—linking through presence, when one character remained on stage while others entered or left. There are, of course, many variations on these types, and not infrequently they are combined.

One of the most important requirements with regard to linking was that each entrance or departure had to be fully justified. For this reason, and also because of the practical need for a delay while oncoming actors made their way from the entrance at the rear of the stage, through the spectators sitting on the stage, and up to the place reserved for acting, the last lines of each scene were usually an announcement of the arrival and/or the decision to leave. It will be seen at once that this latter requirement is directly related to the tempo of the action, for the character who, upon the appearance of another, says even the banal phrase, "Voici le roi," directs the interest toward him, so that the audience is prepared for his first utterance, and there is no pause, either temporal or psychological, in the action.

It is frequently asserted that Racine's first tragedy, *La Thébaïde*, is defective; much less often is an attempt made to discover what particular defects it contains that do not appear in his later works. One of these is Racine's failure to justify consistently his entrances and departures. In I. ii, Antigone's appearance is neither announced nor explained; Etéocle's arrival in Scene iii, although announced by Antigone, seems unmotivated. Four lines from the end of Scene iv, Etéocle brusquely orders Créon to follow him, but as Louis Racine pointed out,[35] the latter remains onstage throughout all of the lengthy Scene v, until, four lines from the end, he announces, "Le roi m'appelle ailleurs, il faut que j'obéisse." This delayed departure is a rather awkward way of permitting Créon to express himself freely to Jocaste. At the end of the act, Antigone, according to the stage directions, follows her mother offstage after an interval which permits her to declaim four lines, which in later plays would have constituted a proper monologue and a seventh scene. The entrances of Olympe, Jocaste's confidante, are never announced, and Racine apparently considered her rôle as messenger sufficient to motivate her frequent but unheralded arrivals. In one instance we never learn when she leaves the stage. She appears unannounced at the beginning of II. ii, delivers the message of the oracle, and says not a word more, although she is presumably present for the rest of the scene. In Scene iii, however, she is not present, and in iv, when news comes of the outbreak of fighting, it is not Olympe who brings it; she has been replaced as messenger by an anonymous soldier. In III. v. there is no real justification for the exit of Etéocle, Jocaste, and Antigone, leaving Créon and Attale alone in Scene vi, since Etéocle has agreed to receive Polynice in the palace. Attale is present in IV. ii, but inexplicably absent in IV. iii. In V. v, Olympe appears only to announce Antigone's death and her exit is unexplained, save by the stage direction, "elle s'en va." Racine's difficulty in controlling the presence or absence of his characters is most glaringly evident in the long third scene of Act IV, during all of which Créon is onstage, although at no time does he utter a word.

But very shortly after *La Thébaïde*, Racine addressed himself to this thorny problem. In the first Preface to *Alexandre* (1666), he asks, concerning the play's critics, "Mais de quoi se plaignent-ils, si toutes mes scènes . . . sont liées nécessairement les unes avec les autres, si tous mes acteurs ne viennent point sur le théâtre, que l'on ne sache la raison

---

[35]Louis Racine, *Remarques sur les tragédies de Jean Racine*, Amsterdam, Rey, 1752, I, p. 56.

qui les y fait venir?" And certainly this second play offers ample proof
of his newly acquired mastery. Oncoming characters are announced,
usually four or five lines before the scene ends, but even more important,
some reference or brief description of the look or attitude of the oncoming actor, or some reflexion concerning him, smoothes the transition, directing our attention toward him, and preparing us for his
opening words, which usually begin the new scene. An interesting
example occurs at the end of I. i, where Cléofile has been attempting
to persuade Taxile to throw in his lot with Alexandre:

> CLÉOFILE
> Porus vous fait servir, il vous fera régner;
> Au lieu que de Porus vous êtes la victime,
> Vous serez... Mais voici ce rival magnanime.
> TAXILE
> Ah! ma sœur, je me trouble; et mon cœur alarmé,
> En voyant mon rival, me dit qu'il est aimé.
> CLÉOFILE
> Le temps vous presse. Adieu. C'est à vous de vous rendre
> L'esclave de Porus ou l'ami d'Alexandre.

There are several interesting things about this scene ending. First,
a naturalness is obtained by the breaking off of Cléofile's words at
"Vous serez," giving the effect of an interruption. Not only is sufficient
time allowed for Porus' approach, but what Taxile reads in his expression determines in part his attitude in the following scene. This tendency of Racine's to make the moment of the change of scene highly
significant dramatically became fully developed in the later plays, and
it affords a further example of his ability to recreate the convention,
to turn it to his own use. He uses the device in the same way, though
with far greater power, when he has Phèdre murmur to Œnone as
Hippolyte approaches, "Dans ses yeux insolents je vois ma perte
écrite."

It was possible to strengthen and deepen in significance even such
stereotyped announcements as "le voici," or "voici le roi," which still
retained, in *Alexandre*, a certain monotony. Hermione, in her despair,
has agreed to accept Oreste's aid:

> Hermione est sensible, Oreste a des vertus.
> Il sait aimer du moins, et même sans qu'on l'aime;

Et peut-être il saura se faire aimer lui-même.
Allons : qu'il vienne enfin.

CLÉONE

Madame, le voici.

HERMIONE

Ah ! je ne croyais pas qu'il fût si près d'ici.

(II. i. 472–6)

Here, in the tiniest of spheres it is true, is nevertheless an evidence of genius. Hermione's sudden cry, which reveals her revulsion at the prospect of seeing Oreste, confirms our impression that her earlier words were no more than rationalization and self-persuasion. Her sudden reversal not only transforms the conventional "le voici"—she is caught off guard—but by revealing her duplicity, prepares the audience for her hypocritical appeals to Oreste's love, granting us that omniscience necessary for the dramatic irony to take effect.

Several examples in the same play illustrate the ability to assimilate or change conventional practice according to the dramatic needs of the action. In one case when Pyrrhus and Phœnix enter unannounced, this is no lapse, for Oreste, delivering his exultant monologue, does not see them (II. iii–iv; V. iv–v). Again, the "liaison de fuite" which becomes a "liaison de présence" when Hermione attempts to leave at the sight of Andromaque but is restrained by the weeping heroine (IV. iii–iv), symbolizes by the arrested movement both the psychological and the physical action, since Andromaque has interrupted Hermione's transports of joy at the news of Pyrrhus' return to her.

In the scenes just preceding the eavesdropping scene in *Britannicus* (II. iv, v), instead of the conventional announcement, we hear first Narcisse's statement that Britannicus is approaching, then, when Néron hides, Junie's frenzied appeal to Narcisse to stop her lover, which is interrupted when she sees him. In this case a simple entrance becomes the symbol of the tragic character's inevitable progress toward his doom.

A glance at the pattern of scenes in *Bérénice* further illustrates the way in which Racine's linking accords with the dramatic action. The first three acts remain essentially static, as the characters watch their situation gradually unfold. With the fourth act, the dramatic conflict begins, the tempo increasing until the *dénouement*. At the beginning and end of each of the first three acts, linkings of presence leave behind a character alone, or with a confidant (I. i–ii, iv–v; II. i–ii, iv–v; III. i–ii, iii–iv). It is obvious that this pattern is appropriate to meditation, to the consideration of the newly discovered facts that precipitate action.

The fourth and fifth acts each contain a greater number of scenes than the first three (acts I and II contain 5 scenes each; Act III, 4; Act IV, 8; Act V, 7), and the linking in every case now conveys the haste, the indecision, the desperation of the characters. First of all, both acts begin with a brief monologue expressing the speaker's impatience to see the person who is to appear in Scene ii. Bérénice's words show how the leisurely pace of the preceding acts has changed:

> Phénice ne vient point ! Moments trop rigoureux,
> Que vous paraissez lents à mes rapides vœux !
> Je m'agite, je cours, languissante, abattue;
> La force m'abandonne, et le repos me tue.
> Phénice ne vient point. Ah ! que cette longueur
> D'un présage funeste épouvante mon cœur !
> Phénice n'aura point de réponse à me rendre,
> Titus, l'ingrat Titus n'a point voulu l'entendre;
> Il fuit, il se dérobe à ma juste fureur.
>
> (IV. i. 953–61)

This impatience with dragging time, the sadly reiterated "Phénice ne vient point," the disconsolate predictions of the result of Phénice's interview with Titus, seem literally to pull the confidante onto the stage. The straining between immobility and action, revealed through Bérénice's gesture and movement in suspension, prepare for the explosive quality of the ensuing action. In V. i, Arsace's monologue beginning "Où pourrai-je trouver ce prince trop fidèle?" with its promise of hope, prepares Antiochus' entrance, the subsequent rising of his hopes, and the bitterly despondent soliloquy after Titus' decision to retain Bérénice.

Other types of linking convey the confusion and heightening of the emotions. The "liaisons de fuite" which occur in the third and fourth acts are more than skilful devices to get the actors off the stage; they are actual flights by people who cannot bear to see or be seen. The dishevelled Bérénice is hurried out by Phénice as Titus enters (IV. ii–iii), and Antiochus at the end of his speech (V. iv), seeing Bérénice and Titus, rushes out, so they will not see his tears.[36] Another effective linking occurs when Bérénice sees Titus for the second time. The latter's monologue is broken off as Bérénice bursts into the room, crying out to the invisible Phénice and her ladies in waiting:

> Non, laissez-moi, vous dis-je.
> En vain tous vos conseils me retiennent ici :
> Il faut que je le voie.
>
> (IV. v. 1040-2)

The brusque interruption of Titus' soliloquy, the words addressed to someone offstage, increase the effect of violence and surprise. This linking should be contrasted with that in II. iii–iv, when Bérénice first confronts her lover. Rutile announces her, there follow three lines of hesitation, and finally, Titus' reluctant "Qu'elle vienne." Bérénice's first words in Scene iv are measured and formal, in contrast to her first words in IV. v.

The transition between scenes may be accelerated by riming the first line of a scene with the last line of the preceding scene. This is not particularly unusual in itself, since it was practised by Corneille and other dramatists. But in Racine, not only is rime-linking very frequent, it is consistently used to suggest rapid or unexpected entrances. It never occurs in "liaisons de fuite." As might be expected, the examples multiply in the last two acts of *Bérénice* (although one is found in III. ii–iii). In other plays the effect is heightened by the echoing of a word in the interior of a line. At Clytemnestre's words "Un Dieu vengeur, un Dieu fait retentir ces coups," Arcas the messenger hastens in with the words, "N'en doutez pas, Madame, un Dieu combat pour vous" (V. iv–v).

We have chosen *Bérénice* as our primary source of examples because the problem of linking must have been extremely difficult in a play so devoid of "action," and indeed, Racine's remarkable use of the device in this instance helps to illustrate how well he succeeded in "making

---

[36]Schérer (*La Dramaturgie classique en France*, pp. 275–6) errs in his comment on this linking when he says that "Antiochus sort après avoir prononcé son monologue, *sans que rien* indique dans le texte qu'il ait vu les deux héros entrant à ce moment-là, ou qu'il ait été vu par eux." The linking is explicitly stressed by Antiochus' exclamation as they enter:

> . . . Bérénice ! Titus !
> Dieux cruels ! de mes pleurs vous ne vous rirez plus.

something out of nothing." But many other examples from all the plays could have been adduced, had there been need, to show that in his approach to the technical problem of linking, Racine's hand was as sure as it was in his treatment of the more abstract elements of structure. His mastery of linking highlights his rapid technical development from the awkward beginning of *La Thébaïde*. In *Alexandre* and *Britannicus* we find the occasional fortuitous or ill-motivated entrance, but these are slips, not to recur.[37] Racine's use of linking reveals anew the conscientious craftsman, deftly moulding the smallest detail of technique to the needs of drama.

An extremely common dramatic device, especially in comedy, was that which theorists have labelled, quite understandably, the *quiproquo*. A *quiproquo* exists when one or more characters think and act on the basis of a misunderstanding; when some thing is taken for something else. Such a misunderstanding may be brought about by various means; by ambiguous language, by a gesture, or even by an expression. Corneille seemed to take a particular delight in displaying his virtuosity in the use of *quiproquos*. In his *Horace*, for example, a common type occurs when the erroneous report of the battle is given. Racine used the *quiproquo* in this fashion in both *La Thébaïde* and *Alexandre*. In the former, Olympe's report in V. ii that Polynice is the victor is comparable to Julie's account of the defeat of Horace; perhaps even more closely similar is Taxile's statement in *Alexandre* that he has seen Porus take to flight (III. ii). In the first case, however, Racine is careful to show that the erroneous report is open to doubt, the result, as Olympe puts it, of "mille rumeurs" rather than an action actually witnessed.

Another type of *quiproquo* is illustrated by Jocaste's assumption, on seeing Etéocle with blood on his clothes, that he has fought his brother. This might be compared to Chimène's conclusion, when Don Sanche returns from the duel with Rodrigue still wearing his sword, that he has slain her lover. But although the device in both cases is similar, in

---

[37]E.g. "Je sais qu'il se dispose à me venir parler" (*Alexandre*, IV. i. 999). The logic of certain entrances, exits, and locations in this play has been questioned by Louis Racine in *Remarques sur les tragédies de Jean Racine*, I, 100–1. In *Britannicus*, Burrhus' "La voici: mon bonheur me l'adresse" (III. ii. 808), recalls the fortuitous entrance in *Horace* (I. i. 128), "Voyez qu'un bon génie à propos nous l'envoie," but in the first case we learn from Agrippine that she had sought Burrhus for a definite reason—to accuse him of Pallas' exile.

Racine's hands it has already become far more naturally a part of the dramatic action. One expects Jocaste to jump at conclusions in this way; her despondency, her earlier conviction that the battle had begun while she slept, prepare us for the misunderstanding. The parallel situation in *Le Cid* is much less acceptable. Aside from the question of whether Chimène could assume so easily the defeat of the stalwart Rodrigue, it is hardly possible that the audience really feels suspense. Corneille employs the device, in this case, as elsewhere, almost for its own sake; it is one of those "grands égarements" he spoke of complacently in the *Examen* of *Mélite*—a surprise package from the prestidigitator's bag of tricks.

In this example from *Le Cid*, and elsewhere in Corneille, the *quiproquo* is frequently prolonged by the excited flow of words of the deceived character, who permits no interruption that might set the situation straight. Significantly, this kind of prolongation occurs nowhere in Racine. In the only similar instance, Britannicus' stubborn assumption that Junie no longer loves him, her silence is enforced by Néron's watchful gaze. Since once again we seem to be well embarked on the eternal parallel, one last comparison may illustrate how skilfully Racine adapted the *quiproquo* to the dramatic needs of his play. It will be remembered that in *Horace*, Sabine fears that Camille has transferred her affections from Curiace to Valère because she has seen her talking to him with a smile:

> Hier, dans sa belle humeur, elle entretint Valère;
> Pour ce rival, sans doute, elle quitte mon frère.
>
> (I. i. 111–12)

Beside this totally unprepared misunderstanding of Camille's and Valère's conversation, we may place Acomat's account of an interview between Roxane and Bajazet:

> ... une esclave à mes yeux s'est offerte,
> Qui m'a conduit sans bruit dans un appartement
> Où Roxane attentive écoutait son amant.
> Tout gardait devant eux un auguste silence.
> Moi-même, résistant à mon impatience
> Et respectant de loin leur secret entretien,
> J'ai longtemps immobile observé leur maintien.
> Enfin, avec des yeux qui découvraient son âme,
> L'une a tendu la main pour gage de sa flamme;

L'autre, avec des regards éloquents, pleins d'amour,
L'a de ses feux, Madame, assurée à son tour.
(III. ii. 878-88)

Unlike Corneille, Racine has made the device integral to his play. In the closed atmosphere of the seraglio the characters in *Bajazet* must continually watch for the revealing gesture, the unguarded expression. The hush, the distance from which Acomat, standing motionless, observes the interview, focus our attention on the mimetic quality of the scene, and because the spoken word becomes merely the movement of the lips seen from afar, a part of the "maintien," there still remains room for doubt, and reason for Zaïre to warn, "Mais ce succès, Madame, est encore incertain." In this case there is a double *quiproquo*; both Acomat and Roxane misinterpret Bajazet's expression.

Racine, it is evident, used the device with greater discretion, and with a greater concern for verisimilitude than his predecessor. The only play in which it may have been used excessively is *Mithridate*. Almost every scene has its *quiproquo*. In II. iv, Mithridate accuses Monime of being in love with what he vaguely designates as "un fils perfide"; this makes her think he means Xipharès, although the audience knows he has Pharnace in mind. Then, still threatening this unnamed son, he suddenly orders, "Appelez Xipharès." The misunderstanding can now extend to the audience, so that we wonder with Monime if the diabolical King has really discovered her secret. Almost immediately, however, he says scornfully that she need not deny an affair with Xipharès, who would never betray his father. This sudden introduction of the name of Xipharès, producing a misunderstanding which is immediately allayed, seems rather artificial.

In the following scene Mithridate tells Xipharès that Pharnace is Monime's lover, creating a further *quiproquo* whereby Xipharès suspects that Monime does in fact love his brother. The confusion persists when Mithridate, finally suspecting Xipharès, is attempting to trap Monime, and pretends to misunderstand when she rejects his proposal that she marry his favourite son. Then she must love Pharnace, he declares, and his angry diatribe continues until her explosive denial, "Je le méprise!" brings her to the edge of confession. In a final *quiproquo*, Xipharès tells Monime he suspects some "secret enemy" has told Mithridate their secret, when it is actually Monime herself who has betrayed him.

Why this plethora of *quiproquos* in *Mithridate*? Are they justified? I believe that they are. In no other play of Racine is the situation of the characters so precarious. Mithridate himself is the most *dépaysé* of Racinian characters. First of all, he is merely pausing at Nymphée before setting off to attack Rome. He has no court, no trusted retainer like Néron's Narcisse. Arbate is less his confidant than that of Xipharès, and deliberately conceals from him what he knows about the latter's feelings for Monime:

> Son frère, au moins jusqu'à ce jour,
> Seigneur, dans ses desseins n'a point marqué d'amour.
>
> (II. iii. 497–8)

The double or triple misunderstandings we discussed above result from the King's constant trickery, and are thus dramatically necessary. Even the two lovers are almost strangers, although as Xipharès tells Arbate, his love is not "un secret de deux jours." He has been less than a week at Nymphée, and has not yet spoken to her when the play begins (I. i. 89–90; II. iii. 483–4). Thus, Xipharès' momentary assumption that Monime may love Pharnace after all is more plausible than, for example, Britannicus' sudden willingness to believe that Junie, whom he has known so long, could have yielded with alacrity to Néron.

In the remaining plays, the device is once again used only sparingly, though at times with telling effect.[38] But in no other tragedy are the characters more naturally susceptible to this type of dramatic misunderstanding than in *Mithridate*.

---

[38]Notably the unforgettable instance in *Iphigénie,* when the girl asks eagerly to be present at the sacrifice, and her father answers sadly, "Vous y serez, ma fille." There is also Athalie's desire for the "hidden treasure" in the temple, which is actually the boy who will dethrone her.

# IV. RACINE'S SYMBOLISM

FROM TIME TO TIME in the course of the present study, I have had occasion to use the words symbol and symbolical. This has been no accident, for I am convinced that the identifying of dominant symbols in a Racinian tragedy greatly strengthens our grasp of the play. But though the validity of studies of symbolism in Shakespearean tragedy has been long established, in general, critics have shown considerable reluctance in applying the term to French classical literature. This is probably due, in part at least, to the rather considerable truth expressed in Gustave Lanson's dictum concerning the *précieux* theory of language: "Elle consiste à ne pas traiter les mots comme des formes concrètes, valant par soi, et possédant certaines propriétés artistiques, mais comme de simples signes, sans valeur ni caractère independamment de leur signification."[1] If this means what I take it to mean, Lanson is precisely denying the possibility of symbol in *précieux* writing.

It is, I believe, only because Racine renovates and recreates the language of preciosity that we are able to find symbolism in his work. This process of renovation, glimpses of which we have caught from time to time during this study, may be briefly summarized. In the Racinian tragic drama, certain words develop through three stages, none of them chronologically or mutually exclusive: (1) words, which through the influence of preciosity have lost their metaphorical or metonymical quality, function primarily as euphemisms; (2) they become "demetaphorized," so that they function concretely; (3) they are "remetaphorized," and they either rediscover an earlier metaphorical meaning, or assume new metaphorical or symbolical force.

Several critics have shown how, as Racine's genius matured, words like "feux," "yeux," and "flamme" developed from stage 1 to stage 2.[2] One may, for example, watch the word "yeux," first as it ranges

[1] G. Lanson, *Histoire de la littérature française*, Paris, Hachette, 1896, p. 399.
[2] See especially G. May, *D'Ovide à Racine*, Paris, Presses Universitaires, 1949, pp. 112–33.

from the empty metonymy of Créon's words addressed to the dead
Antigone in *La Thébaïde* (V. vi. 1480): "Et vous-même, cruelle,
éteignez vos beaux yeux!" then, as it reaches a painful balance between
the euphemistical use and a soupçon of metaphorical quality in Hémon's
declaration to Antigone that she ("vos beaux yeux") is his god and
oracle, more powerful than those that Etéocle is consulting at that very
moment:

> Permettez que mon cœur, en voyant vos beaux yeux,
> De l'état de son sort interroge ses dieux.
>
> (II. i. 317–18)

Finally, in *Andromaque, Britannicus, Bérénice,* and *Iphigénie,* it begins to
serve a dramatic purpose by revealing the characters' feelings through
fierce or mournful or indifferent glances. The warlike Pyrrhus' eyes
flash, Britannicus is made uneasy by beloved eyes full of sadness, and
Antiochus resolves to escape from

> ... des yeux distraits,
> Qui me voyant toujours, ne me voyaient jamais.
>
> (I. v. 277–8)

Eriphile, voicing her suspicions that all is not well at Aulis, says firmly
"J'ai des yeux," and Athalie tells Mathan, "Vous m'ouvrez les yeux."
     Frequently words participate in at least two of the stages. Thus,
when "feux" and "flamme" have regained concrete meaning, this
affects instances in the *précieux* sense when they occur in the same play.
Through the repeated evoking of the scenes of burning Troy, as in the
tableau of Pyrrhus in *Andromaque,*

> ... les yeux étincelants,
> Entrant à la lueur de nos palais brûlants,
>
> (III. vii. 999–1000)

even Hermione's line, "ses feux que je croyais plus ardents que les
miens," where the word is still firmly fixed in stage 1, takes on
heightened colour, while Pyrrhus' famous conceit, "Brûlé de plus de
feux que je n'en allumai," if read in the context of fire and devastation,
actually begins to penetrate stage 3.[3]

---

[3]This fact, added to the ironic interpretation we saw earlier, which depended on the contrast
between heroism and love, increases the richness of this much-belaboured line.

Through this kind of propinquity, words which may actually have come from the author's pen as *précieux* euphemisms, can, for the modern reader, acquire colour and force. Leo Spitzer quite legitimately discovers a bold oxymoron in Phèdre's "flamme si noire." In the same play, as this critic has shown, the symbolic currents with which Racine deliberately charges the word "monstre" flow across into a euphemistical expression like "les monstres dévorants," a mere reference to the dogs that devoured Peirithoüs.[4]

It would be generally agreed that a symbol must not only have metaphorical force, but that it must recur rather frequently in the body of a work: so, for example, Mallarmé's "azur," his "blancheur," his "fard," his "chevelure." Not only do these recur frequently, but unlike the same words in Baudelaire, they begin to assume an identity of their own, beyond their basic meaning and even beyond the thing or idea symbolized. In a play, however, a symbol should be first of all a reinforcement of the theme, and it should remain subservient to it, harmonizing completely with the rest of the structure. Though it is of necessity much less obtrusive in the drama than in lyric poetry, the patient reader who seeks it there will have his reward.

Once Racine has revitalized some key words in the various ways discussed above, he invests them with symbolic significance, both by the frequency with which he uses them, and by linking them closely to the dramatic theme. One such word is "autel," which beginning with the *précieux* sense of "veneration" or "reputation" in *Alexandre*, becomes in *Iphigénie* not only a concrete object, waiting ominously in the invisible scene, but a symbol of love and death toward which the characters are irrestibly drawn.

If we consider briefly how this word develops in three plays, *Alexandre, Andromaque,* and *Iphigénie*, we shall be struck, I think, by the fact that the symbolic word in Racine is actually an important vehicle of dramatic irony. In the first of these plays, the word remains within the boundaries of the kind of general conceit of deification addressed to the beloved, a variant of which we have already noted in *La Thébaïde*. The Greek heroes worshipped in India, says Porus, "ont

---

[4]See L. Spitzer, *Linguistics and Literary History,* Princeton University Press, 1948, pp. 97–9. J. Pommier (*Aspects de Racine,* Paris, Nizet, 1954, p. 260) suggests that "monstres" may not mean dogs, but real monsters, like the fire-breathing horses that Diomedes set upon strangers.

trouvé des autels" and the gallant Alexandre himself vows that for
Cléofile he will "faire dresser des autels" even among godless savages.
In *Andromaque* we can watch the process by which the word takes on
various metaphorical accretions. It is first of all the place in the temple
where the marriage is performed, and

> Andromaque, au travers de mille cris de joie,
> Porte jusqu'aux autels le souvenir de Troie.
>
> (V. ii. 1437-8)

When Andromaque speaks of "recevant la foi sur les autels" (IV. i.
1091), the word suggests not only the place of the marriage rite, but
the sacredness of the oath sworn there. Finally, the altar, in one instance,
takes on the significance of the scene of sacrificial death, when Oreste
pleads with Hermione to be allowed to choose for himself the time and
place where he will kill Pyrrhus:

> Laissez-moi vers l'autel conduire ma victime.
>
> (IV. iii. 1210)

It is traditional to point to the "linear" qualities of the plot of
*Andromaque*, with Oreste–Hermione–Pyrrhus–Andromaque as the
chain of passion, but this is an analytical statement unrelated to structure, since both Oreste and Pyrrhus vacillate until the end of Act IV.
The actual physical movement toward the climax is linked to the
altar. Pyrrhus, unguarded, sets out for the temple: "Sans gardes, sans
défense, il marche à cette fête" (IV. iii. 1218). His inexorable progress
toward the fatal goal is also conveyed by the verbs of motion in
Cléone's description of the wedding procession:

> Je l'ai vu vers le temple, où son hymen s'apprête,
> Mener en conquérant sa nouvelle conquête;
> Et d'un œil où brillaient sa joie et son espoir
> S'enivrer en marchant du plaisir de la voir.
>
> (V. ii. 1433-6)

Pyrrhus' fatal love-frenzy shows in the combination of verbs of movement like "entraîner" and "courir" with "autel":

> L'un par l'autre entraînés, nous courons à l'autel
> Nous jurer, malgré nous, un amour immortel.
>
> (IV. v. 1299-1300)

All of these meanings—the altar as scene of the marriage rite, as the sacred place of the gods, as the sacrificial table, as the goal of the tragic personage—combine in Hermione's wild imprecations:

> Va lui jurer la foi que tu m'avais jurée,
> Va profaner des Dieux la majesté sacrée.
> Ces Dieux, ces justes Dieux n'auront pas oublié
> Que les mêmes serments avec moi t'ont lié.
> Porte aux pieds des autels ce cœur qui m'abandonne;
> Va, cours. Mais crains encor d'y trouver Hermione.
>                                                    (IV. vi. 1381-6)

In the last scenes, the altar is the point at which the protagonists converge. Oreste runs to the temple, where the Greeks, mingling with the crowd, have secretly made their way to the altar: "se sont jusqu'à l'autel dans la foule glissés" (V. iii. 1500). Pyrrhus himself, in a grim echo of Hermione's curses, dies precisely before the altar; after struggling wildly to escape the assassins' blows, "à l'autel il est allé tomber" (V. iii. 1520). His triumphal march ends as he drags himself forward to die. Finally, Hermione, who kills herself upon his corpse, commits a sacrificial act related to the altar symbolism.

This symbolism is of course not fully woven into the play, but remains confined to the latter part of acts IV and V. It is in *Iphigénie* that the altar assumes the full symbolic force that it could not achieve in the earlier plays. Throughout this tragedy, the altar symbolizes death, and the irony derives from its being also a symbol of life and love, the place of man's union with woman. The altar is the goal of Iphigénie's journey both in the pre-dramatic action and in the action proper. Early in the play, Achille points the ironic contrast between the supposed and the actual purpose of her journey:

> On dit qu'Iphigénie, en ces lieux amenée,
> Doit bientôt à son sort unir ma destinée.
>                                                    (I. ii. 177-8)

This ominous significance of the altar, unknown to the heroine, makes more poignant the famous *quiproquo* in which she questions her father about a projected sacrifice of which she has vaguely heard. When she asks if this will take place soon, the King replies, "Plus tôt que je ne veux"; and to her request to be allowed to witness the ceremony—"Verra-t-on à l'autel votre heureuse famille"—he answers painfully, "Vous y serez, ma fille."

But the deepest irony springs from the dual symbolism of love and death, love in the minds of Achille, Iphigénie, and her mother, death in the minds of the audience and the other protagonists. Agamemnon attempts to trick Clytemnestre into letting her daughter go alone to the altar by telling her that it is there Iphigénie is to marry Achille:

> ... Laissez, de vos femmes suivie,
> A cet hymen, sans vous, marcher Iphigénie.
>
> (III. i. 793–4)

In persuading Clytemnestre not to accompany Iphigénie, the King stresses the warlike aspect of the camp, portraying the altar as "hérissé de dards," and thus ill-suited to her presence. In III. iv, we watch the heroine draw closer to the dread site, serenely confident, and praising her lover's magnanimity in terms the unconscious irony of which strikes at the gods themselves:

> Montrez que je vais suivre au pied de nos autels
> Un roi qui non content d'effrayer les mortels,
> A des embrasements ne borne point sa gloire,
> Laisse aux pleurs d'une épouse attendrir sa victoire,
> Et par les malheureux quelquefois désarmé,
> Sait imiter en tout les Dieux qui l'ont formé.
>
> (III. iv. 871–6)

When Arcas reveals the plot two scenes later, Achille bursts out in anger at the subterfuge:

> C'est peu que de vouloir, sous un couteau mortel,
> Me montrer votre cœur fumant sur un autel :
> D'un appareil d'hymen couvrant ce sacrifice,
> Il veut que ce soit moi qui vous mène au supplice ?
>
> (III. vi. 975–8)

In the earlier plays, the noun tended to be used in the plural, which emphasizes the abstract at the expense of the concrete. Of the 34 times the word "autel" is used in *Iphigénie*, it occurs 26 times in the singular, so that it has now acquired greater force as an actual object. Its concrete and symbolic meanings coincide throughout, as they do not in *Andromaque*.[5]

[5]In *Mithridate* the word is used 9 times, in each case signifying the place of marriage. In two instances it is referred to as the place of sacrifice (II. iv. 552; III. v. 1078), but it is not a ruling symbol.

Although Racine could not have found this ironic symbolism in the ancients, who celebrated marriages in the home of the bride's parents, the marriage-death irony may have been suggested by Seneca's *Troades*, where it is very fully developed. Helen is required to prepare Polyxena for the sacrifice as if for a wedding:

> ego Pyrrhi toros
> narrare falsos iubeor, ego cultus dare
> habitusque Graios
>
> (865-7)
>
> [I must forge the tale
> That she shall marry Pyrrhus; I must deck her
> In finest Grecian raiment].

Her speech to Polyxena equivocates between the marriage with Achilles, which means death, and the supposed wedding to Pyrrhus; the word "thalamus" has throughout the symbolic meaning of death.

Aeschylus may have provided another ironic symbol in the bandeau of Monime in *Mithridate*. It will be remembered how, in the *Suppliants*, when the King first confronts the strange visitors to his land, the Chorus Leader tells him darkly, "I have headbands and belts to bind my dress; from them I shall seek a wondrous aid." As Pelasgos answers in puzzlement, "They are doubtless ornaments proper for women," irony hangs heavily in the air, for we recall the maidens' earlier threat to hang themselves upon the altar if they cannot, through the help of their hosts, "escape the embrace of the male." The similarity between this ironic employment of the bandeau and its rôle in *Mithridate* is evident ( it is immaterial whether Racine was inspired by Aeschylus alone, or by the Plutarch of Amyot, where the headband is called "le diadème ou bandeau royal," or by both). Throughout the play, the headband symbolizes bondage and death as well as royalty; there are repeated allusions to it as the "gage" or sign of Mithridate's promise to make Monime his queen, and the audience is aware that it will be the instrument of her attempted suicide.

Whenever Monime appears, she is wearing the bandeau, and either she or the other characters mention it. Pharnace's words are typical:

> ... ce bandeau royal fut mis sur votre front
> Comme un gage assuré de l'empire de Pont.
>
> (I. iii. 233-4)

Mithridate, seeing Monime for the first time after his arrival home, drives home again to her its bitter significance:

> ... vous portez, Madame, un gage de ma foi
> Qui vous dit tous les jours que vous êtes à moi.
>
> (II. iv. 541–2)

But a moment later, the "gage" becomes the ceremonial crown worn by the sacrificial victim—cf. *Iphigénie*: "Mais le fer, le bandeau, la flamme est toute prête" (III. v. 905)—as the old King cries furiously, "Vous n'allez à l'autel que comme une victime" (II. iv. 552). When Monime's attempt at suicide fails with the breaking of the band of which she had tried to make "un affreux lien," her anguished words sum up the ironic meanings of this badge of royalty which has meant only suffering and death:

> Et toi, fatal tissu, malheureux diadème,
> Instrument et témoin de toutes mes douleurs,
> Bandeau, que mille fois j'ai trempé de mes pleurs,
> Au moins, en terminant ma vie et mon supplice,
> Ne pouvais-tu me rendre un funeste service ?
>
> (V. i. 1500–4)

The altar in *Iphigénie* is ominous in part *because* it is invisible and amorphous—in Agamemnon's description, its outlines are broken as it bristles with spears—but the headband, as part of Monime's costume, is a visible symbol of her plight, becoming in a sense a part of the *décor*.[6]

A symbolism which bears an even closer relationship to stage setting is Racine's use of light. It will be recalled that the opening scene in *Iphigénie*, which takes place before dawn, shrouds in darkness the conversation between Agamemnon and his officer, Arcas. The tragic obligations upon which the helpless King has brooded in silence flow forth in darkness, but as the action progresses the scene grows gradually brighter, until at the end, as Ulysse and Achille burst in, the sun has risen. The light of the sun symbolizes the re-emergence of the King's responsibilities; his forebodings and despair must now retreat before the light of day.

---

[6]Jean Cocteau, in his *Machine infernale*, uses the silk scarf with which Jocaste eventually strangles herself, in exactly the same way, drawing attention to it with almost comic insistence. As she enters with Tirésias, the latter inadvertently steps on it, and she exclaims: "Je suis entourée d'objets qui me détestent! Tout le jour cette écharpe m'étrangle."

Discussing the play's spatial depth, we have already indicated the importance of light in *Phèdre*. The heroine's emergence from the shadows, in surrender to the terrible fascination of the light, also underscores symbolically her struggle with her criminal desires. Before her first appearance, we learn that she has been languishing in darkness, "lasse enfin d'elle-même et du jour qui l'éclaire" (I. i. 46). But the pull of fate is too strong, "elle veut voir le jour," and she drags herself, a moment after Œnone speaks these words, into the light, only to shrink back in terror: "Mes yeux sont éblouis du jour que je revoi" (I. iii. 155). From the light that illumines her criminality she shrinks back toward the darkness of concealment:

> Vous vouliez vous montrer et revoir la lumière.
> Vous la voyez, Madame, et prête à vous cacher,
> Vous haïssez le jour que vous veniez chercher ?
>
> (I. iii. 166–8)

This symbolism clarifies the magnificent double image of her dying words, in which her death becomes a purification of the light sullied by her guilt:

> Et la mort, à mes yeux dérobant la clarté,
> Rend au jour, qu'ils souillaient, toute sa pureté.
>
> (V. vii. 1643–4)

The seventeenth-century stage director, Mahelot, prescribed, on the basis of one line of the play, that the scene should be a "palais voûté," and as recently as 1945, J.-L. Barrault obediently sealed up his heroine in a palace with a vaulted ceiling. But the symbolism of light in *Phèdre*, it seems to me, demands a setting bathed in the brilliant glare of noon, above it the actinic blue of the Grecian sky.

One of the dangers, of course, in the quest for symbolism in Racine's or any other theatre, is that we may over-estimate the importance of something which is much more the quarry of the reader than of the spectator. This is true of Cleanth Brooks's brilliant essay on the clothes symbolism in *Macbeth*,[7] which strengthens our understanding of the

---

[7]Cleanth Brooks, "The Naked Babe and the Cloak of Manliness," *The Well-Wrought Urn*, New York, 1947, pp. 21–46.

play, but which perhaps tends to obscure the fact that all the elements of structure, the flesh and blood interpretation of rôles, may overshadow symbols. The striking thing about the symbolism in Racine is that it participates on both the scenic and rhetorical levels; that his symbols, unlike the multi-coloured and multifarious symbols of Shakespeare, are neat and spare, playing their modest part as adjuncts of theme and structure.

# V. THE ESSENCE OF RACINIAN TRAGEDY

### The Tragic Setting: Constraint and Presence

GEORGES LE BIDOIS has remarked, concerning Racine's characters, that "le visage, ce vestibule de l'âme, est . . . sans cesse assiégé de leurs regards ardents."[1] Why so besieged? The Racinian character is, like the Racinian play itself, in the beginning a product of convention. Like his prototype, the seventeenth-century courtier, he has learned that not only his words, gestures, and expressions, but even his reticences and his silences, are the object of constant scrutiny, of endless and varied interpretations. Like the Princèsse de Clèves, so poignantly aware that she is "exposée au milieu de la cour," he feels that silence and deception are forced upon him. In turn, his safety depends upon his ability to interpret correctly the words, gestures, and expressions of his fellows at the same time as he masks his own feelings and intentions. Part of his torment is that he can never be sure of success; the most carefully worded answer, the blandest expression, may prove more damning than the candour that he scrupulously avoids. To pursue the example already quoted (since *La Princèsse de Clèves* best illustrates the particular tension of court society, and the kind of psychological deception and counterdeception Racine transferred to his plays), it will be recalled that when the heroine first dances with her future lover, the Duc de Nemours, she has not been introduced, but has nevertheless recognized him. To the sharp-eyed Dauphine she denies that she knows her partner's identity. Thereupon the Dauphine declares: "il y a même quelque chose d'obligeant pour M. de Nemours, à ne vouloir pas avouer que vous le connaissez sans l'avoir jamais vu." Thus, her refusal to confess having recognized the duke is more damaging than what would have been the height of immodesty, a frank admission that his unusual good looks had convinced her of his identity.

[1]G. Le Bidois, *La Vie dans la tragédie de Racine*, Paris, Gigord, 1922, p. 79.

This dramatic scene depends for its power upon bringing together, under the scrutiny of others, two characters bound to have a considerable effect on one another. Because of the code of manners imposed by an artificial society and because of the attentive onlookers, each must strive not to reveal the impact of the other's presence. The dramatic interest is in the questions: What will they reveal of their feelings? How will they reveal it?

In the course of our discussion in this chapter we shall have occasion to use the terms "presence," "constraint," and "tragic setting." In Racine it is "presence," the electric effect of mere physical proximity, that challenges "constraint" most strongly; situations which instigate that challenge constitute the "tragic setting."

We may first examine the dramatic devices by which Racine strengthens and deepens our awareness of this "tragic setting." Most dramatic devices, the reader will agree, are in themselves completely neutral; their effect, comic, tragic, melodramatic, depends on the nature of the atmospheric structure in which they occur. If, however, they develop logically out of a tragic situation, they serve to confirm and even to heighten our awareness of that situation. To illustrate this, consider the device whereby one character, in order to break through the layers of reserve by which another character protects himself, administers a shock so disturbing that the result is an involuntary betrayal. This is the type of shock treatment used by the Prince de Clèves when, after narrowing his list of suspects to three, and finally eliminating all but Nemours, he tells his wife that the duke will go with them to Spain. Realizing the terrific strain such a journey will impose upon her, the princess confirms her husband's suspicions by showing her excitement and distress.

Despite this appearance in a famous novel, our device is essentially dramatic in nature. An interesting example can be found in Corneille's *Le Cid*, which will help us to demonstrate, by contrast, how Racine made of it an important device of tragedy. In IV. v, the somewhat weary but benevolent Don Fernand decides to trick Chimène into revealing she still loves Rodrigue, despite her untiring clamour for his death. As Rodrigue leaves the stage, she appears, and the King whispers his plan to Don Diègue:

> On m'a dit qu'elle l'aime, et je vais l'éprouver.
> Montrez un œil plus triste.

Don Fernand then announces to Chimène that her lover is dead:

DON FERNAND

Enfin soyez contente,
Chimène, le succès répond à votre attente.
Si de nos ennemis Rodrigue a le dessus,
Il est mort à nos yeux des coups qu'il a reçus;
Rendez grâces au ciel, qui vous en a vengée.
(à don Diègue)
Voyez comme déjà sa couleur est changée.

DON DIÈGUE

Mais voyez qu'elle pâme, et d'un amour parfait,
Dans cette pâmoison, sire, admirez l'effet.
Sa douleur a trahi les secrets de son âme,
Et ne vous permet plus de douter de sa flamme.

CHIMÈNE

Quoi ! Rodrigue est donc mort ?

DON FERNAND

Non, non, il voit le jour,
Et te conserve encore un immuable amour :
Calme cette douleur qui pour lui s'intéresse.

CHIMÈNE

Sire, on pâme de joie, ainsi que de tristesse :
Un excès de plaisir nous rend tous languissants,
Et quand il surprend l'âme, il accable les sens.

DON FERNAND

Tu veux qu'en ta faveur nous croyions l'impossible ?
Chimène, ta douleur a paru trop visible.

Although this is deception, we never feel that great matters are at stake, but only experience a rather detached and tolerant amusement at the effect of the trick. For not only do we known that Chimène's love for Rodrigue is not dead, we know from the tone of indulgence that pervades the scene that nothing dire, either for her or for the perpetrators of the trick, will result from the fact that "Sa douleur a trahi les secrets de son âme." The King and Don Diègue are masters of the situation; it is they who devise the deception, correctly anticipate its result, and put an end to it at will. Chimène's pretense is self-imposed, and may be abandoned without altering either her relationship to the other characters or the course of the drama.

The identical device appears in Racine's *Bajazet* (IV. iii), when Roxane, increasingly suspicious that Atalide loves Bajazet, hands her an order for Bajazet's death, and bids her read it aloud:

ATALIDE (*Elle lit*)
*Avant que Babylone éprouvât ma puissance,*
*Je vous ai fait porter mes ordres absolus.*
*Je ne veux point douter de votre obéissance,*
*Et crois que maintenant Bajazet ne vit plus.*
*Je laisse sous mes lois Babylone asservie,*
*Et confirme en partant mon ordre souverain.*
*Vous, si vous avez soin de votre propre vie,*
*Ne vous montrez à moi que sa tête à la main.*

ROXANE
Hé bien ?

ATALIDE
Cache tes pleurs, malheureuse Atalide.

ROXANE
Que vous semble ?

ATALIDE
Il poursuit son dessein parricide;
Mais il pense proscrire un prince sans appui :
Il ne sait pas l'amour qui vous parle pour lui,
Que vous et Bajazet vous ne faites qu'une âme,
Que plutôt, s'il le faut, vous mourrez...

ROXANE
Moi, Madame ?
Je voudrais le sauver, je ne le puis haïr.
Mais...

ATALIDE
Quoi donc ? Qu'avez-vous résolu ?

ROXANE
D'obéir.

ATALIDE
D'obéir !

ROXANE
Et que faire en ce péril extrême ?
Il le faut.

ATALIDE
Quoi ! ce prince aimable... qui vous aime,
Verra finir ses jours qu'il vous a destinés !

ROXANE
Il le faut. Et déjà mes ordres sont donnés.

ATALIDE

Je me meurs.

ZATIME

Elle tombe, et ne vit plus qu'à peine.

ROXANE

Allez, conduisez-la dans la chambre prochaine.
Mais au moins, observez ses regards, ses discours,
Tout ce qui convaincra leurs perfides amours.

Comparing these two widely different examples of the same dramatic device, one can see at once how much more fully Racine adapted
it to the basic needs of tragedy. The shock administered to Chimène
is an *hors-d'œuvre*, an amusing trick which, revealing something of
which everyone is already aware, has no more momentous result than
to make Chimène appear somewhat less coldly adamant. For Racine,
however, the device becomes the means by which the play's elaborate
structure of deception and intrigue is broken down, the victorious
weapon in a frenzied struggle. Not only does the shock produce the
fainting spell which reveals the secret of Atalide's soul, and precipitates
the catastrophe; it reduces her to a state of helplessness, in which "ses
regards, ses discours" will betray her further in the first moments of
consciousness.

Because of the constraint each character knows his opposite imposes
upon himself, in order to find out the truth he must be on the lookout
for similarly unguarded moments, if he cannot, like Roxane, bring
them about by violent means. Junie naively expresses surprise at the
gap between thought and word, heart and mouth, in Néron's court;
the experienced Agrippine knows well this discrepancy. Gone is the
time, she laments, when she watched the Senate from behind a curtain,
sure in her power to dictate their actions; now she sees her son only in
the presence of his counsellors Burrhus and Sénèque. His replies, and
even his silence, that silence that is so often more eloquent than words,
are dictated by the fact of their presence. That is why she seeks to surprise him in the morning, as he arises from bed; in the "désordre" of
awakening, he will not be on his guard against a sudden question.

We have already, in another connection, referred to the scene in
*Britannicus* described by Agrippine, and adapted by Racine from
Tacitus, in which Néron prevented his mother from taking her place

on the throne.[2] This is another striking instance of "tragic setting."
Néron's anger and hatred flashed involuntarily over his face:

> ... Néron, d'aussi loin qu'il me vit,
> Laissa sur son visage éclater son dépit.

> (I. i. 105-6)

But before the court and the watching ambassadors, such emotions
had to be concealed, and so,

> L'ingrat, d'un faux respect colorant son injure,
> Se leva par avance; et, courant m'embrasser,
> Il m'écarta du trône où je m'allais placer.

> (I. i. 108-10)

The fleeting picture of naked hatred, which appears for a moment,
only to be effaced by a studied gesture, helps to strengthen the portrait
of this "monstre" as "naissant." Throught this play, until the catastrophe, we catch only glimpses of the evil that seethes beneath Néron's
mannered exterior; from time to time the mask is off, but only for a
moment.

Agrippine's remaining power lies wholly in the force of her presence; only the thought of her angry stare restrains Néron, who ima-
gines apprehensively that she may lead Octavie before him:

> Mon amour inquiet déjà se l'imagine
> Qui m'amène Octavie, et d'un œil enflammé...

> (II. ii. 484-5)

In his long speech in answer to Narcisse's insistence that he reign for
himself, he tells how, separated from his mother, he is his own man,
threatening and commanding, plotting against her, heeding his counsellors' advice, but once in her presence, his resolve collapses:

> Eloigné de ses yeux, j'ordonne, je menace,
> J'écoute vos conseils, j'ose les approuver;
> Je m'excite contre elle, et tâche à la braver.
> Mais (je t'expose ici mon âme toute nue)
> Sitôt que mon malheur me ramène à sa vue,
> Soit que je n'ose encor démentir le pouvoir

---

[2]Although this scene is copied closely from Tacitus, in the Latin source it is Seneca who sends
Nero to meet his mother, so that the "scandal" of her taking her place may be avoided. In Racine
the decision is Néron's alone, as is the quickly concealed expression of anger.

De ces yeux où j'ai lu si longtemps mon devoir,
Soit qu'à tant de bienfaits ma mémoire fidèle
Lui soumette en secret tout ce que je tiens d'elle,
Mais enfin mes efforts ne me servent de rien;
Mon génie étonné tremble devant le sien.
Et c'est pour m'affranchir de cette dépendance,
Que je la fuis partout, que même je l'offense,
Et que de temps en temps j'irrite ses ennuis
Afin qu'elle m'évite autant que je la fuis.

(II. ii. 496–510)

One could scarcely find a more explicit statement of the power of presence. The author carefully abstains from assigning any specific cause for this power; Néron's vaguely proffered reasons are hardly more than conjectures, and as his abrupt "Mais enfin," dismisses any further search for an explanation as futile, we realize that the effect he describes lies somewhere beyond reason.

The famous eavesdropping scene in Act II shows us the power of presence upon the stage; this time it is Néron, whose invisible presence controls every action of the helpless Junie. Before going to his hiding-place, he has given her orders to rebuff Britannicus by both word and gesture; a careless glance may cause her lover's death:

Et soit par vos discours, soit par votre silence,
Du moins par vos froideurs, faites-lui concevoir
Qu'il doit porter ailleurs ses vœux et son espoir.

(II. iii. 672–4)

"J'entendrai des regards que vous croirez muets," whispers Néron, as he glides to his place of concealment. Thus Junie's every movement becomes charged with a deadly significance. To Britannicus' astonished exclamations, "Quel accueil! quelle glace," Junie can only hint guardedly at Néron's terrible omnipresence:

Vous êtes en des lieux tout pleins de sa puissance.
Ces murs même, Seigneur, peuvent avoir des yeux;
Et jamais l'Empereur n'est absent de ces lieux.

(II. vi. 712–14)

Her helplessness and the inevitability of Britannicus' doom are conveyed by her hopeless efforts to make him unsay his declaration of enmity for Néron. And finally, as he rushes out in despair, crying in a final formulation of the speaking-glance motif that runs through the scene, that "vos regards ont appris à se taire," Junie, ever conscious of the malevolent puppeteer, must watch him go, with head bowed.

Ironically, her heroic constraint only serves her ill; her strain has been too evident, and her silence, instead of placating the tyrant, only infuriates him:

> ... de leur amour tu vois la violence,
> Narcisse : elle a paru jusque dans son silence.
>
> (II. viii. 747–8)

Eavesdropping scenes were frequent in the literature of the time,[3] but in this case the unusual fact that one of the protagonists knows he is being spied on makes it extremely likely that a scene from Rotrou's *Bélisaire* (1643) was Racine's model.[4] In Rotrou, Queen Théodore similarly warns Antonine, on pain of incurring her displeasure, to rebuff her lover, Bélisaire, who has just returned triumphant from the wars. She then listens from a window to what transpires. A long speech of Bélisaire ends rather tardily by his noticing Antonine's coolness, whereupon she tries guardedly to explain by telling him that her attitude is "important" for him. She then bids him adieu, and he hurries off, threatening suicide.

But unlike Rotrou's play, Racine's has projected from the first line onward an atmosphere of dread, of secret crimes in the making. Néron, the personification of unlimited power slipping from control, dominates every scene; he is truly "invisible et présent." Rotrou's eavesdropping scene is only one in a series of harassing incidents perpetrated by Théodore, who has really no power over Bélisaire's life. Unlike Antonine's interview with her lover, Junie's is not fortuitous, but prearranged by Néron, and its outcome will decide Britannicus' fate.

But the difference in dramatic intensity between the two scenes may perhaps best be shown in the statements of the two eavesdroppers before they hide. Théodore says merely, "Je vous écouterai par cette jalousie"; hers is the conventional function of the eavesdropper. Néron is both

---

[3]As we might have expected, there is a highly significant eavesdropping scene in *La Princesse de Clèves,* when Nemours listens in on the Princess and her husband. In *L'Astrée,* Diane eavesdrops on Sylvandre and the nymph Philis.

[4]This was first pointed out by H. C. Lancaster, *MLN,* XXVII (1912), pp. 226–7.

listener and watcher; his parting shot, "J'entendrai des regards que vous croirez muets," embodying the dual meaning of "entendre" (hear, understand) through the coupling of "muet" with "regard," increases the precariousness and instability of Junie's situation, in which not only her speech, but her gestures and glances must be made in the aura of constraint imposed by Néron's unseen presence.

Like Néron, the aging Mithridate interprets Monime's silence and resignation as proof she loves someone else; ignoring her words, he bases his conclusion on her expression, gestures, and evident self-control. When he first confronts her, he denounces her apathy, and submits her to the closest scrutiny. Beginning with the words "Je vois, malgré vos soins, vos pleurs prêts à couler," he repeats twice in three lines "Je vois," and his statement, "Je vous entends ici mieux que vous ne pensez," is the result of his observation.

Later, in III. v, when by a ruse Mithridate obtains an avowal from Monime of her love for Xipharès, he cannot repress his anger; his expression changes, and she cries in alarm, "Seigneur, vous changez de visage." It is this sudden look, instantly repressed, that causes her forebodings in the following scene. But the King, aware of his lapse, warns himself that he must guard his expression more closely.

> Mais, sans montrer un visage offensé,
> Dissimulons encor, comme j'ai commencé !
>
> (III. vi. 1125-6)

He is unable, however, to disguise his true feelings from his son, who knows him too well:

> Il feint, il me caresse, et cache son dessein;
> Mais moi, qui dès l'enfance élevé dans son sein,
> De tous ses mouvements ai trop d'intelligence,
> J'ai lu dans ses regards sa prochaine vengeance.
>
> (IV. ii. 1189-92)

In *Bajazet*, as in *Mithridate*, the central figure embarks on a campaign of discovery: is Bajazet's love (of which Atalide and Acomat have assured Roxane) really sincere? Despite his protestations, his actions in Roxane's presence are not those of a man in love:

> Je ne retrouvais point ce trouble, cette ardeur,
> Que m'avait tant promis un discours trop flatteur.
>
> (I. iii. 283-4)

It is Roxane's conviction that words do not suffice that makes the action of the play. Bajazet must not merely confirm the eager assurances of his love that she has received indirectly, his expression must corroborate his words:

> Je veux que devant moi sa bouche et son visage
> Me découvrent son cœur, sans me laisser d'ombrage.
>
> (I. iii. 329–30)

And finally, we share Atalide's fears because, before the fatal interview, she has not been able to prepare Bajazet's expression for him.

Racine's concept of the hegemony of expression is nowhere better formulated than in the report of the slave girl, Zaïre, that Bajazet has surely been pardoned because of Acomat's triumphant look:

> Il ne m'ont point parlé; mais mieux qu'aucun langage,
> Le transport du vizir marquait sur son visage...
>
> (III. i. 797–8)

How different is Racine from Shakespeare, whose characters are individuals, confined to no elaborate court ritual of language or expression, and who can freely hide or mask their true feelings. "One can smile and smile, and be a villain," says Hamlet, and Duncan reflects, "There's no art to find the mind's construction in the face." It is part of their tragedy that Racine's hounded creatures, despite the elaborate defences that they set up, never know in what unguarded moment the forces of passion or fear may break through. In a very real sense, Racine's use of expression supports the theme of reason and passion in conflict, with the physical (expression or involuntary gesture) betraying the rational (speech).

In other plays, in which concealment and subterfuge play a less important rôle, the play of expression is less integral to the dramatic action. Where the conflicts are largely internal, the chief struggle is to determine from what appears on the surface what lies beneath it, with the result that tone, gesture, and appearance have a primary function. In any play, however, Racine's characters unfailingly *see*, and make conclusions from what they see. Even in *Alexandre*, Taxile, foreshadowing Phèdre, cries out when Porus appears,

> ... mon cœur alarmé,
> En voyant mon rival, me dit qu'il est aimé.
>
> (I. i. 119–20)

In the same play, Axiane concludes from the "front satisfait" of Taxile that Porus has been defeated, and, as she urges Taxile to redeem himself by attacking Alexandre, declares,

> ... je vois sur ton visage
> Qu'un si noble dessein étonne ton courage.
>
> (IV. iii. 1201-2)

In *Andromaque*, both Pylade and Cléone warn their impulsive master and mistress, "Dissimulez. . . ." (III. i. 800; III. iii. 855).

Many commentators have noted Hermione's feverish questioning of her confidante, Cléone; less often noticed has been the terrible irony of Pyrrhus' final glance of triumph, just before the assassins' daggers thrust home. "Sans changer de face," Oreste relates, "Il semblait que ma vue excitât son audace." In *Bérénice*, the first hint of calamity shows in her lover's appearance, "Muet, chargé de soins, et les larmes aux yeux."

But until *Mithridate* the development of the plot or the tragic outcome does not hinge upon the revelation of glance or movement; to illustrate this, we may note that Bérénice, when Antiochus bids her farewell, repeats almost word for word Monime's cry at Mithridate's ominous glare: "Prince, vous vous troublez et changez de visage." Yet Bérénice's remark holds none of the tragic implications of Monime's fear-stricken cry.

In the Racinian tragic setting, "tous nous trahit, la voix, le silence, les yeux" (*Andromaque*, II. ii. 575). Not only expression, but tone of voice, gestures of head, hands, and arms, even clothing and ornament, have meaning. To realize the wide range in tone of the dialogue, one need not rely on the Abbé Dubos' description of how Racine taught La Champmeslé to lower and raise her voice within the scope of a single Alexandrine; even the average reader, reciting such a speech as Phèdre's confession to Hippolyte, with its checks and hesitancies, its broken rhythms, cannot help but impart to it some of the sensual hymning, the dejection and sudden abandon, of the heroine's plea. The characters themselves are aware of the power of tone, and Phèdre begs Œnone:

> Presse, pleure, gémis; plains-lui Phèdre mourante,
> Ne rougis pas de prendre une voix suppliante.
>
> (III. i. 809-10)

As to the rôle of clothing, we are more conscious of Phèdre's debility when she complains of the weight of veil and headband. In a passage unusual for its blunt realism, we see Bérénice counting on her dishevelled hair and disorderly clothing to move Titus. Phénice remonstrates:

> Mais voulez-vous paraître en ce désordre extrême ?
> Remettez-vous, Madame, et rentrez en vous-même.
> Laissez-moi relever ces voiles détachés,
> Et ces cheveux épars dont vos yeux sont cachés.
> Souffrez que de vos pleurs je répare l'outrage.
> (IV. ii. 967–71)

Bérénice answers simply, "Laisse, laisse, Phénice, il verra son ouvrage."

It is perhaps a further evidence of Racine's realism that he has re-vitalized even ritual gestures. In three plays, *Britannicus, Iphigénie*, and *Phèdre*, a character embraces another's knees in supplication. In the first of these, Junie, weeping, clasps the feet of Augustus' statue, and her gesture takes on symbolic significance, since, as we have seen, Augustus stands for the virtues of the past. In *Iphigénie*, when Clytem-nestre says to Achille, "c'est donc à moi d'embrasser vos genoux" (III. v. 928), the stage direction following reads, "Achille, la relevant." When Œnone conjures Phèdre "Par vos faibles genoux que je tiens embrassés" (I. iii. 244), her mistress replies, "Tu le veux. Lève-toi." In all these cases the statement is accompanied by the act. The whole question of gesture as mere statement or as action or as both in litera-ture is immensely complicated, and deserves more detailed treatment than it can receive here. Yet it may be noted that in *Le Cid* (II. viii. 648) when Chimène tells the King "Je me jette à vos pieds," and Don Diègue tells him, "J'embrasse vos genoux," clearly neither character makes an actual gesture.

As for less monumental gestures, what remarkable effects Racine can obtain by having a character merely turn his head away from the speaker! Polynice and Etéocle are only the first of many who inflict despair by such an action. Though it may mean only discomfiture, to a despairing lover it is infallibly a sign of indifference:

> Perfide, je le voi,
> Tu comptes les moments que tu perds avec moi !

cries Hermione (*Andromaque*, IV. v. 1375–6). Antiochus resolves to escape Bérénice's indifferent glance, and she herself reproaches Titus thus:

Vous détournez les yeux, et semblez vous confondre.
Ne m'offrirez-vous plus qu'un visage interdit ?

(II. iv. 596-7)

In contrast, the inability to turn away may reveal the fascination of fear, and Zacharie says of Athalie, "Ses yeux, comme effrayés, n'osaient se détourner" (II. ii. 413).

So far, we have largely confined our discussion to the various constraints imposed upon the Racinian character, and we have examined with some care various ways in which these constraints, whether self-imposed or not, inevitably produce dramatic conflicts. Concerning the dramatic effect of "presence," its power to intimidate and control, we have seen how, in one striking instance, the eavesdropping scene in *Britannicus*, one character by sheer force of presence can mould another to an artificial mode of conduct. But unique as their use by Racine may be, the eavesdropping scene and the "shock treatment" are devices, employed in one or two plays at most. It remains to determine to what extent Racine made use of the sheer physical impact of characters upon one another as a basic dramatic motive.

For example, the presence of one character, or even his entrance upon the stage, may suffice to alter completely the decision already made by another. In Roxane's first interview with Bajazet, her denunciations speedily give way to a pitiful plea, in which she admits his power over her ("Je te donne, cruel, des armes contre moi") and when he appears before her at Atalide's request, before he utters a word she jumps to the conclusion that he has come to declare his love. A moment before the last meeting in Act V, she admits the hopelessness of seeing him once again, and asks, "Que ne le laissons-nous périr?" But she breaks off as he appears; her resolution is broken, like the ellipsis that precedes her faint "Mais le voici." In the lines that follow, she is no longer in control; we recognize the desperation of appeals that she herself has already analysed as hopeless:

Malgré tout mon amour, si je n'ai pu vous plaire,
Je n'en murmure point. Quoiqu'à ne vous rien taire,
Ce même amour peut-être et ces mêmes bienfaits
Auraient dû suppléer à mes faibles attraits.

(V. iv. 1473-6)

The faint "je n'en murmure point," followed by the concessive "quoiqu'à ne vous rien taire" (which is no cheville, but rather a pathetic attempt to impart a confidential tone), the tentative quality of the suggestion that gratitude might compensate for her lack of attractiveness, show her weakness in the lover's presence. Is her final "Sortez!" the scream of rage it is generally thought to be, or is the word pronounced rather in the dying tones of one for whom time has run out, one finally and irrevocably convinced by the irony of Bajazet's reference to her "bontés" that all hope is dead? The melting of her will in the presence of the loved one suggests the latter interpretation. Only by dismissing him from her presence can she regain her strength and once again envision his death with composure. Now she can say to Atalide, "Je me connais, madame, et je me fais justice." The poor slave has awakened, but too late.

The "Greek" plays, Iphigénie and Phèdre, depend far less on the external evidences of emotions for dramatic effect than the plays discussed above. The characters appear as the victims of supernatural forces; their capacity for concealment is reduced, their reactions more immediate and violent.[5] Phèdre, it is true, keeps silent about Hippolyte's innocence because she misinterprets his expression. But once again, it is for the elemental impact of presence that Phèdre concerns us. When the hero appears, Phèdre completely forgets in that one dazzling moment the reasons she had invented for her summons ("J'oublie en le voyant ce que je viens lui dire"). Although she recovers sufficiently to speak rationally of her helpless son, her control soon begins to slip away again. The structure of the confession scene is that of the crescendo-like breaking of barriers under the terrific weight of the hero's physical proximity.

The intensification of emotion through proximity, for Racine a purely dramatic conception, helps to account for his unusually naturalistic treatment of love. Of the two clichés concerning the effect of absence upon love, idealistic literature evidently preferred to believe that such absence "made the heart grow fonder." Does not the gallant

---

[5]This is also true of Athalie, where there is an almost total absence of references to expression, gesture, and physical appearance. Josabet's words when her son appears: "Où courez-vous, ainsi, tout pâle et hors d'haleine?" (II. ii. 380) are purely descriptive; the boy has rushed in with a message, he is frightened and out of breath, and his mother's statement involves none of the probing, the interpreting, the jumping to false conclusions on the strength of a look or an attitude that we have seen in the earlier plays. Joad's words to the Levites, "Mais je vois que déjà vous brûlez de me suivre" (IV. iii. 1369) are little more than a statement of fact, fulfilling what we have seen to be a secondary function of Racine's references to expression: that of implicating silent personages in the action.

Céladon return more ardent than ever, after having been sent to Italy by his father in the hope that he would forget Astrée?[6] And although as Racine once caustically pointed out, all heroes are not meant to be Céladons, other heroes, not all of them fictitious, shared his attitude in this respect, at least. The amorous Thésée of Corneille's *Œdipe* preferred the dangers of the plague to absence from Dircé. La Fontaine sang, in mock-heroic vein, of the dangers of separation in *Les Deux Pigeons*. Even the cynical La Rochefoucauld found that the depth of a passion was in direct ratio to its perseverance during separation.[7]

What of Racine? Perhaps his most famous unrequited lover, Oreste, returns ·to Hermione his passion redoubled—"ses feux redoublés." But is this because absence has fanned the flames? Not at all. As he tells Pylade, his despair at the news of Hermione's betrothal to Pyrrhus turned to fierce anger; he determined to forget her, and what is more, believed he had succeeded: "Je fis croire and je crus ma victoire certaine." Only the news that Pyrrhus had abandoned her, and the prospect of seeing her again rekindled his fires: "De mes feux mal éteints je reconnus la trace." He decides to pursue his love, to give himself blindly to destiny, not because absence has intensified his passion, but because the possibility of physical contact reawakens it.

Even such ideal lovers as Xipharès and Monime can envisage being separated from one another. Xipharès tells Arbate that he had forgotten her completely until the news of Mithridate's death (I. i. 69, 81–4), and Monime begs him to avoid her:

> Dans ce dessein vous-même il faut me soutenir,
> Et de mon faible cœur m'aider à vous bannir.
> J'attends du moins, j'attends de votre complaisance
> Que désormais partout vous fuirez ma présence.
>
> (II. vi. 701–4)

Monime is aware of the power of presence; the longer she remains with her lover, the weaker is her resolve:

> Je me sens arrêter par un plaisir funeste.
> Plus je vous parle, et plus, trop faible que je suis,
> Je cherche à prolonger le péril que je fuis.
>
> (II. vi. 740–3)

---

[6]See M. Magendie, *Le Roman français au 17e siècle,* Paris, Droz, 1932, p. 102.

[7] "L'absence diminue les médiocres passions, et augmente les grandes, comme le vent éteint les bougies et allume le feu." But see *La Princesse de Clèves*: "Enfin, des années entières s'étant passées, le temps et l'absence ralentirent sa douleur et éteignirent sa passion."

Just as his absence will calm her ardour, his presence may startle her into betraying her passion:

> Je sais qu'en vous voyant, un tendre souvenir
> Peut m'arracher du cœur quelque indigne soupir.
> (II. vi. 729–30)

Similarly, in *Athalie*, Josabet fears that seeing Eliacin she might involuntarily reveal her love:

> Autant que je le puis j'évite sa présence,
> De peur qu'en le voyant, quelque trouble indiscret
> Ne fasse avec mes pleurs échapper mon secret.
> (I. ii. 192–4)

This anti-idealistic attitude toward passion shows also in the steps Phèdre takes to escape her guilty love; she has Hippolyte banished. Once he is gone from Athens, she breathes freely again:

> Je respirais, Œnone; et, depuis son absence,
> Mes jours moins agités coulaient dans l'innocence.
> (I. iii. 297–8)

The wound, with time, might have healed, but destiny intervenes. They meet again at Troezen, and (l. 304),

> Ma blessure trop vive aussitôt a saigné.

Racine was of course perfectly well aware of the conventions of idealistic love, and in *Phèdre* he used them to throw into relief the animality of the heroine's passion. Aricie loves Hippolyte, not for his beauty, but for his purity; the timid hero languishes for love, and like Petrarch's stag, "bears everywhere the barb that smote him."[8] Yet even in the midst of idealism, Racine does not forget his naturalistic bias; the idyllic farewell duets sorrowfully intoned by Titus and Bérénice contain the acknowledgment that ardour cools with separation (IV. v. 1131–4, despite II. iv. 587–8).

It is something of a commonplace that only a fine line divides love and hate in the Racinian psyche. We should thus not be surprised if hatred, as well as "amour-passion," appears to be intensified by proximity. Indeed, much of the effectiveness of one of Racine's greatest scenes derives from this concept: the irony of Jocaste's confront-

[8]See G. May, *D'Ovide à Racine*, Paris, Presses Universitaires, 1949, pp. 127–31, for a full discussion of this particular conceit.

ation of the enemy brothers springs from the premise that their hatred will increase in proportion as they approach one another. An analysis of Jocaste's speech (IV. iii. 973–1000; 1015–32) reveals the dramatic power inherent in such a premise.

There are three movements. First of all, Jocaste's expression of her joy at the meeting which has finally come about

> Et moi, par un bonheur où je n'osais penser,
> L'un et l'autre à la fois je vous puis embrasser;

secondly, her urging that they discover natural affection, both by memories evoked by the place where they are meeting ("ce même palais où vous prîtes naissance"), and by approaching one another so as to recognize the family resemblance in one another's features ("Tous deux dans votre frère envisagez vos traits"); and thirdly, her alarmed reactions to the gestures and glances of her sons

> Loin d'approcher, vous reculez tous deux !
> D'où vient ce sombre accueil et ces regards fâcheux ?

Then comes an attempt to rationalize the brothers' behaviour:

> N'est-ce point que chacun, d'une âme irrésolue,
> Pour saluer son frère attend qu'il le salue ?

Further exhortations end in the appeal with its pitiful rationalization: "venant de si loin, vous devez commencer."

The final revelation is brought about through the propinquity of the tragic trio. We have heard Créon's prediction of the result, and Eté-ocle's words a moment before: "Qu'on hait un ennemi quand il est près de nous." Créon has advised him to dissimulate:

> ... s'il se peut, Seigneur, cachez votre colère;
> Feignez;

Polynice's probable reactions are not known. But the sight of one another is too much; Jocaste's efforts to make the *rapprochement* more complete by urging her sons to embrace cruelly heightens the irony. As she begs them to find affection in one another's glance, in one another's features, and, for that purpose, to draw nearer, she says, "pour en mieux juger, voyez-les de plus près." Here the verb "juger" is highly significant, expressing once again the need of Racine's characters to probe beneath words and actions to the hidden reality. On the stage, the fierce glances, the recoil, are seen; they are stressed by Jocaste's lines which both provide a commentary and implicate her in the action, for even here she is still acting her part as conciliator. And at the last, it is a gesture that reveals her final defeat; the brothers turn away as she repeats her plea to find compassion in the scene of their birth.

It is proof of the sureness of Racine's purpose, and perhaps also of the consistency of his tragic view, that the effects of what we have called constraint and presence appear in his first tragedy. On these effects depend much of the atmosphere of the Racinian play, much of our realization, as spectators, of the plight of the characters, and many of the most memorable scenes. But integral as they may be, "constraint" and "presence" afford us only one set of clues to the nature of Racinian tragedy. To determine other essential characteristics, we must next consider the question of sources. Although, like Shakespeare and Corneille, Racine found subject-matter and tragic themes in history, legend, and contemporary drama, he leaned far more heavily than those playwrights on the classic theatre, not only in his adaptation of actual Greek plays, but in his concept of tragedy. It will be our purpose in the following section to discuss Racine's dependency on these sources, what he assimilated, what he discarded, and how, in the final process of amalgamation, he evolved what we may properly call "Racinian" tragedy.

## RACINE AND THE GREEK DRAMA

Although there is every reason to believe that Racine knew intimately not only the plays for which he has left marginal comments but all the extant work of Aeschylus, Sophocles, and Euripides, the actual proportion of his plays based upon Greek tragedy is small: three out of eleven. The study of literal borrowings, or even the comparison of the plays with their Greek models, thus hardly answers the larger question: what was the impact of Greek tragedy upon Racine? What rôle did it have in forming his concept of the tragic?

A fairly frequent topic of critical discussion has been the presence or absence of a "Greek" quality in Racine's tragedies. Critics have argued that even in the plays in which he avowedly followed a Greek model, his views had nothing Greek about them. But at once a difficulty arises. Just what is the "Greek tragic view"? There is an obvious danger in the rather common tendency to lump all Greek tragedy together, to assign to it certain general characteristics, regardless of who wrote it, and even to neglect essential differences in various plays by the same dramatist. One critic, for example, in an extremely cogent and interesting study, suggests that Racine is not "Greek" because the idea of "measure" or *sophrosyne* does not occur in his plays.[9] But must we not ask further whether all Greek dramatists give equal importance to *sophrosyne*, and therefore whether it can properly be considered a characteristic of "Greek tragedy"? Could a tragic view in a modern, which we might properly consider "Greek," exist without it? Certainly the question remains open. In attempting to answer it, it seems most satisfactory to consider the three major writers of Greek tragedy singly in our attempt to discover Racine's relationship to them.

*Euripides and Racine*

In considering Racine's contact with the Greek tragic drama, one takes as an almost inevitable starting-point his avowed affinity and preference for Euripides. He thought him the most "tragic of poets" and was as outraged at contemporaries who belittled him as if he had been himself the target of attack. Notwithstanding this, the modern critic, reading Euripides with Racine in mind, may wonder if such an affinity really existed. The answer is that it did, but that the affinity is tonal, rather than textual or structural. One has only to read Racine's marginal notes on Euripides (so often more severe than those on Aeschylus or Sophocles, but with the severity of a lover) to see that he almost totally rejects the Euripidean structure in favour of his seventeenth-century principles of unity and progression. Why, for example, does he question the remarkable Parodos of the *Medea*? Because only the nurse and the pedagogue appear, and they are not sufficiently "noble" to start a play. Inevitably, too, certain scenes appear to him to be insufficiently motivated. He complains frequently, "Ceci n'est point de l'action." Of the messenger speech describing at some length the brothers' preparations for battle in the *Phoenician Maidens*, he asks impatiently, "Pourquoi donc avoir fait un si long récit dans un péril si pressant?"[10] We cannot, however, blame Racine for failing to see that neo-Aristotelian principles of logical unity did not apply to Euripides.

[9]P. H. Frye, *Racine*, University of Nebraska Studies, vol. XIX (1919), pp. 173–212; H. Peyre, *RR*, XXXI (1940), p. 297.
[10]*Œuvres,* ed. Picard *et al.*, II, p. 875.

It has taken a good many years for critics to realize that in many of Euripides' plays, of which the *Phoenician Maidens* is one example, he was not developing a tragic theme, but rather creating a kind of dramatic pageant, in which, as Professor Kitto says, "incident is superior to thought."[11]

For the above reasons, Racine seems to have been mistaken even about the character of Phaedra that he praised so highly. In declaring his debt to Euripides, he says he understands why the character should have been so successful. This, he goes on, is because it so admirably fulfils the Aristotelian specifications for tragic heroes. But part of the Sophoclean concept of tragic character, from which Aristotle's theories derive, is that the play should concentrate upon a single hero who prefigures Man; the reasonable Aristotelian laws of necessary or probable sequence are valid for such tragedy because there must be a constant interplay between character and situation. Euripides' play, however, is not the tragedy of a single victim, but of victims; the dramatic situation is only the setting for the outburst of unreason in the natural order which affects all the characters. Therefore, Euripides was less interested in a clash between Phaedra's character and that of Hippolytus, than he was in showing the effect of irresponsible cosmic forces upon a variety of characters. Phaedra can disappear and leave us with Hippolytus before the play is half over without violating "unity," because neither character controls his fate. Their destruction does not arise from any complexity in their characters, but from a tragic singleness. Aphrodite, appearing at the beginning of the play, explains both structurally and morally the real character of the action: she is the agent, and she makes it clear that Hippolytus' tragedy is his refusal to come to terms with her, who represents a potentially disastrous element in our nature. As Kitto has so astutely seen, the very quality in Phaedra which makes her seem Sophoclean, her virtuous struggle against passion, serves actually to prevent Hippolytus from seeming to be her victim rather than the goddess'.[12]

When Racine, impelled by his Aristotelian principles of logical sequence, made Phèdre his central figure, he did not thereby succeed in making her a Sophoclean hero. True, she is no longer the mere

---

[11]H. D. F. Kitto, *Greek Tragedy: A Literary Study*, London, Methuen, revised ed., 1950, 344 ff. I am much indebted to Professor Kitto's brilliant study.

[12]*Ibid.*, p. 204.

instrument of the gods, discarded as soon as she has served her purpose. But despite her eminence, she is still very much a victim. Her debility, her fear, and above all the lucidity with which she sees the hopelessness of her struggle have nothing Sophoclean about them. Paradoxically, Racine's substitution of what he considered a "tragic flaw" for Hippolytus' arrogant neglect of Aphrodite in the Greek play results only in a greater sympathy for him. How could the audience, those avid readers of *L'Astrée*, have failed to sympathize with the love story of Hippolyte and Aricie? As we saw earlier, Racine even carefully idealized their love, in contrast to the sensual passion of the heroine. Despite the fact that lack of "measure" or *sophrosyne* no longer explains Hippolytus' downfall, Racine's play remains Euripidean because its characters are victimized; there is no hint that they have disrupted the ideal "pattern of things" so typical of Sophoclean tragedy.

In part because they are victims, Racine's characters, like those of Euripides, are singularly unheroic. But there are other reasons for their lack of the tragic stature we usually associate with the Sophoclean hero. In our discussion of space in Racine's tragedies, we noted that in widening the unseen area of action, he diminishes the stature of his characters, making them thus the playthings of destiny. But this process of "playing down," of "demolishing" the hero, to borrow Bénichou's term, began long before *Iphigénie*, as we have already seen in our remarks on *Andromaque*. The Euripidean characters, although they bear the great names of legend, are, like Racine's, stripped of much of their grandeur. If we look at the play which Racine followed most closely, the *Iphigeneia*, we see at once how devoid of greatness the characters are. Agamemnon is a sorrowing father, regretful at the unpleasant task he must perform, but there is no majesty in him. His motives, too, are rather questionable. In the heated argument with Menelaus, in which the latter accuses him of the basest political conniving, he comes off a bad second best. He almost founders in the storm of Clytemnestra's denunciations; and the new information we receive about their marital relationship is not at all to his credit; he had taken her by force, after killing her first husband.

Clytemnestra too has little that is noble about her. One finds perhaps the best example in Euripides of that "chatter," abasing the tragic tone, for which Aristotle denounced him, in the second episode, when she drives in on her chariot with her daughter and baby, for all the world like a *bonne bourgeoise* arriving in the country in her limousine, clucking to the servants to hold the baby as she hovers protectively over her daughter who is engaged to the rich country cousin.

As for Achilles, he reminds one of a character in a play by Musset. With the suppliant Clytemnestra at his feet, he can only advise caution; he is hardly put out about the false marriage announcement, since, as he tells us, he is so used to being pursued by young girls.

Similar examples of the lowering of tragic tone could be found in other plays, for example in the *Alcestis*, which Racine admired so greatly. Of course, Racine could not adopt Euripides' method of "humanizing" his characters; to have imitated the Clytemnestra scene discussed above would have been to venture into comedy. For similar reasons, Racine's Achille is Homeric, rather than Euripidean. But the attitude of Euripides in seeing his heroes as human rather than semi-divine is certainly reflected in Racine. In this connection, it is significant that none of the plays of Euripides that Racine either adapted or planned to adapt are considered to be tragedies by modern critics.[13]

The reduction of tragic stature is also linked to the Euripidean hero's defeat by passion. A critic has written that in Euripides' plays, "for the first time in recorded history we meet the realization that emotion may be stronger than reason, and drive men to do what they know to be disastrous merely because they cannot help themselves."[14] This comment might equally well be made of Racine, save for the priority in time. Actually, however, none of the plays from which Racine borrowed exemplifies this triumph of passion over reason as well as the *Medea*. The heroine murders her children, she says, "because her *thumos* [passion] is stronger than her counsels; *thumos* is the cause of man's worst crimes."[15] Hermione, Roxane, or Phèdre could have uttered those words, and although Racine did not, or could not, write a *Médée*, the terrible unreason of the Medean act echoes through his theatre.

Contrary to general belief, Euripides is the only one of the Greek tragedians who posits an irrational element in the universe and in human nature. As E. R. Dodds has shown, his plays run counter to three basic affirmations of Greek rationalist thought as it had finally emerged in his own day: first, that reason (rational discourse, *logos*) is

[13]For Professor Kitto, they are "melodramas."
[14]*The Medea*, tr. D. W. Lucas, London, Cohen and West, 1949, pp. 3-4.
[15]Quoted by D. W. Lucas, *ibid.*

the sole instrument of truth (as opposed to views which lean on sense perception or faith or intuition, or deny that such an instrument exists at all); second, that reality is understandable through reason; and third, that in such a universe, values, as well as facts, will be rational.[16] The basis of such a philosophy is that error, moral and intellectual, is the result of a failure to use the reason we possess and that it can be cured by intellectual processes. The characters of Euripides, in their conception and in their actions, contravene these affirmations. Medea could not have erred through an inability to use reason, since the dramatist is at pains to illustrate her superior intellect, and Phaedra's nurse says that one can be intelligent and desire evil; the conclusion of the *Hecuba* is that the evil in human nature is indestructible, rooted in heredity, rather than the ancestral curse of Aeschylean tragedy. Phaedra, Agave, Heracles, all reveal, in differing degrees of intensity, symptoms of neurosis and insanity.

The lack of any specific divine cause for the tragedies of Racine's Jocaste, his Agamemnon, his Phèdre, is thus essentially Euripidean. Phèdre's disease is hereditary; like Euripides' Kypris, Racine's Venus "haunts the air; in the waves of the sea she hath her dwelling; of her are all things born. She is the sower, she the giver of desire; and children of desire are all we upon the earth."[17] Like Euripides' characters, Racine's condemn the gods, and protest the injustice of their actions.[18] There is no more striking proof that for Racine as well as the Greek dramatist the natural life force is equated with the divine, than the picture of the desperate Phèdre, sacrificing to Venus, yet unable to distinguish, as she makes the offerings, whether it is Hippolyte or Venus she worships. whether she is praying for release from passion, or for its consummation.

An offshoot of Euripides' irrationalism is the way in which his plays seem to question standards, examining from a peculiarly wry and ironic angle beliefs which have an ultimately rational basis, but which have been erected into shibboleths. Two examples may serve as illustration. First of all, we may note the treatment of "sacrifice" in the *Alcestis.* Old Pheres is "expected," because of his age, to be willing to

---

[16]E. R. Dodds, "Euripides the Irrationalist," *CR,* XL (1929), pp. 97–104.

[17]Quoted by Dodds, *ibid.,* p. 102.

[18]Cf. Oreste (*Andromaque,* III. i. 775–6):

> De quelque part sur moi que je tourne les yeux,
> Je ne vois que malheurs qui condamnent ces Dieux.

die in his son's place. But he unexpectedly refuses, because he loves life more than ever in his old age, and he rejects the beautiful deed it would have been for him to sacrifice himself for his son and wife. Even the central character (whom Racine thought so tragic) seems to have questionable motives in dying for her husband. There is an implication that she has lost her beauty and desires a spectacular end, that her "sacrifice" is tinged with vainglory.

An even better example of Euripides' vision that things are not what they seem is the children motif in the *Medea*. The forces of disorder that prey on the characters reveal themselves in the series of paradoxes built upon this theme. Besides the central irony of a mother who hates and destroys her children, we have a Creon who loves his children more than his kingdom, but would pitilessly exile Medea's innocent sons. Children are past and present instruments of evil; beloved and cherished by their parents, they yet prove their undoing. Medea has caused Pelias to be killed by his own daughters; Creusa, Jason's betrothed, accepts the deadly gifts from the hands of Medea's children, and Creon dies because he embraces his daughter in her agony. Medea declares that had she been childless, she would have spared Jason; her refuge in Athens is assured because she promises by her spells to end Aegeus' childlessness; the natural desire for children thus protects a murderess.[19] The wry little ode of the Chorus in praise of childlessness summarizes the idea: since the natural, i.e., the bearing of children we love, inevitably brings, at the very least, sorrow and pain, the unnatural, childlessness, may be preferable. Yet the implication is plain: human beings will go on having children, moved by natural forces which in turn bring disaster.

As we have already seen, Racinian tragedy rings various changes on this theme. *La Thébaïde, Britannicus, Mithridate, Iphigénie, Phèdre,* all treat, in one form or another, the woes visited by children upon parents.

Discussing the way in which certain seventeenth-century philosophers resolutely reject any duality in human nature, Paul Bénichou has remarked that for such writers the word "nature" has a single meaning: the domain of morally indifferent, brute necessity.[20] In discussing

---

[19] I am not aware whether this explanation of the "fortuitous" arrival of Aegeus has ever been offered. Since his journey is for the purpose of consulting the oracle concerning his childlessness, if we consider the children theme a unifying motif, then neither his arrival nor his promise of refuge to Medea need be considered extraneous.

[20] *Morales du grand siècle*, Paris, Gallimard, 1948, p. 103.

*Andromaque* we have shown how this applies to Racine. The doubt he casts on such standards as "honour," "reputation," "noble-heartedness," by showing them to be pretexts for acts that gratify passion, reflects the Euripidean denial that the good can be clearly distinguished from the bad. This denial of fixed standards extends to Euripides' portrayal of the gods. They are not merely dramatic fictions, but they personify the forces of necessity to which man must yield. As Dodds puts it, "for Euripides Man is the slave, not the favorite child, of the gods; and the name of the 'ageless order' is Necessity."[21]

At times, as in the case of *Phèdre*, Racine comes very close to this view. More often, however, his way of following Euripides is to generalize the gods; not only will he never bring Artemis to the stage, but he will submerge her influence in a concert of divine forces. It is to Neptune that Thésée prays, but Hippolyte appeals, not only to the unnamed god of the temple where he is to wed Aricie, but to

> Et la chaste Diane, et l'auguste Junon,
> Et tous les Dieux enfin...
>
> (V. i. 1404-5)

As to actual doubt, one may place Clytemnestra's bitter inquiry, in Euripides' *Iphigeneia at Aulis*, whether the story of Artemis' substitution of a hind for her daughter is not simply a fable to console her, alongside the Racinian scepticism, which seems directed at the motives of the gods rather than at their existence. On hearing of the gods' demand that he sacrifice Iphigénie, Agamemnon's first reaction is to denounce them; his second thought is that it is all a trick, and that if he obeyed, he would be punished. At the same time, however, he identifies the gods with ignorant superstition, and in his gloomy prediction that once Iphigénie sets foots in Aulis she is lost, we already hear the accents of Voltaire:

> Calchas, qui l'attend en ces lieux,
> Fera taire nos pleurs, fera parler les Dieux;
> Et la religion, contre nous irritée,
> Par les timides Grecs sera seule écoutée.
>
> (I. i. 135-8)

Evidently, then, the traditional view that Racine "resembled" Euripides holds good, though perhaps not for the usual reasons ad-

---

[21]"Euripides the Irrationalist," p. 101.

vanced.[22] The Greek writer's structure could only have seemed erratic to the Frenchman. And compared to the highly inventive Euripides, who added to or changed the established stories at will, Racine was extremely cautious, requiring a precedent for almost every innovation. Nor can we say, as some critics have suggested, that it was through some peculiarly "human" quality of his characters that Euripides appealed to Racine; one hardly thinks of his Medea or Electra in that light.[23] Euripides' characters are not "human" in the sense that they are "like us"; if, by his questioning of rational motives and standards, he reduces his heroes to mere humans, it is in order to find the impetus for their acts in the dark and irrational side that to Euripides is inseparably part of the "human." It has often been said that Euripides' rationality elicited Racine's response to his works; this is so only in so far as Racinian, like Euripidean rationality presupposes the irrational. But certainly the chief clue to their affinity lies in a common rationality which is a far wider concept than logical deductibility or scientific verifiability. I have no doubt that in their vision of a precarious equilibrium between an order connoting fitness, propriety, and adjustability, and a contrasting unreasonableness, the two are most akin.

*Sophocles and Racine*

In our comment on Euripides, we mentioned the fact that the Euripidean structure, with its lack of logical sequence, could not have appealed to Racine. Conversely, and not merely because the Aristotelian principles derive from Sophocles, the tragic rhythm of that writer resembles Racine's ordering of the dramatic action. Reading the *Oedipus Rex,* one cannot fail to be struck by the relentless forward movement of the drama, in which, little by little, incident is heaped

[22]Cf. the statement of Longepierre, "Disons que M. Corneille approche davantage de Sophocle, & que M. Racine ressemble plus à Euripide," discussed by G. May, *Tragédie cornélienne, tragédie racinienne,* University of Illinois Press, 1947, p. 188.

[23]In his extremely thoughtful discussion of Euripides and Racine, G. May suggests that the "humanity" of Euripides and what he calls the "familiarité totale du public avec les thèmes et les personnages" explain the affinity. But certain of his examples are questionable. One could make out a case for Sophocles' Electra as more "human" than Euripides'. It seems probable that Euripides depended for much of his interest not upon "total familiarity" but upon the independence with which he treated known legends and characters; that is, his spectator did not say "Ah! these are the characters I know," but "How is the dramatist going to recreate these familiar characters and situations?" Racinian drama produces a similar interest of curiosity. The question of the influence of conventional depiction of legendary characters on Racine has been interestingly broached by W. B. Stanford, "On Some References to Ulysses in French Literature from Du Bellay to Fénelon," *SP,* L (1953), pp. 446–56.

upon incident until the edifice of appalling guilt is constructed. Even such a formal device as "linking" has its counterpart in Sophocles; just as Racine's characters are propelled by skilful linking devices through each succeeding stage of the action, so in the *Oedipus*, for example, different characters approaching to add their weight to the testimony are announced by the Chorus.[24]

But far more important than such similarities is the fact that in both Sophocles and Racine, structure may be viewed as symbolic. Sophoclean tragic irony is closely related to the march of the action. Una Ellis-Fermor's fruitful suggestion that the form of the Sophoclean tragedy symbolizes the forces of order (*logos*)[25] could also be applied, in an indirect way, to Racine. As we saw in an earlier chapter, there is an inexorable logic in Racine's ordering of scene, act, and incident. And although it goes without saying that the laws of Racine's universe have nothing of the Sophoclean serenity and immutability, nevertheless the fine-edged precision and brilliance of the Racinian structure may be set, in ironic contrast, over against the collapse of reason in the dramatic action.

As a specific example within a play, again taking the *Oedipus*, one finds a striking use by Sophocles of what we have called "sculptural" groupings in Racine. In the opening scene of the Prologue, Oedipus receives as suppliants the people of Thebes. From the majesty of this grouping—the King enthroned before his people—stems an irony, for the scene portrays the stability of leadership and power which will be progressively undermined by the dramatic action. Racine develops irony in a similar manner in the scene of Mithridate's announcement of his plans to his sons.

Sophocles and Racine closely parallel one another in their use of irony. Sophoclean irony derives from the spectators' possessing a knowledge that is not shared by the protagonist. The possession of this knowledge, coupled with the agonized impotency of the spectator-actor relationship, accounts for some of the tensest moments in the dramas of both playwrights. In the *Oedipus*, for example, Sophocles makes us aware of the hero's guilt from the beginning, relaying the

[24]In the Prologos and succeeding stasimons. There are frequent parallels; to instance only one, Creon's joyous expression, as he approaches with the "good" news that Thebes has only to banish the man who is contaminating the city. A similar ironic linking occurs in *Mithridate*, IV. i.

[25]In *Frontiers of Drama*, p. 133, quoted by Kitto, *Greek Tragedy*, p. 140.

secret to the audience in a remarkable *tour de force* which has Tiresias
bursting angrily forth with the truth, which Oedipus cannot, however,
in his anger believe. There is no need to dwell on the many examples
of this kind of enlightenment of the spectator in Racine's tragedies.[26]
These are his careful revelation of the true identity of Eriphile in the
first act of *Iphigénie*, the early announcement of the pending arrival
of the Roman army in *Mithridate*, the care with which doubt is cast
on the rumour of Thésée's death in *Phèdre*, the specific nature of the
divine promise in *Athalie*, and, on a smaller scale, the audience's fore-
knowledge in such scenes as the interview between Britannicus and
Junie, Agamemnon's meeting with Iphigénie, and the agon between
Athalie and Eliacin.

Racine's appreciation of Sophocles' technical powers is evident in
the way in which he could single out with unerring taste some of the
Greek writer's most dazzling effects. An example is the scene in the
*Electra* where Orestes first speaks to his sister, as he holds the urn which
is supposed to contain her brother's ashes. "Il n'y a rien de plus beau
sur le théatre," writes Racine, "que de voir Electra pleurer son frère
mort en sa présence, qui en étant lui-même attendri, est obligé de
se découvrir." As R. Picard has pointed out, Racine not only appreciates
the pathos of the scene, he admires the dramatic movement which
brings about the actual recognition by a steady progression from word
to word.[27]

As I said earlier, our purpose is not to consider textual borrowings,
but affinities.[28] In fact, too careful a search for the exact resemblance
may lead one to ignore what is actually an imitation even where the
texts themselves are dissimilar. For example, Racine enthusiastically
praises Sophocles' habit of carefully establishing the setting at the
beginning of the play. He gives three examples:

Sophocle a un soin merveilleux d'établir d'abord le lieu de la scène. Il se sert ici
[in the *Electra*] pour cela d'un artifice très agréable, en introduisant un vieillard qui
montre les environs du palais d'Argos à Oreste, qui en avait été enlevé tout jeune. Le
*Philoctète* commence à peu près de même : c'est Ulysse qui montre à Pyrrhus tout

---

[26]See his repeated references, in the marginalia, to "bel artifice d'instruire le spectateur, sans
éclaircir l'acteur."

[27]*Œuvres*, ed. R. Picard *et al.*, II, p. 1123.

[28]For an exhaustive study of the first type, see R. C. Knight, *Racine et la Grèce*, Paris, Boivin,
1950, *passim*.

jeune l'île de Lemnos, où ils sont, et par où l'armée avait passé. L'*Œdipe Colonéen* s'ouvre par Œdipe aveugle qui se fait décrire par Antigone le lieu où il est. Ces trois ouvertures, quoiqu'un peu semblables, ne laissent pas d'avoir une très agréable diversité et des couleurs merveilleuses.[29]

R. C. Knight has claimed that despite this evident admiration, Racine did not emulate this method of establishing the setting, since in *Athalie*, the one tragedy whose setting is both familiar to the audience and full of religious and historical associations, he did not have the characters describe Jerusalem.[30] However, the technique, as Racine admired it, not only required that a character describe the setting, but that he should describe it to another character who for some reason had not seen it. In *Athalie* there is obviously no need for Joad to describe city or temple to Abner. But at least one Racinian exposition, that of *Bérénice*, in which Antiochus shows Arsace "la pompe de ces lieux," follows the Sophoclean pattern closely. Perhaps it would not be inexact to say that in general, the concern for setting we noticed in our discussion of Racine's exposition and his treatment of space, like his use of irony, owes much to the example of Sophocles.

## Aeschylus and Racine

Although we have only one play of Aeschylus annotated by Racine, there is no reason to believe that he had not read the other works, nor, at least on the basis of his remarks concerning the *Choephori*, that he underestimated him.[31] He seems to owe nothing of his structure or technique to the first of the great Greek tragedians, yet it is possible that he studied Aeschylus' use of the Chorus after determining to use it in the religious tragedies.[32]

Aeschylus, of the three tragic writers, may be the least close to Racine. We have already noted, however, a similarity in the two dramatists' treatment of pre- and post-dramatic time. As so often with Racine's characters, Aeschylus' are enveloped in their past, which Chorus and secondary characters evoke poetically. In the *Agamemnon*, the King's past walks with him onto the grim red carpet that leads to the site of his death. And the play ends with the Chorus' defiance of Clytemnes-

[29]*Œuvres*, ed. R. Picard *et al.*, II, p. 861.
[30]Knight, *Racine et la Grèce*, p. 223.
[31]As Knight remarks, *ibid.*, p. 224.
[32]On Aeschylus' use of the Chorus as distinct from Sophocles', see Kitto, *Greek Tragedy*, pp. 49 ff.

tra, summoning the future action: "unless, by chance, a god should guide Orestes to us." Other parts of the trilogy similarly project the action beyond the close of the play, recalling the Racinian post-dramatic time.

On more than one occasion, the famous Aeschylean "foreboding" recalls Racine. In the first scene of the *Agamemnon*, the Watchman, who is not dramatically necessary, helps to project the action forward by the foreboding he creates; he cannot speak of what has been going on, he tells us, yet there is much to be told: "This house, if it had a voice. . . ."[33]

Elsewhere in this chapter, I shall discuss similarities in the use of symbol, and one possible structural borrowing. But the resemblances we have noted are rather slight, and it is impossible to say definitely whether they were inspired by Aeschylus. One gathers from this, as one does from Racine's notes on the *Choephori*, which consist, for the most part, of paraphrases of certain lines whose aptness of poetic quality impressed him, that in reading Aeschylus, our playwright did not feel the sense of participation in the work of a kindred spirit that he experienced in his study of Euripides and Sophocles.

## The Process of Re-Creation

Although Racine's sources have been exhaustively treated, it will be our purpose at this point to consider them from perhaps a slightly different angle than is usual in Racinian criticism. Racine's relationship to his richest source, classical literature, and especially Greek literature, has of course been studied thoroughly. In the majority of cases with which I am familiar, however, critics have been concerned with textual parallels, with what has been directly imitated. No attempt will be made here to take note of all these borrowings, nor even to find new ones, but to consider instead what Racine did with some of them.[34] To this end, I shall attempt a work of demonstration, rather than discovery or history. We have already seen how, out of dramatic conventions firmly rooted in the theatre of the seventeenth century, certain new structural concepts were developed. In the same way it may be

[33]An interesting comparison might be made of Aeschylean and Racinian evocation of space, especially in connection with the Prologos of the *Agamemnon*.

[34]Almost all may be found in the footnotes to the Mesnard edition of Racine's complete works.

shown how Racine wove certain strands from Greek, Roman, and contemporary literature into a new and unique fabric.

In order to do this, I shall discuss three famous passages, the first two inspired by or even closely transcribed from the sources, the third selection one which we might call "original" since it is impossible to find any single model on which it is based.

### The Récit de Théramène (V. vi. 1498–1592)

THÉRAMÈNE

A peine nous sortions des portes de Trézène,
Il était sur son char. Ses gardes affligés
Imitaient son silence, autour de lui rangés;        1500
Il suivait tout pensif le chemin de Mycènes;
Sa main sur ses chevaux laissait flotter les rênes.
Ses superbes coursiers, qu'on voyait autrefois
Pleins d'une ardeur si noble obéir à sa voix,
L'œil morne maintenant et la tête baissée,        1505
Semblaient se conformer à sa triste pensée.
Un effroyable cri, sorti du fond des flots,
Des airs en ce moment a troublé le repos;
Et du sein de la terre une voix formidable
Répond en gémissant à ce cri redoutable.        1510
Jusqu'au fond de nos cœurs notre sang s'est glacé;
Des coursiers attentifs le crin s'est hérissé.
Cependant sur le dos de la plaine liquide
S'élève à gros bouillons une montagne humide;
L'onde s'approche, se brise, et vomit à nos yeux,        1515
Parmi des flots d'écume, un monstre furieux.
Son front large est armé de cornes menaçantes;
Tout son corps est couvert d'écailles jaunissantes;
Indomptable taureau, dragon impétueux,
Sa croupe se recourbe en replis tortueux.        1520
Ses longs mugissements font trembler le rivage.
Le ciel avec horreur voit ce monstre sauvage;
La terre s'en émeut, l'air en est infecté;
Le flot qui l'apporta recule épouvanté.
Tout fuit; et sans s'armer d'un courage inutile,        1525
Dans le temple voisin chacun cherche un asile.
Hippolyte lui seul, digne fils d'un héros,
Arrête ses coursiers, saisit ses javelots,
Pousse au monstre, et d'un dard lancé d'une main sûre,
Il lui fait dans le flanc une large blessure.        1530
De rage et de douleur le monstre bondissant
Vient aux pieds des chevaux tomber en mugissant,

Se roule, et leur présente une gueule enflammée,
Qui les couvre de feu, de sang et de fumée.
La frayeur les emporte, et sourds à cette fois,                    1535
Ils ne connaissent plus ni le frein ni la voix.
En efforts impuissants leur maître se consume;
Ils rougissent le mors d'une sanglante écume.
On dit qu'on a vu même, en ce désordre affreux,
Un Dieu qui d'aiguillons pressait leur flanc poudreux.    1540
A travers des rochers la peur les précipite.
L'essieu crie et se rompt. L'intrépide Hippolyte
Voit voler en éclats tout son char fracassé;
Dans les rênes lui-même il tombe embarrassé.
Excusez ma douleur. Cette image cruelle                      1545
Sera pour moi de pleurs une source éternelle.
J'ai vu, Seigneur, j'ai vu votre malheureux fils
Traîné par les chevaux que sa main a nourris.
Il veut les rappeler, et sa voix les effraie;
Ils courent. Tout son corps n'est bientôt qu'une plaie.    1550
De nos cris douloureux la plaine retentit;
Leur fougue impétueuse enfin se ralentit :
Ils s'arrêtent, non loin de ces tombeaux antiques
Où des rois ses aïeux sont les froides reliques.
J'y cours en soupirant, et sa garde me suit.                   1555
De son généreux sang la trace nous conduit :
Les rochers en sont teints; les ronces dégouttantes
Portent de ses cheveux les dépouilles sanglantes.
J'arrive, je l'appelle, et me tendant la main,
Il ouvre un œil mourant, qu'il referme soudain.             1560
*Le ciel*, dit-il, *m'arrache une innocente vie.*
*Prends soin après ma mort de la triste Aricie.*
*Cher ami, si mon père un jour désabusé*
*Plaint le malheur d'un fils faussement accusé,*
*Pour apaiser mon sang et mon ombre plaintive,*         1565
*Dis-lui qu'avec douceur il traite sa captive,*
*Qu'il lui rende...* A ce mot ce héros expiré
N'a laissé dans mes bras qu'un corps défiguré,
Triste objet, où des Dieux triomphe la colère,
Et que méconnaîtrait l'œil même de son père.              1570
                    THÉSÉE
O mon fils ! cher espoir que je me suis ravi !
Inexorables Dieux, qui m'avez trop servi !
A quels mortels regrets ma vie est réservée !
                    THÉRAMÈNE
La timide Aricie est alors arrivée.
Elle venait, Seigneur, fuyant votre courroux,              1575
A la face des Dieux l'accepter pour époux.

Elle approche : elle voit l'herbe rouge et fumante;
Elle voit (quel objet pour les yeux d'une amante !)
Hippolyte étendu, sans forme et sans couleur.
Elle veut quelque temps douter de son malheur,　　　1580
Et ne connaissant plus ce héros qu'elle adore,
Elle voit Hippolyte, et le demande encore.
Mais trop sûre à la fin qu'il est devant ses yeux,
Par un triste regard elle accuse les Dieux;
Et froide, gémissante, et presque inanimée,　　　1585
Aux pieds de son amant elle tombe pâmée.
Ismène est auprès d'elle; Ismène, toute en pleurs,
La rappelle à la vie, ou plutôt aux douleurs.
Et moi, je suis venu, détestant la lumière,
Vous dire d'un héros la volonté dernière,　　　1590
Et m'acquitter, Seigneur, du malheureux emploi
Dont son cœur expirant s'est reposé sur moi.

This peroration on Hippolyte's death, in the final act of *Phèdre*, has perhaps incurred more critical displeasure than any other passage in Racine. The objections have tended to group themselves under three headings: (1) that it is dramatically superfluous; (2) that it is too ornate; and (3) that it is too long. One may reject out of hand Fénelon's rationalistic protest that no one as moved as Théramène could do more than gasp out the bare news of his master's death, since such strictures could equally well apply to the other *récits* of which we have already considered the dramatic function. Racine has made the *récit* an essential part of his drama, and one cannot wish it otherwise.

It is nevertheless true that such an account might have been briefer. The story of Britannicus' death, of Bajazet's, is brief enough in comparison. Thus, if the first two objections seem to stem from that excessively rationalistic approach that culminates in J.-J. Bernard's so-called "Theatre of Silence," the third has to be taken into account in any study of this most famous of *récits*.

As far as the actual decision to retain the *récit* is concerned, remembering Racine's insistence on following the "fable," we must recognize that tradition plays an important rôle. All earlier versions, Greek, Roman, and French, included it, in even lengthier form than Racine's. But the mathematical precision of the play itself (the announcement of the return of Thésée occurs at almost the exact middle)[35] suggests

---

[35]Act I is equal in length to Act II, and Act IV to Act V.

that Racine may have been influenced by the plain necessity of avoiding too short a final act. Once he had decided for various reasons to use the passage, it remained for him to fit it to the play, to make it a part of the dramatic whole.

Euripides, Seneca, Quinault, and Bidar provided Racine with almost all the essential elements.[36] The description of the monster's appearance, the flight of the horses, and the hero dragged to his death over rocks and through brambles follows Seneca's version closely. The appearance of Aricie at the scene, Hippolyte's attack on the monster, and his dying speech were inspired by the obscure Bidar. But despite his evident debt to his predecessors, Racine put his *récit* to a use which none of them did. If it had been merely the magnificent piece of poetry that it is, it would have been justified. But Racine, with the remarkable sense of unity we have already discussed, went farther; he used the *récit de Théramène* as a means of impressing upon the audience the tragedy of Hippolyte, for not only is it an account of the awful death of the fleeing youth, it becomes the spectacle of his final frustration, producing the most ironic of paradoxes, the would-be slayer of monsters who faces, in the form of a monster, his certain destruction.

In order to achieve this, Racine makes the passage stem logically from the foregoing action by appealing to our memory of the "fils de l'Amazone." We know from the Preface that he took pains to stir compassion for Hippolyte. But his theory that the young hero is possessed of a "tragic fault" because he disobeys Thésée's order that no one should court Aricie is unconvincing.[37] The public of the time must have approved Hippolyte's action; the triumph of love over filial duty would delight an audience nourished on the *Grand Cyrus* and *Clélie*. Punishment for disobedience is certainly not a Racinian theme, and probably the comment in the Preface is no more than an elaborate justification after the fact. Actually, his way of arousing sympathy was to "humanize" Hippolytus, making his famous chastity the result of timidity and inexperience rather than arrogant pride. Hippolyte has a character quite different from his earlier counterparts. True, he remains athletic; he loves horses and the chase; but in Racine he is ambitious (to emulate his father), youthful and shy, noble and self-

---

[36]See Knight, *Racine et la Grèce*, p. 361.

[37]Although it might have satisfied the pedantic critics of his time. Thésée is absent when his ruling is discussed, and it is represented as unfeeling and illogical.

denying. The first scene stresses his "farouche" qualities, contrasting his stiffness and embarrassment with the knowing and paternal manner of his companion and tutor, who twits him slyly on yielding to Venus:

> Pourriez-vous n'être plus ce superbe Hippolyte,
> Implacable ennemi des amoureuses lois...
> Aimeriez-vous, Seigneur ?
>
> (I. i. 58-9, 65)

We note the ironical force of the conditional tense, and the over-emphatic adjective "implacable." Théramène listens in silent amusement to the youth's lengthy and over-declamatory protest, and in reply, speaks for the audience, those experts on love:

> Ah ! Seigneur, si votre heure est une fois marquée,
> Le Ciel de nos raisons ne sait point s'informer.
>
> (I. i. 114-15)

The important shift in the possessive pronouns, suggesting that now Hippolyte has joined the generality of love's victims, helps to render him more human in the eyes of the audience. After the youth's bombast, his mentor's words are matter-of-fact, even prosy; he is the older, experienced counsellor, nudging the shy young man, and saying, in effect, "Where would you be today, my lad, if your father and mother hadn't. . . ."

> Vous-même où seriez-vous, vous qui la combattez,
> Si toujours Antiope à ses lois opposée,
> D'une pudique ardeur n'eût brûlé pour Thésée ?
>
> (I. i. 124-6)

His kindly brusqueness:

> Mais que sert d'affecter un superbe discours ?
> Avouez-le, tout change,
>
> (I. i. 127-8)

his humorous indulgence, with which the spectators identify themselves, permit them to feel the paternal fondness of experience for youthful inexperience.

In the *récit* itself, skilfully placed "echoes" recall these traits which have been brought out earlier. Beginning his oration, Théramène describes how the proud steeds, with head hanging and dulled eyes, seem to reflect their master's sorrow. This original addition by Racine reminds us of the bond between master and animal, heightening the

irony of his death by their agency. There is pathos in the fact that a
horseman of such prowess, one who can so skilfully "rendre docile au
frein un coursier indompté," should be trampled by his own horses,
but perhaps the deepest irony of all stems from his ambition to emulate
his father, the slayer of monsters. Developing a suggestion in Seneca
(*Hippolytus*, 1066–7), Racine has made of Hippolyte a youth eager for
a chance to prove his mettle. In the early scenes of the play, we have
heard how the story of Thésée's deeds, related by Théramène, stirred
his ardour; we have heard him speak impatiently of "aucuns monstres
par moi domptés jusqu'aujourd'hui." And just before setting out on
his fatal journey, he has told his father of his proud resolve to dip his
spear in "un sang plus glorieux."

The words "digne fils d'un héros," with which Théramène begins
his description of the battle, stress again the parallel between Hippolyte
and Thésée. Racine's innovations serve to stress the unequal odds.
Bidar was the first to show the youth attacking the monster, but his
Hippolyte's spear shatters against the scaly hide. Picking up the suggestion, Racine sublimely increases the irony by having Hippolyte
actually wound the monster gravely. Ironically, it is his victory that
helps to bring about his undoing; the bull-dragon falls roaring at the
horses' feet, and, as if we might forget that the monster's attack is god-
provoked, Racine has Neptune appear to goad the frightened horses,
and it is only then that they bolt.

Other additions or modifications jog our memory. The passage
describing Aricie recalls the earlier scene in which the lovers had
chosen their rendezvous at the very spot where Hippolyte meets his
death. His promise to meet Aricie (the irony that he should choose a
cemetery!)

> Aux portes de Trézène, et parmi ces tombeaux
> Des princes de ma race antiques sépultures,
> > (V. i. 1392–3)

echoes in our ears as Théramène describes the place to which the horses
had dragged their master:

> Ils s'arrêtent, non loin de ces tombeaux antiques
> Où des rois ses aïeux sont les froides reliques.
> > (V. vi. 1553–4)

The wheel has come full circle; the audience, through the *récit*, can

watch the scene in which "la triste Aricie" hastening to her lover, finds
him mangled and dying at the place destined for their marriage. His
last thought is for her, and his words, "si mon père *un jour* désabusé,"
recall his desire to spare Thésée ignominy.

The *récit* has thus been woven into the fabric of the play, and far
from being superfluous, deepens and confirms the spectator's experience
of tragedy. Moreover, once the dramatic necessity of the passage is
established, its "ornateness" and length seem to need little explanation.
What Fénelon called the "enflure" of the description of the sea-monster
(which shows Seneca's influence)[38] can now be seen as an effort to make
us visualize Hippolyte's death, a case of metaphor becoming an
auxiliary of tragic pity. And finally, its length is due to Racine's
emphasis on the elements calculated to inspire tragic pity, as a glance
at the disposition of the various parts of the *récit* reveals: out of 92 lines,
8 are devoted to Hippolyte's sadness (1499–1506), 16 to the hopeless
fight (1527–42), 18 to the death scene (1553–70), and 10 to Aricie's
grief (1577–86).

*Phèdre's Confession* (II. v)

PHÈDRE
Le voici. Vers mon cœur tout mon sang se retire.
J'oublie, en le voyant, ce que je viens lui dire.
ŒNONE
Souvenez-vous d'un fils qui n'espère qu'en vous.
PHÈDRE
On dit qu'un prompt départ vous éloigne de nous,
Seigneur. A vos douleurs je viens joindre mes larmes.          585
Je vous viens pour un fils expliquer mes alarmes.
Mon fils n'a plus de père, et le jour n'est pas loin
Qui de ma mort encor doit le rendre témoin.
Déjà mille ennemis attaquent son enfance;
Vous seul pouvez contre eux embrasser sa défense.              590
Mais un secret remords agite mes esprits.
Je crains d'avoir fermé votre oreille à ses cris.
Je tremble que sur lui votre juste colère
Ne poursuive bientôt une odieuse mère.
HIPPOLYTE
Madame, je n'ai point des sentiments si bas.                   595
PHÈDRE
Quand vous me haïriez, je ne m'en plaindrais pas,

---

[38]One significant difference is that Seneca's imagery is that of a monstrous birth, while Racine
has the sea, which in the Roman version "followed its monster," recoil in horror.

Seigneur. Vous m'avez vue attachée à vous nuire;
Dans le fond de mon cœur vous ne pouviez pas lire.
A votre inimitié j'ai pris soin de m'offrir.
Aux bords que j'habitais je n'ai pu vous souffrir. 600
En public, en secret, contre vous déclarée,
J'ai voulu par des mers en être séparée;
J'ai même défendu par une expresse loi
Qu'on osât prononcer votre nom devant moi.
Si pourtant à l'offense on mesure la peine, 605
Si la haine peut seule attirer votre haine,
Jamais femme ne fut plus digne de pitié,
Et moins digne, Seigneur, de votre inimitié.

HIPPOLYTE

Des droits de ses enfants une mère jalouse
Pardonne rarement au fils d'une autre épouse. 610
Madame, je le sais. Les soupçons importuns
Sont d'un second hymen les fruits les plus communs.
Toute autre aurait pour moi pris les mêmes ombrages,
Et j'en aurais peut-être essuyé plus d'outrages.

PHÈDRE

Ah ! Seigneur, que le Ciel, j'ose ici l'attester, 615
De cette loi commune a voulu m'excepter !
Qu'un soin bien différent me trouble et me dévore !

HIPPOLYTE

Madame, il n'est pas temps de vous troubler encore.
Peut-être votre époux voit encore le jour;
Le Ciel peut à nospleurs accorder son retour. 620
Neptune le protège, et ce Dieu tutélaire
Ne sera pas en vain imploré par mon père.

PHÈDRE

On ne voit point deux fois le rivage des morts,
Seigneur. Puisque Thésée a vu les sombres bords,
En vain vous espérez qu'un Dieu vous le renvoie, 625
Et l'avare Achéron ne lâche point sa proie.
Que dis-je ? Il n'est point mort, puisqu'il respire en vous.
Toujours devant mes yeux je crois voir mon époux.
Je le vois, je lui parle, et mon cœur... Je m'égare,
Seigneur; ma folle ardeur malgré moi se déclare. 630

HIPPOLYTE

Je vois de votre amour l'effet prodigieux.
Tout mort qu'il est, Thésée est présent à vos yeux;
Toujours de son amour votre âme est embrasée.

PHÈDRE

Oui, Prince, je languis, je brûle pour Thésée.
Je l'aime, non point tel que l'ont vu les enfers, 635

Volage adorateur de mille objets divers,
Qui va du Dieu des morts déshonorer la couche;
Mais fidèle, mais fier, et même un peu farouche,
Charmant, jeune, traînant tous les cœurs après soi,
Tel qu'on dépeint nos Dieux, ou tel que je vous voi.          640
Il avait votre port, vos yeux, votre langage,
Cette noble pudeur colorait son visage,
Lorsque de notre Crète il traversa les flots,
Digne sujet des vœux des filles de Minos.
Que faisiez-vous alors ?  Pourquoi, sans Hippolyte,          645
Des héros de la Grèce assembla-t-il l'élite ?
Pourquoi, trop jeune encor, ne pûtes-vous alors
Entrer dans le vaisseau qui le mit sur nos bords ?
Par vous aurait péri le monstre de la Crète,
Malgré tous les détours de sa vaste retraite.          650
Pour en développer l'embarras incertain,
Ma sœur du fil fatal eût armé votre main.
Mais non, dans ce dessein je l'aurais devancée :
L'amour m'en eût d'abord inspiré la pensée.
C'est moi, Prince, c'est moi dont l'utile secours          655
Vous eût du Labyrinthe enseigné les détours.
Que de soins m'eût coûtés cette tête charmante !
Un fil n'eût point assez rassuré votre amante.
Compagne du péril qu'il vous fallait chercher,
Moi-même devant vous j'aurais voulu marcher;          660
Et Phèdre, au Labyrinthe avec vous descendue,
Se serait avec vous retrouvée, ou perdue.

HIPPOLYTE

Dieux ! qu'est-ce que j'entends ?  Madame, oubliez-vous
Que Thésée est mon père, et qu'il est votre époux ?

PHÈDRE

Et sur quoi jugez-vous que j'en perds la mémoire,          665
Prince ?  Aurais-je perdu tout le soin de ma gloire ?

HIPPOLYTE

Madame, pardonnez. J'avoue, en rougissant,
Que j'accusais à tort un discours innocent.
Ma honte ne peut plus soutenir votre vue;
Et je vais...

PHÈDRE

              Ah ! cruel, tu m'as trop entendue.          670
Je t'en ai dit assez pour te tirer d'erreur.
Hé bien ! connais donc Phèdre et toute sa fureur.
J'aime. Ne pense pas qu'au moment que je t'aime,
Innocente à mes yeux, je m'approuve moi-même,

Ni que du fol amour qui trouble ma raison                    675
Ma lâche complaisance ait nourri le poison.
Objet infortuné des vengeances célestes,
Je m'abhorre encor plus que tu ne me détestes.
Les Dieux m'en sont témoins, ces Dieux qui dans mon flanc
Ont allumé le feu fatal à tout mon sang,                     680
Ces Dieux qui se sont fait une gloire cruelle
De séduire le cœur d'une faible mortelle.
Toi-même en ton esprit rappelle le passé.
C'est peu de t'avoir fui, cruel, je t'ai chassé.
J'ai voulu te paraître odieuse, inhumaine.                   685
Pour mieux te résister, j'ai recherché ta haine.
De quoi m'ont profité mes inutiles soins ?
Tu me haïssais plus, je ne t'aimais pas moins.
Tes malheurs te prêtaient encor de nouveaux charmes.
J'ai langui, j'ai séché, dans les feux, dans les larmes.     690
Il suffit de tes yeux pour t'en persuader,
Si tes yeux un moment pouvaient me regarder.
Que dis-je ? Cet aveu que je te viens de faire,
Cet aveu si honteux, le crois-tu volontaire ?
Tremblante pour un fils que je n'osais trahir,               695
Je te venais prier de ne le point haïr.
Faibles projets d'un cœur trop plein de ce qu'il aime !
Hélas ! je ne t'ai pu parler que de toi-même.
Venge-toi, punis-moi d'un odieux amour.
Digne fils du héros qui t'a donné le jour,                   700
Délivre l'univers d'un monstre qui t'irrite.
La veuve de Thésée ose aimer Hippolyte !
Crois-moi, ce monstre affreux ne doit point t'échapper.
Voilà mon cœur. C'est là que ta main doit frapper.
Impatient déjà d'expier son offense,                         705
Au-devant de ton bras je le sens qui s'avance.
Frappe. Ou si tu le crois indigne de tes coups,
Si ta haine m'envie un supplice si doux,
Ou si d'un sang trop vil ta main serait trempée,
Au défaut de ton bras prête-moi ton épée.                    710
Donne.

In perhaps the most powerful scene in Racinian tragedy, a mighty
agon through which range almost every degree of fear and sensual
passion, Racine's dramatic and poetic inspiration are almost wholly
Senecan. Seneca was the first to confront the tragic pair, and of the
most lyrical moments, almost all are his. This is the only case I know of

where a scene of considerable length, involving two main characters, closely follows an earlier model.[39] For this reason, a detailed comparison should be revealing. It ought to demonstrate how Racine preserved Seneca's poetry and insight, embellishing them with his own, yet carefully refraining from imitating his coarseness and bombast. Finally, it should illustrate in another way that integrative process we have already found to be a basic element in the Racinian genius. We shall see how the reaction of the characters has logically developed from what we knew of them before, how their every word, attitude, and action, whether imitated directly from Seneca or not, both provide a necessary climax to the earlier action and commit the protagonists irrevocably for the future.

Racine's first major change is one of proportion. What is in Seneca's version a scene of both confession and reaction, with approximately equal attention paid to both Hippolytus and Phaedra, becomes in Racine's a carefully graduated crescendo of confession alone. Taking as his basis the Senecan Phaedra's momentary restraint (for an instant or two she cannot speak, calling her woes "too weighty" to bring forth) but surely also remembering the conventional reluctance of woman to confess her love, Racine divides Phèdre's confession into four clearly distinguished movements.

In the first of these, lines 584–94, Phèdre gives her reason for seeking the interview: her desire that Hippolyte serve as protector, even as father for her sons. Racine thus adapts the cruder request of the Roman heroine who, in asking that Hippolytus take the throne, calls upon him to "pity her womanhood" and "take her in his arms." The Roman heroine makes no mention of her children; it is Hippolytus who, in innocent misunderstanding of this request, answers her that he will gladly care for his two brothers. By transferring this concern for the children to his heroine, Racine provides her with a motive plausible even to herself, yet there nevertheless remains in the French heroine's words, though deeply submerged, an awareness of equivocation in her request that Hippolyte protect her son.[40]

In the second movement (ll. 596–608) Phèdre actually begins her avowal in the guise of an attempt to convince her stepson that her

---

[39]They are even almost identical in length; Seneca's being 135 lines, Racine's 131.
[40]Cf. III. i. 804–5,

> Il instruira mon fils dans l'art de commander;
> Peut-être il voudra bien lui tenir lieu de père.

apparent animosity was not real. Initiates in the audience would understand her statement that she did not hate him as an admission of love,[41]
but not, of course, the timid Hippolyte (ll. 606–8). At least the starting-
point of Hippolyte's placating answer that it is natural for a stepmother
to dislike the children of another wife was probably suggested by
Phaedra's remark that hers is "a trouble thou wouldst scarce believe
could befall a stepmother." But his words excite Racine's heroine to
take a further step toward revelation; she declares that she is an exception to this general law, and the exclamatory form of the sentence quite
clearly says that her feeling is the opposite (ll. 615–17). Hippolyte's
brief reply, with its reference to stepmothers, has given her the cue to
swing the pendulum, by her two statements, from hatred to love.

This provokes a further reassurance that takes the same form as in
Seneca: Hippolyte's belief that Thésée will return from Hell. But
instead of the "kindly deities" that the Roman youth believes will
protect his father, Racine has Hippolyte specifically mention Neptune
(ll. 621–2). This reference helps to link the confession to the preceding
and ensuing action; we know the involvement of Neptune in the
destinies of both father and son. It further provides an ironic echo for
the later scene in which the father invokes the god of the sea and of
horses against his son.

In answer, Phèdre, like her Roman ancestor, protests that he who
sees the dread realm never returns. Here Racine combines Seneca's
lines 219–21 and 625–6; to her nurse, Phaedra had answered:

> non unquam amplius
> cónvexa tetigit supera qui mersus semel
> adiit silentem nocte perpetua domum.

> [Nevermore shall he
> See o'er his head the blue of vaulted skies,
> After the endless night of the silent home.]

To Hippolytus she said,

> regni tenacis dominus et tacitae Stygis
> nullam relictos fecit ad superos viam.

> [From that tenacious realm and silent Styx,
> Its lord has built no road to the upper world.]

[41]Cf. Monime (*Mithridate*, III. ii. 221–2):
> Pour me faire, Seigneur, consentir à vous voir,
> Vour n'aurez pas besoin d'un injuste pouvoir.

Racine transfers "tenacis," with a slight change of meaning, to the name of another river of Hell, producing the line "l'avare Achéron ne lâche point sa proie." The image is made consistent by his reference to "les sombres bords," rather than the "perpetual night" of the Latin.

In Racine, her protest leads naturally into the third movement of the confession; she suddenly reverses herself, her rational conclusion yielding to a hallucinatory confusion of Hippolyte with his father. "Il n'est point mort, puisqu'il respire en vous," she cries. A momentary recovery of her control—"ma folle ardeur malgré moi se déclare"— only prompts Hippolyte, once again following his Roman counterpart, to interpret this as passion for his father. His obtuseness launches the heroine on her wild speech in which she transposes the identity of son and father.

This speech in Racine closely resembles, even in length,[42] its counterpart in Seneca. In both speeches, the heroine compares in some detail her stepson's beauty with his father's when he first came to Crete, and remarks that had he accompanied his father, Ariadne would have spun the thread for him. But the French version is far more subtly graduated; it is a crescendo within a crescendo. And unlike the Latin speech, which after eighteen lines arrives promptly at an explicit confession, Racine's makes use of the Hippolytus–Theseus transposition to preserve a last vestige of concealment. Although Phèdre is speaking more openly of her love than before, her references to Thésée add just enough ambiguity to justify Hippolyte's ready admission that he had misunderstood her (l. 667). Where Phaedra says "Thesei *vultus* amo"—"Theseus' *features* I love," Phèdre moans, "Oui, prince, je languis, je brûle pour Thésée." The effect of hallucination occurs only in the French. Just as in sacrificing to Venus Phèdre had seemed to be sacrificing to Hippolyte instead, here the youth standing before her, by Racine's marvellous grasp of the psychology of love, *is* Thésée.[43]

Her first lines state his superiority, not in terms of his beauty, as in Seneca, but of his shyness, timidity, freshness, and innocence. True,

[42] It has 29 lines, 3 more than Seneca's.

[43] As L. Spitzer pertinently remarks, Racine realizes that love is "typologically monogamic," so that matrimonial infidelity can be a form of faithfulness to the original.—*Linguistics and Literary History*, Princeton University Press, 1948, p. 98. Here there is also an echo of Phèdre's earlier confession to Œnone: "Mes yeux le retrouvaient dans les traits de son père" (I. iii. 290). In fact, Phèdre's actions in the confession scene are in large part a re-enactment of her past actions as recounted to the nurse in I. iii.

the germ is in the Latin, half way through the speech (l. 660) "in ore Graio Scythicus apparet rigor"— "on your Grecian face shows a Scythian austerity," but Racine makes it the main theme of the comparison. The Latin Phaedra's sensual references to his smooth cheeks and muscular arms are gone; only "pudor" remains.[44]

Most striking of all is Racine's addition to Phaedra's declaration that her sister would have aided Hippolytus to return from the labyrinth: "tibi fila potius nostra nevisset soror"—"for thee my sister would have spun her thread." At this point, Seneca breaks off. But from this statement to Phèdre's magnificent "Mais non," is one step, and Racine takes it, in what seems the product of a kind of natural momentum inherent in Racine's way of constructing the passage. Until line 647, Phèdre maintains the half-ambiguous parallel. In the reference to her sister, she still preserves a layer of restraint—it is she who would have loved him—until the final "Mais non" is torn from her, and the following nine lines spill forth in a torrent.

Again, Seneca suggests the spirit, if not the letter, of these powerful lines. Phèdre first declares that not Ariadne, but she would have spun the thread, even more, that she would have gone with him into the labyrinth, sharing all his perils, and even walking ahead of him to make sure of his safety. The same idea of sacrifice for the loved one animates the Roman heroine's offer to be his slave, to walk through "deep drifted snows" for him, over the cold peaks of Pindus, through fire or battle, although Seneca places these lines at the beginning of the interview.[45] Phaedra's identification of her sister's cause with hers— "invoco ad causam parem"—may also have helped suggest the transition. But when these parallels are duly noted, there remains Racine's skill in developing this part of the speech as the last stage before the climax, the final agonized moment before the painful baring of Phèdre's feelings.

As we said earlier, these vestiges of restraint make it plausible enough that Hippolyte should first recoil in horror, and then, upon Phèdre's swift rejoinder, stammer his apologies (ll. 667-9). If Hippolyte appears somewhat too obtuse, one should remember that he is not only com-

[44]For both Aricie and Phèdre his appeal is in his virginal qualities, but for what different reasons!

[45]An earlier hint of the same idea may be found in Phaedra's talk with the nurse, lines 233-5.

pletely unskilled in the subtleties of love, but that he thinks of Phèdre as a person who is mentally and physically disturbed. As her prompt denial shows, she has recovered momentarily, but it is Hippolyte's turning to go (ll. 669–70) that precipitates her final, naked and irrevocable avowal. Her last iota of reserve vanishes; she is desperate to keep him there at all costs. The forty-line *tirade* that follows replaces Hippolytus' shrill denunciation in Seneca. Racine's hero is rooted to the spot; he can neither move, nor look at her, as her pathetic words, "Si tes yeux un moment pouvaient me regarder," tell us.

This last movement of the confession, after the frenzied cry in lines 672–3 with its violent shift to *tutoiement*, takes the form of a recapitulation, whose dramatic uses we have already discussed. First evoking the distant and immediate past, she tells how the jealous gods (and note again the plural, with its implication of a malevolent concert of deities) have pursued her (ll. 681–2). She recalls briefly the steps she has taken to free herself: her exiling of Hippolyte, and at Troezen her persecution of him, which had the opposite effect (l. 689), for as in the case of Néron's love for Junie, and even Hippolyte's for Aricie, the distress and misfortune of the loved one only increased the attraction (cf. I. i. 117–18).

This recapitulation, aside from its unifying effect, lends an instantaneous quality to the whole scene. The position is now clear; Hippolyte can recall every moment as part of an avowal he was slow to comprehend, and Phèdre can make her final plea (l. 699). Her next two lines, besides once again linking the confession to the monster motif that runs through the play, provide an echo for the recital of Hippolyte's death (cf. V. vi. 1527).

It is difficult to imagine Hippolyte's actions in the next few moments, as Phèdre advances her breast for him to strike her down. The Senecan Hippolytus had drawn his sword: "Out, sword, to deal her just punishment!" But this violent gesture would have been out of keeping with Hippolyte's character as we now know it. Moreover, the transition from his attitude of horror-stricken immobility would seem strange. In Seneca, Hippolytus throws down his sword in disgust, declaring that it has been polluted by Phaedra's touch; in Racine, it is Phèdre who, in the following scene, suggests this repugnance as the reason he did not take back his sword when she drew it from his scabbard.

Her desire for death at this moment is in Seneca, but her proud gesture, with breast thrown forward to tempt the sword, may have been inspired by Polyxena's defiance of Neoptolemus in Euripides' *Hecuba*.[46]

In the foregoing discussion of Racine's sublime transformation of Seneca, we have noted his delicate reconstruction, his transfer of certain words, phrases, and gestures to the character they suit best, his linking the scene with the rest of the action through highly charged allusions, but we have touched only in passing upon the dramatic principle that animates the whole. This, once again, is "presence," a concept purely Racinian. As we have seen, Racine's Hippolyte is reticent, his reaction to Phèdre's final admission is one of frozen immobility. Yet the keynote, carefully established in the opening lines (581–2) is sustained throughout. Phèdre's confession not only takes the form of a crescendo, it is a breaking down of her control under the continuous assault of the hero's mere presence. That is why it is so important that Hippolyte should remain absolutely immobile[47] throughout the scene, save for the one moment when he turns to go. Racine's version is thus a far more compelling demonstration of the force of physical passion than Seneca's. His mute and motionless hero yet appears invested with a strange power that the aggressive hero of the Roman play lacks and his heroine is much more agonizingly the prey of passion.

*Athalie's Dream* (II. v. 490–514)

ATHALIE

C'était pendant l'horreur d'une profonde nuit.                490
Ma mère Jézabel devant moi s'est montrée,
Comme au jour de sa mort pompeusement parée.
Ses malheurs n'avaient point abattu sa fierté;
Même elle avait encor cet éclat emprunté
Dont elle eut soin de peindre et d'orner son visage,     495
Pour réparer des ans l'irréparable outrage.
*Tremble*, m'a-t-elle dit, *fille digne de moi;*
*Le cruel Dieu des Juifs l'emporte aussi sur toi.*
*Je te plains de tomber dans ses mains redoutables,*

---

[46]G. May, "A propos de quatre vers de *Phèdre*," *MLN*, XLI (1946), pp. 334–6.

[47]See *Phèdre*, ed. J.-L. Barrault, Paris, Ed. du Seuil, 1946, p. 129: "Hippolyte est absolument sans réaction."

*Ma fille.* En achevant ces mots épouvantables,      500
Son ombre vers mon lit a paru se baisser;
Et moi, je lui tendais les mains pour l'embrasser.
Mais je n'ai plus trouvé qu'un horrible mélange
D'os et de chairs meurtris et traînés dans la fange,
Des lambeaux pleins de sang et des membres affreux      505
Que des chiens dévorants se disputaient entre eux.

         ABNER

Grand Dieu !

         ATHALIE

         Dans ce désordre à mes yeux se présente
Un jeune enfant couvert d'une robe éclatante,
Tels qu'on voit des Hébreux les prêtres revêtus.
Sa vue a ranimé mes esprits abattus;      510
Mais, lorsque revenant de mon trouble funeste,
J'admirais sa douceur, son air noble et modeste,
J'ai senti tout à coup un homicide acier
Que le traître en mon sein a plongé tout entier.

Although the prophetic dream is a literary device as old as Homer, it is extremely rare in French tragedy of the seventeenth century. There are only two examples in Corneille, and in Racine, beside the dream in *Athalie*, only Agamemnon's statement in *Iphigénie* that the gods had threatened him in dreams, and Assuérus' dramatically super-fluous warning dream, mentioned by a secondary character, in *Esther*.[48] Athalie's dream is the only example I know in French tragedy of an actual dream vision of genuine structural importance, both because it provides an incentive to action, and because its plastic quality, present-ing as it does a vision clearly seen, felt, and heard, is integral to the action and atmosphere of the play.

What inspired Racine to make such striking use of this device, for which there was no precedent either in his biblical sources or in the two dramatic versions of the Athaliah story that preceded his own?[49] He seems to owe little or nothing to his contemporaries, yet knowing his habits of composition, and in the case of *Athalie*, his desire to emu-late Greek tragedy formally, we might expect him to have looked for guidance to classical, and ultimately Greek, sources. We would not

[48]Corneille, *Horace*, I. ii. 215–22, and *Polyeucte*, I. iii. 221–41; Racine, *Iphigénie*, I. i. 83–8, and *Esther*, II. i. 384–91. There is a striking dream in Tristan's *La Mariane*, I. iii, which Racine un-doubtedly knew, but it bears no resemblance to Athalie's.

[49]For summaries of the two Athaliah plays, see R. Lebègue, "Une représentation d'*Athalie* en 1658," *Revue bleue*, LXXIV (1936), pp. 357–9, and V. L. Saulnier, "Racine et la tragédie scolaire: une *Athalie* française de 1683," *RHL*, XLIX (1949), pp. 62–6.

expect to find, of course, clear-cut "imitations," but rather earlier treatments of the dream device which Racine could transmute with that Midas touch we have seen him apply to borrowings from the greatest or humblest of sources: an Euripides or a Mathieu Bidar.

One of the few critics to discuss the dream as a technical device has made an interesting comparison between the dream of Athalie and Clytemnestra's dream in Sophocles' *Electra*.[50] Certainly in each case the dream motivates an action, which in turn brings about an important discovery. After her nocturnal vision of Agamemnon, Clytemnestra sends her daughter, Chrysothemis, to the King's tomb, where she discovers the lock of Orestes' hair; Athalie is prompted by her dream to visit the temple in the hope of appeasing Jehovah. But in form and content the two could scarcely be more different. First of all, the dream in Sophocles has none of the structural prominence it assumes in Racine. It is the secondary character Chrysothemis, not her mother, who relates the dream, and it is she who goes to the tomb. Agamemnon is not described; in Clytemnestra's dream he had planted his sceptre on the hearth and out of it had grown a branch that overshadowed all Mycenae. No words had been exchanged between dreamer and dream figure; the prophecy remains allegorical. The dream is mentioned only once, and almost casually introduced, rather late in the play, in a speech of six lines.

Actually, Clytemnestra's dream in Aeschylus' *Choephori*, which instigates an identical action and discovery, could have influenced Racine more strongly. Just as he did for the *Electra*, he noted in his marginal comments on this play that the dream provided a motive for Clytemnestra to send the Chorus with offerings to the tomb of her husband. He seems also to have been struck by the antipathy of the Chorus to the Queen; their words, which he translates and underlines: "cette femme impie," recall those of his own Chorus, which has a similar feeling for Athalie, and which thrice calls her "l'impie étrangère."[51] More important still, although in content Aeschylus' dream bears no resemblance to Racine's, in his structural employment of the device Racine is closer to Aeschylus than to Sophocles. In the *Choephori*, the dream is closely woven into the action; scarcely has the play

[50]See G. May, *Tragédie cornélienne, tragédie racinienne*, pp. 186–7. Louis Racine (*Remarques sur les tragédies de Jean Racine*, Amsterdam, Rey, 1752, II, pp. 293–4) had already made the comparison, as May notes.

[51]See *Œuvres*, ed. Picard *et al.*, II, pp. 840, 845.

begun when the Chorus explains the reason it has been sent to make funeral offerings. It speaks, however, only in the vaguest terms; we learn merely that the Queen has had a terrifying dream, which the priests have interpreted as a sign of the murdered man's displeasure (ll. 22–41). This may be compared to Zacharie's description of Athalie's visit to the temple, and her strange terror on seeing Eliacin, which remain without explanation until the dream is related. In the Greek play, only much later does the Chorus tell Orestes of Clytemnestra's dream that she was suckling a serpent that drew blood. Orestes at once interprets this as a sign that he will kill his mother, and it spurs his resolve to do so (ll. 527–51). Similarly, Athalie's account suggests that action be taken against Eliacin. Finally, as Orestes raises his sword to kill Clytemnestra, she identifies the symbol of her dream, crying out that she has borne and nourished a serpent (ll. 929–34), just as Athalie cries on recognizing Joas as the youth who had stabbed her in her dream: "Qu'on lui fasse en mon sein enfoncer le couteau" (V. vi. 1782).

But even if we grant that he was inspired by Aeschylus' use of the device, how did Racine's narration take the form it did? Far from using the symbolic dream of the Greek dramatists, Racine presents two visions clearly seen and described, first of the dead Jezebel, then of the living Joas, and the prophecy of the former is rendered explicit by the dagger thrust of the latter.

What pre-existing structures could Racine have found on which to set this unique neo-classical façade? If we glance from the tragedy to the epic, we see at once that Athalie's dream has all the general characteristics of the Homeric dream vision. First of all, unlike Aeschylus or Sophocles, the Homeric poets in most of their descriptions of dreams treat what is seen and heard as "objective fact." The dreamer is almost completely passive, and a single dream figure, usually a relative or friend, appears, whom he watches, and to whom he listens. Sometimes, though rarely, the dreamer answers, and on occasion will attempt to embrace the vision.[52] In the *Iliad* (xxiii. 99), Patroclus, appearing before the sleeping Achilles, tells his friend he is about to die, and when Achilles tries to embrace him vanishes to earth like a vapour, with a thin cry. Both the futile attempt to embrace the apparition and the manner of its disappearance seem early to take on a conventional

---

[52]I am indebted here to E. R. Dodds, *The Greeks and the Irrational*, University of California Press, 1951, pp. 104–5.

quality. The same gesture and the same smoke-like disappearance occur when Ulysses sees his mother's shade (*Odyssey*, xi. 206–9) and in the *Aeneid* (ii. 792–3; vi. 701–2), both when Aeneas meets Creusa's ghost as he leaves Troy, and when he encounters Anchises in the underworld, suggesting that neither Homer nor Vergil made much distinction between dreams and the appearance of shades to mortals in their waking hours. In these latter cases, the swift disappearance of the shade, avoiding the outstretched arms of the dreamer, is compared to a "winged dream."

Evidently Racine conceived of Athalie's dream in this general Homeric-Vergilian tradition. Analysis of the passage itself and an examination of the elements he inherited show how he set about adapting the dream both to his tragic concept and to the demands of his theme.

The first line reveals a fundamental difference between Racine and classical sources; here as elsewhere in his tragedies,[53] night is horrible, the opposite of Vergil's happy and calm hour of repose ("Nox erat et terras animalis fessa . . ."—*Aeneid*, viii. 26), or of Seneca's peaceful night (cf. Andromache's dream of Hector, *Troades*, 438 ff., "Nox alma . . ."). Racine's Athalie, like his Agamemnon, is harried by remorse, and the night for her is a time of terror.

"Devant moi s'est montrée," (l. 491) corresponds to a stock phrase of Latin dream narrations, "ante oculos stetit," found in Vergil, Seneca, and Ovid, rather than in the Greek versions, in which the dream figure stands over the head of the sleeper.[54] By employing it here, Racine further suggests a dramatic confrontation, rather than a mere awareness of presence.

Line 492 embodies the masterful fusion of biblical and classic sources which makes of the dream recital a reduction *in nuce* of the whole play. Jezebel, like Patroclus, wears the same garb as on the day of her death. The horrible nature of that death is known to us (I. i. 115–18), so that Racine can depend for plastic effect on an appeal to memory at the same time as he projects us backward to the pre-dramatic sources of the action. We have already discussed the cyclic nature of the play.

---

[53]Cf. *Mithridate*, II. iii. 440–6; *Esther*, II. i. 384–91; *Andromaque*, I. ii. 211–12. Tristan's Herod dreamed he was in a dark wood, "où l'horreur habitoit avec l'obscurité." Such a horror of darkness is typical of baroque classicism.

[54]See J. B. Stearns, *Studies of the Dream as a Technical Device in Latin Epic and Drama*, Princeton University Press, 1927, p. 21, n. 65.

The fate of the central figure is the result of earlier crimes committed by herself and her dynasty; her destruction will in turn bring about the destruction of the new king. Athalie's dream, with its vision out of the bloody past, supports this cyclic quality.

The lines following describe the doomed woman as she prepared to meet Jehu. The past definite of line 495 emphasizes the fact that it was for that specific occasion that she painted and bedecked herself; she is thus not only the warning dream figure, but a symbol of death.

Line 496 suggests once again the theme of the decline of majesty. Jezebel, like Mithridate, knew the ravages of time, and so, by extension, will Athalie; Racine's kings and queens are no longer the sublime and immutable figures of earlier tragedy; they age, they are wracked by passion; they are, in a word, human.

The three lines of prophecy (497–9) bear a slight external resemblance to the warning lines spoken by the ghost of Armida's mother in *Gerusalemme liberata*; unlike them, however, they have a grim fatality, suggesting no means of escape.[55] This fact, and the words "cruel" and "redoutable" applied to Jehovah, arouse sympathy for both Jezebel and Athalie.

As I noted earlier, the Homeric dreamer is usually passive, except for occasional attempts to speak or to embrace the dream figure. There is no instance in Homer where the figure itself gestures. Jezebel, however, bends down over her daughter's bed, after pronouncing the warning. In Ovid's *Metamorphoses*, Morpheus in the form of Ceyx appears to the latter's wife, Alcyone, to tell her that he has been drowned. He bends over her bed ("incumbens lecto"), and after he has spoken, she tries to embrace him, but with the usual result grasps only the air ("corpusque petens amplectitur auras"—*Metamorphoses*, XI. 657, 675). In Ovid, however, the gesture precedes the speech; in Racine, it follows, adding pathos, and becoming, instead of a simple movement toward the dreamer, a gesture of compassion and love which in turn incites Athalie's attempted embrace. Thus, by making the futile embrace of tradition the response to the dream figure's gesture, Racine both

[55]IV. xli:

> Fuggi, figlia, dicea, morte sí ria
> Che ti sovrasta omai, pártiti retto:
> Già reggio il tósco e'l ferro in tuo sol danno
> Aparecchiar dal perfido tiranno.

These lines, first mentioned in this connection in the Bernardin edition of Racine's works, are also noted by G. May (*D'Ovide à Racine*, pp. 111–12) but he does not explore the parallel.

increases the humanity of his characters and imparts a logical sequence to the actions.

Of the word "ombre" Louis Racine wrote that "ombre, en parlant d'une personne morte ne convient que dans la bouche d'un Grec ou d'un Romain," but concluded indulgently, "ici, ombre veut dire fantôme."[56] The fact is, of course, that conceiving of his dream in the classical tradition, Racine chose the word quite naturally.

In stating that the shade *appeared* to bend down, Racine maintains the reserve with which he usually describes miraculous or super-natural events, but by this means he also reasserts the speaker's indivi-duality. And by making her express, both before and after her narra-tion, vestiges of a scepticism finally overcome only by the double recurrence of the dream,

> ... me devrais-je inquiéter d'un songe ?...
> ... honteuse de ma peur
> Je l'ai pris pour l'effet d'une sombre vapeur,[57]
> (II. v. 487, 517-18)

by making her grudgingly reject the suggestion that her dream has a physical origin, the dramatist is able to emphasize its supernatural nature.

Athalie's fruitless gesture (l. 502) is of course more "natural" because Racine discarded the ritual thrice-made effort to embrace. Most sig-nificant of all, Racine's dreamer horribly grasps bones and rotted flesh, instead of the wisp of smoke or empty air into which the vision traditionally dissolves, for the verb "trouver" following immediately upon "je lui tendais" suggests that the dreamer actually touches the putrid remains; horror becomes tactile. Again the biblical source is fused with the classical, not only suggesting the dreamer's feeling of desolation, but providing, through this metamorphosis, a symbol of Athalie's destruction. This skilful mingling of biblical subject-matter with the attributes of the prophetic dream of antiquity offers a further example of that "fusion" characteristic of the classico-baroque style.[58]

---

[56]L. Racine, *Remarques sur les tragédies de Jean Racine*, II, pp. 293-4.

[57]Cf. "Les médecins tiennent que les personnes fort mélancholiques sont sujetes à faire des songes espouventables; pour ce que les vapeurs qui s'exhalent de ceste humeur terrestre & noire, ne peuvent guere produire que de tristes & funestes imaginations." Tristan, *Les Plaintes d'Acaste*, quoted in *La Mariane*, ed. J. Madeleine, Paris, STFM, Hachette, 1917, p. 19.

[58]See H. Hatzfeld, "A Clarification of the Baroque Problem in the Romance Literatures," CL, I (1949), pp. 123-32.

There is more subtle evidence of the poet's skill. The body disintegrates, not into the clearly defined members of the biblical version (skull, feet, and palms of hands—II Kings, ix. 35), but into a "horrible mélange," an ill-defined mass of bones, blood-stained shreds of cloth, and flesh. Here the classical plurals help to convey a sense of confusion and blurred outline. The image not only becomes confused, it withdraws momentarily in space, the frame widening to portray the voracious dogs. Thus the fading of the vision becomes a device of spectacle; it not only implies disintegration and death, it provides a transition, a "dissolve," like the wave of a magician's wand, which introduces the second part of the vision and which prefigures imagistically Racine's use of the "ferme" in the last act, when the theatre opens to reveal Joas enthroned.[59] The "désordre" of line 507, which here means confusion, rather than trouble of mind,[60] recalls the "images brouillées" of Pauline's dream in *Polyeucte*, or the jumbled visions of Camille in *Horace*, which "s'effaçaient l'un l'autre," but only superficially. Corneille's dreams are as chaotic and as prismatically broken as his metaphors; they serve only to convey a vague unease, to increase suspense by beclouding the outcome. Racine's blurring of the picture is a deliberate part of the structure.

The play's theme: the renewal and the revitalizing of the race through divine intervention, is supported imagistically through the rising up of Joas, phoenix-like, from the mangled remains of his great-grandmother. Purity replaces corruption: visually, through the dazzling whiteness of the child's garment; intellectually, through the clarity which the apparition restores to the dream vision. The transition also provides a basis for irony. The second apparition produces in the dreamer a relaxed calm, in contrast to her earlier terror. The suddenness of the dagger thrust, brutally interrupting this euphoria, this murderous blow inflicted by a radiant figure of purity, symbolizes the baroque disquietude underlying the theme, and later summed up in Joad's prophetic question, "Comment en un plomb vil l'or pur est-il changé"

[59]In indicating the use of this spectacular device, Racine may have been thinking of the "machines" of opera, as J. Pommier has remarked (*Aspects de Racine*, Paris, Nizet, 1954, p. 64). On the "ferme," see G. R. Kernodle, *From Art to Theatre*, University of Chicago Press [1944], pp. 210–11; and on the influence of operatic staging in Racine, J. Vanuxem, "Racine, les machines et les fêtes," *RHL*, LIV (1954), pp. 295–319.

[60]Racine used the word in both its meanings, though more frequently in the second.

(III. vii. 1142)? In *Athalie*, as elsewhere in Racinian tragedy, tension is provided by the two-sidedness of concepts; here the corruption in purity, elsewhere the weakness in majesty, the fallibility in power.

The vision's surprise attack may have been suggested by two totally disparate sources. In Pauline's warning dream in *Polyeucte*, she first sees a triumphant Sévère, who predicts her husband's death; a mob of Christians then throw Polyeucte at his feet, and when Pauline cries out to her father for help, Felix appears, his dagger raised to plunge it into Polyeucte's breast. This attack from a totally unexpected source may have suggested the surprise of Joas' dagger thrust. In *Gerusalemme liberata*, Armida tells how her mother's ghost warned her of death. Her fear and dismay are like those of a man who dreads assassination; anticipating death, he already feels the murderous blade:

> Qual uom ch'aspetti che su'l collo ignudo
> Ad or ad or gli caggia il ferro crudo.
>
> (IV. xli)

Only Racine could so skilfully combine and adapt the two suggestions: the one of an attack unexpected because of the victim's trust in the attacker; the other of a fear so acute that the blow is physically felt.

Analysis thus confirms the uniqueness of Racine's handling of the dream device. Retaining certain conventional aspects of the classical dream—the appearance of the shade as in life, the warning prophecy, the dreamer's attempted embrace, he adds new qualities or subtly changes and adapts such elements as the gesture of the shade itself. By its humanizing of dreamer and dream figure, by its supernatural origin, by its evocation of past and future, by its spectacular quality, the dream becomes an essential element of the dramatic action, skilfully woven into the play. In his Preface, Racine acknowledges that he created chorus and chorus leader in imitation of ancient tragedy. Athalie's dream, though closer to Homer than to Aeschylus or Sophocles, may be seen as further evidence of his attempt to impart a specifically "Greek" quality to his tragedy. Whether he succeeded there is a moot question. There is no doubt, however, that out of literary tradition and the vast resources of his reading, his genius had fashioned a passage which was, in Voltaire's words, "sublime, vraisemblable, intéressant, et nécessaire."

# VI. CONCLUSION

THE LAST CHAPTER was boldly labelled "The Essence of Racinian Tragedy" in the hope of arriving, through the various lines of investigation set up there, at some point from which it might be finally possible to discover the elusive nature of that tragedy. Although, as I have already warned the reader (and myself), generalizations about Racine are dangerous, after our examination of his structure, tragic themes, symbolism, and sources, certain generalizations have now, I believe, become possible.

One of these is that the Racinian character is hardly tragic in the traditional sense that has developed out of neo-Aristotelian theory. We have seen how Racine, though Euripidean in his attitude toward the hero, seems to have found in Euripides rather a splendid confirmation than an inspiration. Instead of solitary and splendid figures, brought low through some error of judgment or character, Racine creates characters who carry within them the tares common to human nature. The standards whereby men live, which are often elaborate structures of conduct and manners, fail them in a crucial moment of their destiny, collapsing when the elemental forces of nature make their demands.

This conflict permeates every aspect of Racine's work. On this point, his two failures, *La Thébaïde* and *Alexandre*, are instructive. The brutality, the naked force which he had attained in the first was never to reappear again on so sustained a level. Realizing, as he acquired skill and range, that greater effect could be achieved by varying the emotional pitch, he created a Néron, a Roxane, a Hermione, who strike us more forcibly than Jocaste or Etéocle because of the control beneath which we can yet sense smouldering fires. In his second play, he had responded more accurately to his public's taste to produce the "tendre" *Alexandre*. It is, I believe, by means of a combination of the techniques of the two early works that Racine achieved his inimitable tragic pattern, for throughout the canon, beneath the mannered courtesy that characterizes *Alexandre* lies half-hidden the ferocity, the fear and despair of the harried figures of *La Thébaïde*.

Control and abandon. The control of the two-four two-four beat of the Alexandrine, with its neatly riming couplets, suddenly broken and sprawling; the control of the softly spoken "Madame" or "Seigneur" suddenly forgotten; the control of "vous" overwhelmed by the naked violence of "toi". The control inherent in the mastery of all the brittle elements of the play: line, scene, *entr'acte*, act, in an indestructible unity that symbolizes the entrapment of the characters; the control of time, in a momentum which sweeps them relentlessly onward, despite their feeble gestures of protest.

In *La Thébaïde*, to which one may always return for the bare enunciations which the playwright was later to assimilate and interweave, so that they emerged instead from the total action, four lines of Jocaste summarize Racine's concept of the tragic predicament:

> Connaissez mieux du ciel la vengeance fatale.
> Toujours à ma douleur il met quelque intervalle;
> Mais, hélas ! quand sa main semble me secourir,
> C'est alors qu'il s'apprête à me faire périr.
> (III. iii. 675–8)

These lines describe not only the action of *Phèdre*, but of *Bajazet*, for it matters little, in the end, whether the sadistic forces of which Jocaste speaks be supernatural or simply the product of a fatal juxtaposition of characters.

In his predicament the Racinian character is alone. Not solitary in the Oedipean sense, planing above others, a superior mortal, but alone because he cannot communicate with his fellows. We have seen how much of the tension lies in the characters' attempts to break through the façade of manners, through the screen of mere words to the real meaning beneath.

Communication ... is an exchange of responses. It is not a one-way affair. It is a complex of interaction—you say something to me; the expression on my face, or my answer, makes you change your next statement; my feeling at the moment determines how completely I comprehend your intellectual and emotional meaning; the situation in which we both find ourselves determines how we respond; you—as a human being with powers of abstract thought and generalization—are able partly to guess how I will respond even before you speak to me, and therefore you revise or edit your words ahead of time, anticipating my response; and so on, indefinitely.[1]

We recognize at once how fully Racine was aware of this interaction, this interdependence of situation and mode of speech. Yet the important thing is not to praise his undoubted psychological acuity, but to realize how fully he exploited the intense drama of this constant duel, how he related it to the seesaw of control and abandon, reason and passion.

Perhaps only one other French writer was as conscious of man's tragic muteness. This, paradoxically, was Flaubert, who was far closer to Racine than he could have dreamed, and who beautifully expressed the idea in the following lines from *Madame Bovary*:

... personne, jamais, ne peut donner l'exacte mesure de ses besoins, ni de ses conceptions, ni de ses douleurs, et... la parole humaine est comme un chaudron fêlé où nous battons des mélodies à faire danser les ours, quand on voudrait attendrir les étoiles.

Like Flaubert's Emma, Racine's tragic figures are eternally misunderstood. Phèdre's "enmity" for Hippolyte is misunderstood from beginning to end; Œnone, her companion from childhood, can never comprehend the enormity of her mistress' passion-malady and remorse. At the news of Thésée's death, she can announce, blandly confident, "Votre flamme devient une flamme ordinaire." Only the audience knows better. After the disastrous confession and rebuff, she declares, with oblivious firmness, "Vous nourrissez un feu qu'il vous faudrait éteindre," and suggests that Phèdre bury herself in affairs of state. When Thésée returns from the dead, she blunders in officiously,

Il faut d'un vain amour étouffer la pensée,
Madame. Rappelez votre vertu passée.[2]

(III. iii. 825–6)

Our pity is the greater because of our intimate and unshared knowledge of Phèdre's perturbed spirit.

Like this tragic incommunicability, the agony and tension resulting from the mere placing of characters together upon the stage makes Racine essentially a modern. For the Racinian character, nearly three

[1]G. H. Mead, quoted in K. Macrorie, "Two-Campism in Education," *AAUP Bulletin*, XXXVIII (1952), pp. 299–300.

[2]Note that earlier, the news of Thésée's death had been announced by Panope. The irony is the greater that both the news of his return, and the advice to Phèdre to repress her passion, should be brought by Œnone.

hundred years before Sartre, Hell is already "other people," and in *Huis clos*, when Sartre's Garcin, shut up in a drawing-room Hell with two others, tells the Lesbian Inès, "Si vous faites le moindre geste, si vous levez la main pour vous éventer, Estelle et moi nous sentons la secousse," he might be describing the predicament of the Racinian character, for whom the mere presence of another can have the impact of a blow.

But Racine, a modern? What of the periwig and ruffles that an able critic invokes to declare Racinian tragedy old-fashioned?[3] Strangely enough, in those very perukes, ruffles, and high heels lies a clue, not only to his modernity, but to his universality. The sketches by such seventeenth-century costume designers as Jean Bérain clearly demonstrate that the costumes worn at the time artfully combined the Roman costume (which, like the Roman names for the gods, also served plays with a Greek setting), the military tunic and helmet, with the dress of the time. "Even when devising clothes of legendary characters, the artist's line is brought back to the dress of his own day." To the helmet, the designer adds plumes; the wig is subdued, sometimes covered; the tunic suggests both armour-plate and the panelled jacket of the court.[4]

Thus Racine's actors played their rôles, not in court dress, but rather in a costume that was a skilful amalgam of the classic and the contemporary. May we not see in this, one more example of the way in which Racine, through the juxtaposition of the ancient and modern world, achieved timelessness and an eternal quality? Like Bérain, the present-day designer of costumes for a Racine play need not seek archaeological exactness, but may create a costume suggesting the classic in a stylized manner that retains elements of modern costume. The periwig and ruffles, like the famous "anachronisms" critics have so often ferreted out, are no mere accident, but part of the plan.

But may Racine not be too "modern" to have a tragic view? Although we have seen how the rhythm of his action is based on the involvement of his characters in a fatal momentum, and how the statements of Jocaste come to be realized thematically and structurally

[3]Francis Fergusson, *The Idea of a Theater*, Princeton University Press, 1949, p. 57. My disagreement with the author on this point in no way reduces my admiration for this remarkable study.
[4]James Laver, *Drama: Its Costume and Décor*, London, Studio Publications, 1951, pp. 150–6.

in the masterpieces, it has been asserted that "the perfidy of the gods could not have occurred to Racine."[5] Perhaps not, if we take the statement literally, but certainly the tragedy of modern man, trapped in a society of his own making, caught in the eternal tug between civilization and elemental emotion, could and did occur to him. Perhaps not the perfidy of the gods, but the perfidy that Ibsen and Hardy also saw, with which an unnamable complex of forces, if not a "President of the Immortals," could combine to thwart man's existence despite his near perfection.

Yet although Racine's tragedy is pessimistic, and one does not, as in Sophocles or Shakespeare, feel an essential "rightness" in the fate of his characters, the perfection of their form affords a kind of vindication of humanity. The Racinian catharsis lies in an aesthetic, rather than a moral rightness; as André Gide, who loved Racine, expressed it, "Shakespeare, sans doute, est plus humain; mais il s'agit ici de bien autre chose: c'est le triomphe d'une convenance sublime, c'est une ravissante harmonie où tout entre en jeu et concourt, qui comble de satisfaction à la fois intelligence, cœur, et sens. Homme et nature, dans ses pièces ouvertes aux vents, toute la poésie rit, pleure et frémit dans Shakespeare; Racine est au sommet de l'art."[6]

[5]Jean Hytier, "La Méthode de M. L. Spitzer," RR, XLI (1950), p. 52.
[6]André Gide, Journal (1889–1939), Editions de la Pléiade, 1940, p. 1187.

# INDEX